Palestinian Music and Song

Public Cultures of the Middle East and North Africa
Paul Silverstein, Susan Slyomovics, and Ted Swedenburg, editors

Palestinian Music and Song

Expression and Resistance since 1900

Edited by Moslih Kanaaneh, Stig-Magnus Thorsén,
Heather Bursheh, and David A. McDonald

Indiana University Press
Bloomington and Indianapolis

This book is a publication of

Indiana University Press
Office of Scholarly Publishing
Herman B. Wells Library 350
1320 East 10th Street
Bloomington, Indiana 47405 USA

www.iupress.indiana.edu

Telephone orders 800-842-6796
Fax orders 812-855-7931

© 2013 by Indiana University Press
All rights reserved

No part of this book may be reproduced or utilized in any form or by any means, electronic or mechanical, including photocopying and recording, or by any information storage and retrieval system, without permission in writing from the publisher. The Association of American University Presses' Resolution on Permissions constitutes the only exception to this prohibition.

♾ The paper used in this publication meets the minimum requirements of the American National Standard for Information Sciences—Permanence of Paper for Printed Library Materials, ANSI Z39.48–1992.

Manufactured in the United States of America

Library of Congress Cataloging-in-Publication Data

Palestinian music and song : expression and resistance since 1900 / edited by Moslih Kanaaneh, Stig-Magnus Thorsén, Heather Bursheh, and David A. McDonald.
pages cm — (Public cultures of the Middle East and North Africa)
Includes bibliographical references and index.
ISBN 978-0-253-01098-8 (cloth : alkaline paper) — ISBN 978-0-253-01106-0 (paperback : alkaline paper) — ISBN 978-0-253-01113-8 (e-book) 1. Palestinian Arabs—Music—History and criticism. 2. Music—Palestine—20th century—History and criticism. 3. Music—Political aspects—Palestine. I. Kana'inah, Muslih, editor. II. Thorsén, Stig-Magnus, editor. III. Bursheh, Heather, 1975– editor. IV. McDonald, David A., 1976– editor. V. Series: Public cultures of the Middle East and North Africa.
ML3754.5.P35 2013
780.89'9274—dc23

2013022924

1 2 3 4 5 18 17 16 15 14 13

Contents

Preface

The story behind this anthology on Palestinian music and song commenced in the fall of 2007, following a number of meetings between Stig-Magnus Thorsén, a musicologist from the University of Gothenburg in Sweden; Heather Bursheh, a music educator from Edward Said National Conservatory of Music in Ramallah; Ahmad Al Khatib, a Palestinian *ʿūd* (lute) player and teacher based in Sweden; and Moslih Kanaaneh, an anthropologist from Birzeit University. These four initiators were motivated by their close familiarity with Palestinian society and culture resulting from many years of academic engagement in the Palestinian sociocultural context. They shared in common the awareness of the crucial role that music and song have played in the lives of Palestinians as well as in their national-political cause. At the same time the initiators were strongly aware of, and puzzled by, the unfamiliarity (or sometimes ideologically motivated negligence) of Western scholars and the general public with this particular component of Palestinian reality, due to the lack of scholarly work on Palestinian music and song in English or any other European language. The initiators were thus in agreement on the urgent need for a long-term multidisciplinary project aimed at the publication of a collection of scholarly essays in English on Palestinian music and song.

This realization and determination coincided with the Swedish Research Council's expressed interest in promoting cooperation between institutions of higher education in Sweden and Palestine. In early 2008 the initiators submitted to the Swedish Research Council a proposal for funding for a three-year scholarly project that would culminate in the publication of an English anthology on Palestinian music and song. In December 2008 the Swedish Research Council accepted our proposal and awarded the project a grant that was sufficient for arranging and administering a limited number of meetings and symposia that would ultimately lead to the production of the anthology. With all the major pieces falling into place, a project management committee was formed, a cooperation agreement between the Department of Music and Drama at the University of Gothenburg and the Department of Sociology and Anthropology at Birzeit University was signed, and the project was officially launched with the title "Exploring Song and Music among Palestinians."

It took the project's management committee a whole year to locate, contact, and recruit the participants and bring them together for exploring the potentials and possibilities. On February 19, 2010, a three-day symposium convened in Jerash, Jordan, hosting twenty prominent musicologists, anthropologists, folklorists, and musicians from around the world, ten of whom were Palestinians residing either in Palestine or elsewhere in the Palestinian diaspora. The reason behind choosing Jordan as the place for the symposium was to facilitate the attendance of Palestinian and Arab participants who were prevented or banned by the Israeli authorities from entering the Occupied Palestinian Territories, and at the same time to facilitate the attendance of Palestinians with Israeli citizenship (the so-called '48 Palestinians) who are banned from traveling to any Arab country aside from Jordan and Egypt. This symposium was the first of its kind, bringing together scholars, artists, composers, and performers of Palestinian music who shared in common an academic interest in Palestinian music and song and a willingness to contribute a research-based essay to the anthology. Each participant came to the symposium prepared to present a brief proposal based on ongoing or previously unpublished research for discussion by the group. After three days of intensive and highly productive discussions, the participants left the symposium to develop and complete their individual research projects.

From the outset the project was designed to achieve two major goals: (1) developing and publishing an edited volume of research essays on Palestinian music and song, and (2) establishing a platform for a permanent worldwide network of scholars, music composers, and performers interested in investigating various aspects of Palestinian music and song within the context of Palestinian politics, society, and culture. For this purpose, and for facilitating continuous collaborative communication between the contributors to the anthology, the project's management committee launched a website through which contributors could read and discuss one another's papers and exchange ideas, thoughts, comments, and advice.

Through this website and other media of communication, the project's management committee was engaged in editorial work with the contributors, collectively and individually, for approximately two years. Once mature versions of the essays were submitted, the committee called for a second symposium, this time in Jericho, on January 20–22, 2012, for the purpose of discussing the essays and moving forward to the submission of the final draft. In this symposium each participant was assigned to present to the group the essay of another participant along with insightful and constructive critique, and each presentation was followed by an open discussion by all participants. At the very least the committee members can say that this activity was an exemplary case of multidisciplinary teamwork, the result of which we hope readers will find expressed in the quality of the essays in this volume. The combination of scholars and performers, of musicologists and musicians, of music composers and music analysts, was indeed unique and inspiring. In the concluding meeting of the project's administrative committee toward the end of this symposium, the committee decided to establish an editorial committee for the anthology, comprised of project initiators Moslih Kanaaneh, Stig-Magnus Thorsén, and Heather Bursheh, with the addition of music anthropologist David A. McDonald from Indiana University.

This anthology is thus undoubtedly the first of its kind, drawing together some of the world's leading researchers, performers, and composers of Palestinian music and song. It offers readers a unique opportunity for hearing the inquisitive and performative voices of native and non-native scholars and music makers analytically reflecting on the dialectics and developments of Palestinian music throughout the twentieth and twenty-first centuries. Moreover, it provides a diverse and dynamic account of Palestinian music as an inseparable component of Palestinian social, cultural, economic and political life. As such, it is unlike anything currently available in the fields of ethnomusicology, anthropology, cultural studies, or interdisciplinary Middle Eastern studies.

Acknowledgments

This anthology is the result of a three-year project that would not have been possible without the generous grant from the Swedish Research Council, to whom we are greatly indebted.

The project leading to the publication of this book was run within the framework of a cooperation agreement between the Department of Music and Drama at the University of Gothenburg and the Department of Sociology and Anthropology at Birzeit University. We owe special thanks to both departments, as well as to the administration of both universities for facilitating the various activities of the project, including first and foremost the travel arrangements for the project's managing team.

Sincere thanks go to all the authors who contributed articles to this book. Without exception they have been energetic, devoted to the project, and gracious in debating ideas and accepting revisions.

During the four years of our work, many scholars and music performers joined the project for certain periods, attending and contributing to the two symposia and/or contributing ideas for articles. Those people are Sana Moussa, Sunania Maira, Magid Shihade, Sharif Kanaana, Jennifer Sinnamon, Saher Yaseen, Abaher Elsakka, and Martin Stokes. To each of them, we extend our thanks for their outstanding contributions. Special thanks go to Ahmad Al Khatib for his inspiration and input right from the start, as part of the project steering committee.

Much appreciation is due to Fares Mansour, who designed the website to facilitate communication between the authors throughout the project. We also appreciate the assistance of Heather Mousa with translations at various stages.

Finally, our huge gratitude goes to Rebecca Tolen and the team at Indiana University Press, for their enthusiasm, their commitment, and their patience, from the time we first approached them until the final stages of the project.

Moslih Kanaaneh, Stig-Magnus Thorsén,
Heather Bursheh, and David A. McDonald

Note on Transliteration

In our transliterations of the many Arabic words in this book, we have opted to use the Library of Congress transliteration system as a general rule, which uses the diacritical symbols *ā, ī, ū, ṣ, ḍ, ḥ, ṭ, ẓ,* ʿ, and ʾ to represent various letters/sounds in Arabic, and contains detailed guidelines about usage. The full guidelines can be found on the Library of Congress website. There are, however, certain exceptions in the book, which are as follows.

Proper Nouns: Names of people, major towns, and organizations have been written with their common English spellings, or where possible, the preferred spellings of the individuals concerned. For example, the city of Haifa would be written *Ḥayfā* using the Library of Congress system, but we have chosen to use the more common spelling. Likewise, we have taken the spelling of Simon Shaheen's name from his website rather than using the transliteration system, which would result in the rather awkward *Simawn Shahīn*. The names of smaller, lesser-known villages, however, have followed the transliteration system to aid the reader with their pronunciation.

Common Words: Certain Arabic words associated with the Palestinian situation have entered the English lexicon to such an extent that we felt it would be superfluous to change their common spellings. Thus, *Nakba, Intifada, Fatah,* and *Hamas* have also not followed the Library of Congress transliterations.

Colloquial Pronunciations: There are several words that, when spoken in the Palestinian dialect, look strange when written on the page with the Library of Congress transliteration system (which is designed for classical or Modern Standard Arabic). Therefore, words like *ghurbaih* (expatriation/foreignness), *taqīyyaih* (hat), and *ḥurrīyyaih* (freedom) have been given their Palestinian *-aih* ending, rather than the classical *-ah,* in situations where the colloquialism is inherent to the meaning.

Palestinian Music and Song

Introduction: Do Palestinian Musicians Play Music or Politics?

Moslih Kanaaneh

Why Music? And Why Palestinian Music?

While theoreticians, philosophers, and empirical researchers may debate the ontological and epistemological relationships between culture and music (see Middleton 2003), the importance of music in the lives of humans and human collectivities cannot be denied. All human groups around the world and throughout human history have had music in one form or another, and music has been a fundamentally significant element in their cultural life and mode of being. As Philip Bohlman has observed:

> Music represented culture in two ways, as a form of expression common to humanity, and as one of the most extreme manifestations of difference. On the one hand, the essence of universal culture was borne by music; that is, the commonness that the colonizer and the colonized shared. On the other hand, the fact that music might embody profound differences accounted for the way it was totally incompatible with the culture of the colonizer." (2003, 47)

In war and in peace, in turmoil and in tranquility, human collectivities of all kinds and sizes constantly produce and consume music in their everyday life. In the colonial condition, the colonizers sing their triumph while the colonized sing their way to the hoped-for triumph. The difference, however, is that the colonizers always try to silence the colonized, arguing (and perhaps truly believing) that the music of the colonized is nothing but a "primitive" tool for incitement and resistance against "the purveyors of civilization." This becomes like a self-fulfilling prophecy: the colonizers use music and other cultural practices as a tool for labeling the colonized as "primitive," and then this constructed notion of "primitivity" becomes a justification for colonizing "the primitive" in the name of modernity and civilization.

The significance of the Palestinian case for musicologists, anthropologists, and political analysts lies in the fact that it provides an outstanding opportunity for a generative analysis of the interactive relationship between music as a form of expressive culture and the use, abuse, and misuse of power, externally as well as internally. On the one hand, Palestinians share the same discourses and sociocultural, political, and economic characteristics of all the deprived, oppressed, and marginalized peoples of the third world, whether in Asia, Africa, Latin America, or elsewhere. On the other hand, Palestinians are a unique case in that while the rest of the world has moved to the postcolonial condition, Palestinians are still stuck in the colonial condition and seemingly have a long way to go in struggling for survival, resisting occupation, and fighting for liberation and national independence.

Researchers and analysts therefore have to be exceedingly careful when applying postcolonial frames of analysis to the Palestinian situation. Nothing informs the Palestinians' mode of being and ways of life more than their being subjugated to the aggressive, all-encroaching Israeli occupation that penetrates into the most minute details of their lives. An inseparable part of this condition is the permanent temporality of the exile of more than six million Palestinians who have been uprooted and displaced and still are denied the right to return to their homes and lands in Palestine. "All that has been happening to the Palestinians since 1948, whether in the occupied homeland or in exile, is nothing but the ramifications of the tragedy of uprootedness; uprootedness of human beings from their home, uprootedness of homes from their land, uprootedness of land from its history, and uprootedness of history from its humanity" (Kanaaneh 2008, 181).

Since music is an integral part of culture, and culture is, in the final analysis, the mode of humans' innovative adaptation to events and their consequences in time, music is thus inevitably organically tied to history such that one can read history in music, and, at the same time, one always has to understand music and musical works in their historical context. This may sound odd when taking into consideration the common conviction that music as a system of signification and expression is universal and eternal, defying the dividing boundaries of space and time. True as it may be, this universalism and eternality of music should not blind us to the particularity of music and musical works in space and time; that is why we distinguish between ancient, medieval, modern, and contemporary music, and that is why we distinguish among types of music associated with different geographic regions.

This applies equally to Palestinian music and its relation to history. In fact, due to the intensity, severity, and distinctiveness of Palestinian history under successive occupations, this organic bond between music and history is more palpable and tangible in the Palestinian case than in most other cases. At least in the Palestinian case, one has to understand how history affects music in order to understand how music reflects history.

Palestinian music has been both strengthened and weakened by its long engagement with colonialism, occupation, and foreign rule. On the one hand, the experience of subjugation to foreign occupation (Persian, Hellenistic, Roman, Byzantine, Arabic, Turkish, British, or Israeli) has given birth to increased musical activity and the development of various genres and repertoires. On the other hand, sustained structures of domination, censorship, and control have equally hampered the possibilities for composing, performing, and listening to Palestinian music. Nevertheless, musical development has continued both within diverse Palestinian communities and in dialogue with other communities (local, regional, and transnational), resulting in a vibrant tapestry of musical production. Each one of the essays in this volume addresses and elaborates certain aspects of this relationship between Palestinian music and the history of subjugation to occupation.

Palestinian music as it is today is the cumulative outcome of the dialectical relationship between a long intrinsic tradition and a long history of occupation and subjugation to foreign rule. The influence of surrounding cultures and music traditions on Palestinian music has also been marked by cultural intrusion resulting from the asymmetrical power relation between Palestine and its neighboring cultures and countries.

There is hardly any culture anywhere in the world that has been left alone to develop by its own and according to its own dynamics. This obviously applies to Palestinian culture as well. Yet no other culture than the Palestinian one has developed throughout its entire history under foreign occupation and dispossession. This intricacy is truer now than ever before. When considering the situation of Palestinian music in the present (i.e., during the last thirty years or so), the long history of subjugation to foreign rule and the present condition of subjugation to the suppressive and oppressive Israeli occupation have to be further problematized by the addition of four more processes of cultural intrusion that have been decisively shaping and determining Palestinian music's course of development.

The first process is globalization, which blurs and almost erases the cultural boundaries between countries, cultures, and nations, encroaching upon local cultures and music traditions. Palestinian music is profoundly influenced by this sweeping process, and the most eye-catching manifestation of this influence is the rapidly increasing popularity of hip-hop music in Palestinian society, as is the case in most Arab and third-world societies. This subject is extensively dealt with in two essays in this volume, those of Randa Safieh and Janne Louise Andersen.

The second process that has recently been shaping Palestinian music's course of development is the rise of political Islam in Palestine and the overwhelming Islamization of Palestinian society, especially since the early 1990s following the rise of Hamas (the Islamic Resistance Movement) in the Occupied Palestinian Territories and of the Islamic Movement in the '48-area (i.e., inside the State of Israel). Politically, Islamization tends to blur the boundaries between the various Muslim peoples and countries by replacing local patriotism with pan-Islamic *jihād* (holy struggle), replacing secular laws and codes of behavior with the Islamic *Sharīʿah* (Islamic law), and opting for the unification of all Muslims and Muslim countries in one national entity called "the Islamic *Ummah*" embodied in an overall political institution called the *Khilāfah* (caliphate). This is even truer when it comes to music and expressive culture in general, with the potential of blurring, and even neutralizing, the national distinctiveness of local music traditions in the various countries of the Islamic world. In terms of melody, lyrics, and instrumentation, Islamic music in Palestine is more Islamic than Palestinian, and it is much more similar to Islamic music outside Palestine than to traditional Palestinian music. When you listen to Islamic *anāshīd* (anthems) in the Gaza Strip, Egypt, Saudi Arabia, or Afghanistan, you will surely be struck by the similarities rather than by the differences, the differences stemming only from the specificities of the contemporary sociopolitical state of affairs akin to each place or country.

Islamization of Palestinian music is addressed briefly in the essay contributed to this volume by David A. McDonald and in detail in the essay by Carin Berg and Michael Schulz. Although Schulz and Berg concentrate their analysis on the Palestinian (anti-Israeli) content of Hamas songs, considering Hamas's Islamic music as one of the many forms of contemporary Palestinian music, their analysis, in fact, deals with the Palestinian specificities of the Islamic songs of Hamas rather than with the Palestinian cultural identity of these songs. As anthropologists, folklorists, and musicologists specializing in Palestinian music, we cannot help but infer from Berg and Schulz's extensive description and analysis how deeply and profoundly Islamized Hamas songs and music are, while legitimately wondering what remains of the Palestinian cultural identity of these songs and music. It is worth mentioning here that this proclivity of Islamization to neutralize the local cultural identity of music in Palestine is equivalent to the proclivity of globalization to levy a similar impact through hip-hop and other imported Western music genres, although the case of hip-hop is less detrimental to Palestinian music, due to Palestinian hip-hop singers' efforts to integrate traditional Palestinian tones and melodic forms into their songs, which is hardly the case in Islamic anāshīd.

This proclivity to reduce the local cultural particularity of music in Palestine is also one of the far-reaching repercussions of Arabization, the third process that is currently shaping Palestinian music's course of development. Truly the Arab characteristics of music are deeply engrained in the music of Palestinian society as a result of the cultural Arabization of the population in Palestine ever since the integration of Palestine and its population into the Arab nation in the seventh century AD. When Palestine was part of the Levant and of Greater Syria, one could hardly distinguish between music in Palestine and music in the surrounding regions, such as Mount Lebanon, Aleppo, Damascus, and the Jordanian desert (see, for instance, the essay by Issa Boulos in this volume), while being influenced to various degrees by the neighboring regions of Egypt and Iraq. However, just as the music of the Levant preserved its distinctiveness from the "pure" Arabic music of the Arabian Peninsula and the Gulf area (which is still the case today), Palestinian music (or, more accurately, Palestinian song) preserved certain characteristics that distinguished it from music in Syria, Lebanon, and Jordan, with this distinctiveness stemming from the unique historical experiences of the Arab inhabitants of Palestine. In the course of the nineteenth and twentieth centuries, however, the more the fate of Palestine and Palestinians diverged from that of the neighboring regions (due to the special regulations and policies applied by the Ottoman government in Palestine, intensive European missionary activities, and the colonial-settler project of the Zionist movement under the auspices of European colonialism), the more the distinctiveness of Palestinian culture and music grew clearer, firmer, and more substantive. Yara El-Ghadban and Kiven Strohm, in their essay in this volume, refer to a number of old and new sources substantiating this development. We also find a vivid illustration of this in Rachel Beckles Willson's essay, which shows us that the German theologian and linguist Gustaf Dalman had no problem in ascertaining the Palestinian distinctiveness of the collection of songs and melodies he collected and published in *Palästinischer Diwan* (Palestinian Diwan) in the year 1901, although the borders of Dalman's Palestine did not precisely overlap with those of today's Palestine. Various instances of this interactive tension between Arabism and "Palestinianness" before and immediately after the *Nakba* (catastrophe) in 1948 are accounted for in the essay of the Palestinian musician and music analyst Issa Boulos, and partially in the essay of Yara El-Ghadban and Kiven Strohm and in Heather Bursheh's interview with Issa Boulos and Nader Jalal.

With all this being said, the Arabization of Palestinian music that has been taking place during the last twenty-five years is of quite different nature and dimensions. Rather than only affecting and shaping Palestinian music, as was the case in earlier Arabization, the current process actually has the effect of replacing Palestinian music with the Arab music of Egypt, Lebanon, Syria, Iraq, and even Saudi Arabia and the Gulf countries. This takes place mainly through Arab satellite music channels, such as those of Rotana (from Saudi Arabia), Melody and Mazzika (from Egypt), and Nojoom (from Dubai), that are received all over Palestine and the Palestinian diaspora, in which the presence of Palestinian music is equal to nil. This process has had a profound impact on music making in Palestine, and in the essay by Issa Boulos in this volume we see how musicians from Lebanon and Egypt have set the standard of professionalism and musical sophistication that Palestinian composers, singers, and musicians try to live up to and imitate and integrate into their musical production.

The crucial impact of recent Arabization, however, is on the general Palestinian public, modifying and even altering its musical taste, preferences, and actual usage. Throughout Palestine and the Palestinian diaspora (perhaps apart from certain Islamist circles in Gaza), the overwhelming majority of the music and songs that Palestinians play, listen to, and fervently dance to in weddings and other happy occasions is Arabic music from Egypt, Lebanon, Syria, and Iraq rather than from Palestine, whereas some traditional Palestinian folk songs such as *ᶜatābā* and *dalᶜūnā* are rarely performed or listened to. Furthermore, today's average Palestinians in their daily lives and along their daily activities listen to Fairuz and Nancy Ajram (Lebanese), Shireen (Egyptian), Kathem Al-Saher (Iraqi), Mohammad Abdo (Saudi Arabian), and many others from among the hundreds of old and contemporary Arab singers, rather than to Palestinian singers such as Mustafa al-Kurd, Reem Talhami or Al-ᶜAshiqeen group, who actually do not exist on TV channels but only on quite expensive CDs that are not easy to find in the local market. Hence, although the essays in this volume may leave the reader with the impression that Palestine "bubbles" with Palestinian music, or that the music produced and consumed in Palestinian society is all Palestinian music, this impression is far from corresponding to the situation on the ground, except in times of national upheaval such as the two Intifadas and the competition between Palestinian political factions and parties before the elections. Instead, this anthology focuses on music produced in Palestinian society and from the tendency of the contributors to view music from the viewpoint of music makers, performers, and manipulators rather than from the viewpoint of listeners and consumers. The consuming audience, the millions of Palestinian music devotees, appear in this collection only sporadically and ephemerally, mentioned in the essays of Stig-Magnus Thorsén, Janne Louise Andersen, and Heather Bursheh's interview with Reem Talhami.

Like all other forms of expressive culture, the "message" expressed and conveyed though music is determined by the receiver as much as by the sender, and by the decoder as much as by the encoder. And as a "cultural text"—to use James Clifford's (1986) terminology—a musical work is never completely written before it is read, since the act of reading itself inevitably participates in the writing and rewriting of the text. This points toward a direction for future investigations of Palestinian music and of music in general.

The fourth process that has recently been shaping Palestinian music's course of development is the involvement of Western governments and nongovernmental actors and brokers in Palestinian culture and Palestinian music. This involvement began with the outburst of the first Intifada in 1987 and substantially increased in 1994 following the Oslo Accords and the establishment of the Palestinian National Authority in the Occupied Territories, but it was radically intensified in 2003 in the aftermath of the second Intifada. This has been done through channeling a significant portion of humanitarian funds to cultural activities such as music, dance, fine arts, literature, and folklore, with the aim of helping Palestinian society to move from a society of fighters resisting occupation and struggling for liberation to a "normal" human society engaged in building itself as part of the normal world. In their essay in this volume, El-Ghadban and Strohm provide reference to a substantial number of Palestinian and international researchers (such as Sara Hanafi, Linda Tabar, Khalil Nakhleh, Dina Craissati, Mufid Qassoum, Didier Fassin, and Ilana Feldman) who try to uncover the long-term negative impact on culture and sociopolitical situation of this shift in the policy of Western aid to Palestinians. There is, thus, a growing suspicion that the political conviction behind this vehement Western interest in Palestinian culture is that Palestinians should renounce resistance, accept the status quo, and feel, act, and live as if they are in the postcolonial era rather than in the colonial condition. That is what El-Ghadban and Strohm eloquently call "culture as a substitute for political resolution." They further argue that this Western donors' reconceptualization of Palestinian culture "provides an effective alibi for the international community to keep deferring a lasting and just resolution to the political situation of the Palestinians."

The severe impact of this shift in international aid policy on contemporary Palestinian music is extensively addressed in El-Ghadban and Strohm's essay, and to a lesser extent in the essays of Sylvia Alajaji, Randa Safieh, and Stig-Magnus Thorsén. Janne Louise Andersen's essay, on the other hand, can be taken as a vivid firsthand journalistic narration of a typical case of Western intervention in Palestinian music's course of development. In this context Rachel Beckles Willson's analytical reflections on Dalman's *Palästinischer Diwan* reveal some of the old seeds of today's Western governments' treatment of Palestinian culture and music as means for the pacification of Palestinians under Israeli occupation.

Needless to say, music among Palestinians has never been static, always being given to influences from other cultures and dynamically interacting with other musical traditions. The cultural distinctiveness of Palestinian music should thus be dealt with not as a "pure substance," but rather as a dynamic, ever changing quality that is not necessarily altered whenever it gains or loses some of its attributes. With this background in mind, we should comprehend the workings of the abovementioned processes that shape Palestinian music's development and challenge its cultural distinctiveness. Moreover, it is clear that these four processes are directly related to, informed by, or intertwined with colonialism and the colonial Israeli occupation of Palestine. Israeli occupation is thus the overall, omnipresent, and all-embracing condition that directly or indirectly influences all discourses and process in Palestinian reality, whether in the Occupied Territories, inside Israel, or in the Palestinian diaspora.

The life of an occupied population is inherently comprised of two interrelated components: the first is *subjugation* to occupation, with all that entails of oppression, harassment, deprivation, loss, and life hardships in general; and the second is *resistance* to occupation, with all that entails of suffering, sacrifices, loss, and life hardships in general. As action leads to reaction and power leads to resistance in the physical world, occupation leads to resistance in human societies, simply because occupation, like slavery, is by definition the antithesis of freedom and humanity. Resistance to occupation can be direct and active, or indirect and passive. Armed resistance and violence against violence are only some of the forms that resistance to occupation can take. Resistance to occupation can also be carried out through demonstrations, strikes, boycotts, and refusal to pay taxes and revenues, as happened in the Occupied Palestinian Territories during the first Intifada. People can resist occupation even through survival, through refusal to vanish, through retaining their humanity, through remaining normal and living normal lives in spite of all the abnormalities, and even by singing love songs and playing romantic music. This is so because in all of these endeavors the occupied people counteract the occupier's intentions, thwart its ideology and agenda, and undermine its colonial objectives. As the late Palestinian poet Tawfiq Zayyad from Nazareth expressed it in one of his poems, titled "Here We Shall Stay":

We hunger
Have no clothes
We defy
Sing our songs
Sweep the sick streets with our angry dances
Saturate the prisons with dignity and pride
Keep on making children
One revolutionary generation
After another
As though we were twenty impossibilities
In Lydda, Ramla, and Galilee.

Thus, the reality of an occupied people always has two complimentary sides: subjugation to occupation, and resistance to occupation. One always finds a few people leaning to the first side and a few leaning to the other, but the vast majority keep walking the tightrope stretched between both. People under occupation may cease to resist only if they are pacified by somehow becoming convinced that they are no longer under occupation, which appears to be the objective that major international donors aim at and try to achieve in the Occupied Palestinian Territories.

Stig-Magnus Thorsén, in his essay in this volume, argues for this broader definition of resistance, following his well-informed Palestinian informant Omar Barghouti, formerly of the renowned El-Funoun dance group in Ramallah. In this sense, resistance to occupation is the very mode of existence of people under occupation, shaping and determining all aspects of their lives and all components of their culture.

It logically follows that since music is an integral component of culture, music produced under occupation is inevitably music of resistance, whether it is political or not, politicized or not. This is not a philosophical postulation or a theoretical assumption; rather, it is inherent in the nature of things and can logically be inferred when our definitions of reality correspond to reality instead of our theoretical convictions, political affiliations, or ideological orientations. In this sense Palestinian music as resistance is to be considered a given fact that needs not be discussed, disputed, or reified. That is why we have dealt with Palestinian music as a music of resistance from the outset of our project leading to this anthology, and that is why authors in this anthology axiomatically treat it as a premise underlying their investigations. The differences among the various contributions to this anthology, however, lie in their treatment of the role that Palestinian music plays in Palestinian resistance and the form of resistance that Palestinian music takes.

Although the contributors somewhat agree that Palestinian music is potentially music of resistance, not all of them agree that *all* Palestinian music is music of resistance, thus drawing a distinction between music as resistance and music as music, or between music for politics and music for musical enjoyment. David A. McDonald, for instance, distinguishes between Palestinian music and songs as a "popular folklore," part of the "Palestinian cultural heritage . . . rooted in the land and preserved over time," a sort of an "indigenous culture," on the one hand, and on the other, as Palestinian music and songs that are deliberately manipulated and worked out by competing Palestinian political factions that are ideologically struggling for position in order to be used as "a powerful means of articulating national sentiments and legitimacy." Thus, when traditional Palestinian songs are sung by peasants in the field, they are just part of the Palestinian repertoire of cultural heritage. But when the same songs are sung by protesting young men walking the streets wearing the black-and-white-checkered *kūfiyyah,* or by "young, powerful, masculine voices singing in tight unison and low tessitura," they become resistance songs capable of "uniting people for political ends." Underlying this distinction is the view that resistance is only active resistance undertaken by political activists and politically motivated actors in politically charged spaces. Carin Berg and Michael Schulz hold a similar view, distinguishing between music per se and music as deliberately used "in the context of occupation, resistance, and the articulation of Palestinian national identity." For them, music becomes music of resistance when it is used "to mobilize resistance against oppressive power, [and] also to gain external support." This view implies a certain "instrumentalist" perception of the nature of the relationship between expressive culture and politics, according to which politics and politicians strategically use expressive culture as means to their ends, whereas expressive culture has the potential and liability to be used by politics and politicians. At the other end of this continuum we find Stig-Magnus Thorsén, who, distinguishing between defensive and evolutionary art, clearly states that "music and politics are dialectically intertwined" and brilliantly gives voice to a young Palestinian musician who is disillusioned about the institutionalized politicization of Palestinian music: "The political issues are consuming the artistry to a degree that is becoming really annoying . . . For me, resistance is being able to continue your creativity, not to surrender and be a victim of circumstances . . . to always be able to go on playing music, producing, and performing."

This leads us to another crucial issue that differentiates between the various contributors to this anthology—that is, the issue of the functionality of music as resistance: what does music do as a mode of resistance?

The complexity of music lies in the fact that it is both a work of art and a cultural text. Music is a form of expressive culture, yet it is not only that. Music also has an aesthetic aspect or component that directly appeals to our subjectivity and interacts with our inner self in a manner that cannot simply be subjected to semantic or connotative analysis. Furthermore, music as an expressive culture has different layers of connotations with different degrees of semantic immediacy or meaning transparency, consequently performing different functions at different levels. Rhythm and tone combinations are the deepest and least transparent layer, immediately speaking to our emotional self rather than to our analytical intellect, whereas song texts are the nearest and most transparent layer. Nevertheless, even in song texts there are multiple layers of meanings and connotations conveying different messages and performing different functions. Mixing between these various layers in music necessarily generates confusion and ambiguity in identifying what function or functions music performs as an expressive culture in a political discourse.

Beyond expressing meaning and conveying messages, what does music as resistance do? At one end of a continuum are Carin Berg and Michael Schulz, who argue in their essay in this volume that music incites, provokes, mobilizes, and brings people to action, even to extreme actions such as carrying out a suicidal terror operation. For David A. McDonald, music generates sentiments; forms national and political identities; and shapes party affiliations, goals, tactics, and ideologies. At the same time, politically and ideologically manipulated folklore songs signify "a return to the folk, the embodied 'pure' Palestine." For Randa Safieh, music is a significant tool through which Palestinians construct, preserve, and assert their identity, but it is also a tool for resisting Israeli occupation without specifying how this tool is used. Safieh also considers hip-hop music as a new tool providing Palestinian youth with "a therapeutic and creative outlet for their frustration." Janne Louise Andersen emphasizes the communicative function of music, considering that music, and hip-hop in particular, provides "a connection for new generations of physically segregated Palestinians seeking unity and new sources of representation." Issa Boulos argues that revived and reconstructed folklore songs function as markers of Palestinian identity and struggle and help Palestinian musicians to function as political mediators. Sylvia Alajaji perceives music as a channel through which identity is mediated and negotiated and the self is "imagined and performed into being." For her, music is one of the bearers of "the burden of representation" of Palestine and its identity. Stig-Magnus Thorsén believes that Palestinian music expresses "the distinctive nature of Palestinians as individuals as well as their belonging to humankind." Yet he perceives music as a flexible system of representation, shifting meaning as well as function: "[The music of resistance] does not sound unique, but it functions in a unique way." Finally, Yara El-Ghadban and Kiven Strohm add to the discourse on art and music as resistance the discourse of art and music "as survival, as catharsis and most recently as a humanitarian project."

As we can see from the above, while much of this volume casts light on the various aspects and functions of Palestinian music, it also casts light on the various ways of looking at Palestinian music and analyzing it from an academic perspective. We consider this variation to be an inspiring and thought-provoking richness that may benefit ethnomusicological investigations and theorizations as a whole.

In addition to the research-based scholarly essays, this volume includes two interview transcriptions conducted by Heather Bursheh: one with Palestinian music researchers and analysts Issa Boulos and Nader Jalal on the direct impact of the Nakba on Palestinian musicians and musical life, and the other with the Palestinian singer Reem Talhami on the practicalities of being a singer in Palestine. We must mention here that the three interviewees in these two transcriptions joined our project from the very beginning and took part in its two symposia. These interview transcriptions give readers who are not familiar with the Palestinian music scene the possibility to hear some voices from the field—the voices of music makers, performers, and researchers who actually constitute the heart of the subject matter of this volume's analytical essays.

References

Bohlman, Philip V. 2003. "Music and Culture: Historiographies of Disjuncture." In *The Cultural Study of Music: A Critical Introduction,* edited by Martin Clayton, Trevor Herbert, and Richard Middleton, 45–56. New York: Routledge.

Clifford, James. 1986. "Introduction: Partial Truths." In *Writing Culture: The Poetics of Ethnography,* edited by James Clifford and George E. Marcus, 1–26. Berkeley: University of California Press.

Kanaaneh, Moslih. 2008. *Talking Stones and Yearning Ruins.* Ramallah, Palestine: Adwa'.

Middleton, Richard. 2003. "Introduction: Music Studies and the Idea of Culture." In *The Cultural Study of Music: A Critical Introduction,* edited by Martin Clayton, Trevor Herbert, and Richard Middleton, 1–19. New York: Routledge.

Part 1

Background

1

Palestinian Song, European Revelation, and Mission

Rachel Beckles Willson

One of the earliest—perhaps the very earliest—publications of Palestinian song is a book of 360 pages produced in Germany in 1901 titled *Palästinischer Diwan* (Palestinian Diwan).[1] The collector and editor was German theologian and linguist Gustaf Dalman (1855–1941), who went on to become one of the leading commentators on Palestine in the early twentieth century. At first glance the volume seems to be a rather limited source of actual song of the time, because the bulk of the material presented consists of song texts alone. Only thirty-two melodies are provided and many of these are rather minimal. The traces it offers could nevertheless be of enormous value to folklorists seeking a history for poetry and song in the region. And the book's wide geographical source base—most of the songs with melodies stem from as far afield as Madaba (now Jordan), Aleppo (now Syria), and what is now southern Lebanon—reminds us of the scope of conceptions of Palestine at the turn of the twentieth century.

My main concern here, however, is not a folkloristic one. Rather, I discuss the intellectual and ideological frameworks that led Dalman's book to be researched and published in the form that it eventually took. This would seem a crucial process to contextualize the song material, but it is also a valuable inquiry in itself, because it contributes to broader debates about Europe's relationship with the so-called Orient. On one level the *Diwan* must certainly be seen as an Orientalist product of some kind, but on another it challenges the primary models we have. Edward Said's landmark study *Orientalism* addressed nineteenth-century European prejudices and fantasies about Arabs in apparently general terms, but his work tended to focus primarily on the colonization of Egypt, and the majority of subsequent writers have followed suit. As recent scholars have begun to indicate, however, and as I will elaborate further through the example of Dalman's *Diwan,* in the nineteenth century the Palestinian region was viewed and treated quite differently from Egypt, received different types of researchers and travelers, and—because of how it was depicted in the Bible—had a very different place in the European imagination (Goren 2003; Kirchhoff 2005; Nassar 1997; Marchand 2009). Such theologically inspired work deserves fuller research today and may indeed set in motion further revisions to theories of Orientalism.

In the main part of the article I discuss how *Palästinischer Diwan* can be understood through three dominant facets of German Orientalist thought: linguistics, theology, and a field outside academia—namely, mission. In my fourth section I discuss Dalman's actual collecting processes and indeed his contact with singing Palestinians. I close by reflecting briefly on the legacy of the type of research practiced by Dalman and others of his time that has remained alive in conceptions of Palestine ever since.

The Orientalist Diwan

Most obviously, *Palästinischer Diwan* is a collection of song texts gathered in the "Oriental" field. It is apparently, then, exemplary of Oriental linguistics, in which Dalman was well schooled and highly productive. He was indeed already an authority in classical Hebrew and Aramaic when he decided to study Arabic with the Swiss scholar Albert Socin in Leipzig. Socin, who had considerable pedigree as an Orientalist, had settled in Leipzig following a professorship in Oriental languages at Tübingen (1876–1889), had been instrumental in setting up the Deutscher Palästina Verein (German Society for the Exploration of Palestine) in 1877, and had published extensively and regularly in its journal. His Baedecker travel guide was regarded as a standard work for several decades. At the time that he was consulted by Dalman, he was working on the final stages of his monumental collection and analysis of Arabic poetry titled *Diwan aus Centralarabien* (Divan from Central Arabia, 1900), a classic piece of Orientalist linguistic philology. It can serve here as a useful window on that approach and as one context for Dalman's book.

The 300 pages of its part 1 present 112 texts (a combination of poems, prose pieces, and stories collected by Socin in the field) and reproduces seven poems already in the public domain, with the addition of some corrections. Each of the texts is printed in Arabic script, with a transliteration on the opposite page, and is annotated with detailed notes about meter, language, dialect, and occasionally authorship and textual sources. The texts appear, almost without exception, in the order in which Socin collected them and are thus grouped according to the place of collection (Baghdad, Suk al-Shuyukh, Baghdad again, and Mardin). Also included in the volume is an "Excursus," which consists of detailed notes about some objects and concepts encountered in the poems (camels and saddles, for instance, which are also provided with illustrations). Although some of this section relates to use of language, it is primarily contextual in a more material sense, thus offering quasi-ethnographic support for the reader.

Part 2, a further 146 pages, offers German translations of all the texts, with some annotations relating to the meanings of those texts. Part 3, another 350 pages, consists of the introduction, the glossary, indexes, bibliography, and an afterword by the book's editor, Hans Stumme, a student of Socin who took over the final preparations for the publication directly after Socin's death in 1899. Socin's introduction gives an account of existing literature, his sources, and his method, and then goes on to analyze the corpus he has presented in terms of content, form, grammar, pronunciation, prosody, and syntax. Although it contains anecdotes about difficulties in collecting (with deprecating remarks about his informants), its emphasis is formal and focuses on the construction of a system through which the corpus can be rationally categorized. All of this is representative of German Orientalist scholarship of the time.

Dalman acknowledged Socin's help in the introduction to his own *Diwan,* which comes in line with that of Socin by constructing a corpus. Additionally, conforming to Socin's method, it includes materials from a combination of oral and textual sources. In obvious respects Dalman's aim was analogous to that of Socin—namely, preservation and archive creation, a project that he understood as urgent in the context of European colonization of the region. Like Socin, Dalman provided an account of his methods, gave the locations of collection, and offered a classification of his results in terms of poetic content, song types, form, and language. All of this was positioned clearly with reference to scholarly work on Arabic poetry.

The first significant distinction between Socin and Dalman emerges from their selection of texts. Whereas Socin's focus was on city poetry and posited an uncorrupted "original" composition for each of the elaborated poems he gathered from informants, Dalman presented the poetic practices of people he hoped were least influenced by composed poetry, art song, or city life. He sought out material from peasants and Bedouins and constructed it as a permanent accompaniment to their lives from cradle to grave. Where Socin valued original composition (art, even), Dalman sought nature. A second major difference between the two poets is that Dalman's collection could actually contribute very little—perhaps not at all—to the detailed philological research represented by Socin's *Diwan.* Not only is Dalman's main commentary comparatively short (less than thirty-four pages), but also he does not present the poems in Arabic script, just in a transliteration and in German translation. Footnote annotations refer not to scholarly questions of dialect, but specifically to meaning. The textual content is also the basis for thematic groupings of poems.

Part 1, for instance, begins with "Auf Feld und Tenne" (In field and barn), moves through "Beim Pflügen" (Ploughing), "Bei der Ernte" (At harvest), "Beim

Dreschen" (Threshing), toward the final "Auf der Pilgerfahrt" (Making a pilgrimage); part 2 passes through stages of human life from birth to death. Each individual song is also furnished with an individual title in its German version—titles that describe the songs' content as if they were part of a *Lieder* song collection. The place where Dalman collected the song from is provided above the title, sometimes accompanied by the name of the informant, sometimes with the more general descriptor "farmer," "Bedouin," or "leper." On occasion an anecdote is also included, something that would be completely out of place in Socin's work. For instance, the song "Es ging mir unter die Sonne, dunkel ward mir die Nacht" (The sun went down for me, the night became dark) is presented by Dalman with the title "Liebesweh" (Lovesickness) and with a note that he heard a shepherd boy singing it near Essalt, at dusk (1901, 33). In other words, the book is user-friendly to the extent of being almost populist rather than scholarly.

There is yet one more obvious difference between the two works, one where Dalman pushes beyond Socin. This is their treatment of music, for whereas Socin limited himself to the song texts and to describing sounds with words, Dalman did not. Orientalist study of music was not developed to a level that came close to that of language and literature. Nevertheless, Dalman had consulted the several key authorities of the time, both those depending on contemporary experience such as Edward Lane (who wrote on Egypt [1836]) and the philologically based Kiesewetter's *Musik der Araber* (Music of the Arabs, 1842). As mentioned above, Dalman included thirty-two melodies in his collection, two modes or *maqāms* (*bayāt* and *ḥijāz*) in the form of scales, and even provided the tones available on specific instruments (the notes of flute and the double flute, the range of the zither, the open strings of the *ʿūd,* violin, and *rabāb*). See figure 1.1 for the listing of maqāms and instrumental ranges, along with the first five melodies.

In three sections of his introduction devoted to "Poetic Forms," "Rhythm," and "Melodies," Dalman presents some general comments about the material collected. He identified no less than eighteen categories, for instance, including *qaṣīda, mawwāl, ʿatābā, zajal,* and *zalghūtah,* each of which he described briefly in terms of form and context (1901, xiv–xxii). He refrained, however, from attempting to examine the rhythmic nature of most of the songs he heard, explaining that it did not serve the interests of his book and that its challenges would necessitate extensive commentary. He limited himself to some basic observations about syllable counts, meters, and beats in songs where it was clear to him, also noting that poetic meters were often different from the beats in the melody (xxiv).

When it came to melody, Dalman reveals that he had attempted to identify the seventeen pitch levels within the octave that Arabic music theory claimed, but found that musicians in Aleppo came into difficulty when showing him them in practice (xxv–xxvi). Perhaps in response to this result, and his doubt that there really were so many identifiable pitches involved, his own strategy was to seek out similarity, arguing that Arabic intonation was "not far" (*nicht weit*) from West-

— 354 —
I. Tonleitern und Stimmungen.
1. Tonleiter (Bajāt).
2. Tonleiter (Hidğāz).
3. Tonleiter der einfachen Flöte.
4. Doppelflöte.
5. Doppelflöte mit Grundton.
Grundtöne (je nach Verlängerung d. Rohrs).
6. Zither (Ḳānūn).
von
bis
7. Mandoline (ʿŪd).
8. Violine.
9. Bauerngeige (Rabābi).
II. Melodien.
1. Hirtenweise (Belka).
s. 33. Ṛābat ʿa - lai - ji esch - schems waẓlamʿa - lai - ji el - - lēl.
2. Hirtenweise (Belḳa).
3. Schnitterweise (ʿAğlūn).
s. 39. Eḥ-lub la - frē-ğa jā wa - lad
weḥlub la - ha zīd el - ḥa - līb.
s. 7. Jā nā - i - ma nōm eṭ - ṭu - li
wuddaggaʿalburṭum ḥe - li.
4. Tränklied (ʿAğlūn).
Gemächlich.
5. Tränklied (ʿAğlūn).
Rasch.
s. 45. Ğe - dā - li
maschā - riʿ
wēn tar-dīn
mā fīhum ṭīn.
s. 48. Ḥaijhin jōm ğen haij ḥelwāt el - le -
Figure 1.1. Gustaf Dalman's *Palästinischer Diwan* (1901), p. 354.

ern tuning, because some of its instruments were tuned so similarly. He claimed this of the *qānūn and mijwiz,* regional types of zither and flute, and peasant violin (*Bauerngeige*). He then differentiated between instrumental and vocal styles, stating that the intervals of singers varied immensely, and that local informants had told him that they were a matter of "taste" (*Geschmack*).

In consequence of this vagueness, even while Dalman presented interesting observations, his transcriptions are somewhat primitive for their time, not really exploring the nature of the Arabic intonation, rhythm, or ornamentation. To be sure, as he points out in other sections of the introduction, much of what he heard was spontaneous rather than crafted, because he looked mainly for peasant and Bedouin song as opposed to schooled song of urban regions; and it was presumably extremely flexible in terms of pitch, harder to pin down. In one respect his observations are in line with the broader experience of ethnomusicologists and musicians from both his time and our own: Arabic intonation practices have been, and remain, variable and individual (Marcus 1993, 40). Additionally, there are distinctions to be observed between "learned" practices (repertoires of *samāᶜī* and *bashraf*) and oral traditions developed in rural communities (Marcus 1992, 189).

Nevertheless, with respect to historical evidence of Palestinian song, what Dalman's melodies leave us today is rather in question.[2] Songs 23 and 24 are exceptional in that they are notations of a song that remains popular today and that can indeed even be heard sung by Fairouz, "Al-Zaynu" (see figure 1.2). Such a trace may add to discussions of this song's history. Some of the others are recognizable in broad terms as rather typical examples of genres that are still familiar today ("ᶜatābā," for instance). In general, however, Dalman has left us with traces of music that we can access only with great difficulty. The representation of the maqām bayāt as a tempered scale (see figure 1.1 again), for instance, points us in two directions. Most specifically, it indicates that one of Dalman's signs—the F sharp—should actually be taken to represent a different note—namely, an F *half* sharp (for without this, the row of notes would not be maqām bayāt). Indeed the very first song makes sense if read in this way (replacing the F sharp with F half sharp), with a result that it seems to be based on a maqām from the *sīkah* family.

The broader point is that we can read Dalman's notes only extremely loosely. The melodic characters of the first five songs suggest that they draw on members of the maqām sīkah family, and this interpretation can be made to work if we read Dalman's B naturals as B half flats, and his E naturals as E half flats. In other words, we have to change his notation substantially. In effect, we are creating our own musical texts to displace the primary research sources that Dalman offers us. Put differently, we are not using these as historical sources of music, but only witnessing them as signs of a serious struggle between Dalman's knowledge and skill, on the one hand, and the sounds he encountered, on the other. But of course the accurate notation of music was not his fundamental aim.

Figure 1.2. Gustaf Dalman's *Palästinischer Diwan* (1901), p. 360.

The *Diwan* of Revelation

Dalman's initial research was a response to one of the most pressing German debates about the Bible, which concerned the identity of the Song of Songs. An article by the German consul to Damascus, Johann Gottfried Wetzstein, had questioned the canonical status of this book. Basing his argument on songs he had heard at weddings in Syria, Wetzstein asserted that the book was essentially a collection of (secular) wedding songs. (The idea had already been put forward by Johann Gottfried von Herder, but Wetzstein seemed to provide material support [Wetzstein 1873].) Dalman explained in the introduction to his *Diwan* that he had traveled to Palestine with the explicit hope of engaging with this controversy; he intended to compare the Song of Songs with songs in the Palestine region.

The upshot of his research was that he dismissed Wetzstein's thesis. First, while there was no homogeneous practice of love-song singing at weddings in the region, love songs were sung by all groups (including Muslims). Second, he found no specific genre of "wedding song"; love songs were sung often and were associated only with weddings. Third, the content of songs did not correspond neatly to that of the Song of Songs; although bride and groom were occasionally invoked as queen and king, threshing was not mentioned in this connection and indeed for very practical reasons—namely, that weddings tended to happen in the autumn—when threshing was over (Dalman 1901, xi–xii).

Underlying the debate about the Song of Songs, however, was a supposition that Dalman did not relinquish. This is my second point. By the time that Dalman undertook his research, the exact identity of the people on the land had been a subject of (biblically inspired) speculation in Europe and the United States for several decades. Many proposals had been put forward that they were direct descendants of the people who lived on the land *prior to the arrival of the Hebrews* (Goren 2003; Kirchhoff 2005; Löffler 2008). From this perspective, Dalman's interest in people in apparently undeveloped rural areas (as opposed to Socin's preference for urban populations) has more to it than a Rousseau-inspired fascination with the primitive. Although Dalman was opposed to the simplistic connections between Canaanite tribes and the present-day population that circulated in Anglophone circles in particular, he nevertheless argued in his introduction to *Palästinischer Diwan* that the locals would give access to the Bible because they had not been subject to the changes brought about by modernity.

> Even while these [the mind-set and customs of local people] cannot be considered the direct heir or continuation of ancient Israelite or even Canaanite folklore, the tribal relationship and similarity in general life-circumstances have brought such a far-reaching analogy to ways of thinking, living and working, that biblical research cannot find any supporting object-lesson more effective that than of Palestinian folklore. (Dalman 1901, v)

The point of studying the people, then, was to understand the Bible better. In a sense this projected European theology onto the Palestinian population—and then sought to research that projection. But it was more peculiar than that, because the projection was also a real imposition. This is my third point.

In the most basic terms, the projection was an imposition of Christian belief on non-Christians. This third point of intersection with the Bible is in some contradiction to the second, given that it involves imposition upon the people of Palestine (rather than learning from them as they are). It assumed the supremacy of the Bible above all other texts and indeed all cultural practices, and to a large extent it conformed to the New Lutheran movement that had been centered in Leipzig since the 1860s, which struggled to reconcile the historical nature of the Bible with its still-adhered- to transcendence. The key concern had nothing to do with Muslims (Palestine's majority population) but a lot to do with Jews and much to do with the relationship between the Old and New Testaments. Dalman argued that the Old Testament must be approached with historical questions but must never lose its *revelatory* quality (*Offenbarung*). The balance between the two, he argued, could be found by building a particular link between the New and the Old Testaments—namely, by observing that the Old Testament had prophesized Jesus, the community had recognized Jesus as Christ, and Jesus had called the community "Christian." Today's "Christian" community should therefore understand its historically prophesied nature and regard the entire body of scripture as the word of God. This circular process affirming the incontestable truth of Jesus was essentially a rehearsal of his statement some ten years earlier, according to which the history of ancient Israel was a "*revelatory* history" (*Offenbarungs geschichte*), which could not (even in academic work) be separated from belief (*Glaube*) (Männchen 1987, 28, 67).

This point is crucial to the history of Palestine, because it illuminates how early nineteenth-century Christian-Jewish relations in Europe and North America were to have such an impact on the Middle East. At the end of the eighteenth century, a resurgence in religious activity in Europe and North America saw the growth of missionary organizations desirous of converting Jews to Christianity, and this was interconnected with discussions among Protestants about moving Jews to Palestine. Inspired by interpretations of the biblical books of Isaiah (59:20), Jeremiah (31:33), Romans (9–11) and Revelation (20–21), there were proposals that Jews should be gathered together and brought to the Holy Land. The aim was to accelerate a Second Coming (Kirchhoff 2005, 90–92; Löffler 2008, 56; Vreté 1972). Even while the projected date of the Second Coming passed, by the end of the nineteenth century there was a range of settlement projects in Palestine, some commercial, some missionary, some philanthropic or protective (in reaction to persecution of Jews), and some anti-Semitic. This was a Protestant-led movement that focused initially on Jews but predated and fed into Zionism. And as its religious workers spread through Palestine (where the few Jews living there were not interested in converting to Christianity), they adapted and moved opportunistically to gather converts from among Eastern Christian and Catholic churches. One Swiss writer observing the consequent transformation referred to it as a "peaceful crusade" (Tobler 1868, 321–22; for discussion, see Schölch 1986, 68–73).

In line with this broad phenomenon, Dalman's convictions meant that he sought a spiritual transformation of the people of Palestine. For Dalman, Jesus transcended all qualities of the region: "the land that was consecrated by His life, passion, death, and resurrection. All other memories from the time of the Patriarchs to the Crusades pale before this fact, which is comparable in significance only with the creation of the world itself" (1900a, 90–91). And he elaborated the Gospels of Matthew, Mark, and Luke to make clear what he wished would happen: "When will the time come, in which the hidden candle will be placed in the candlestick, and Christians, Jews and Mohammedans will find the bond in the person of Jesus of Nazareth that unites all people?" (175).[3] Although this utopia may seem to take us some way from the *Diwan,* in fact the opposite is the case. Despite its close link with linguistics as discussed above, the *Diwan* could come into being only through

Dalman's concern with the connection between Christians and Jews. He was able to make the trip to Palestine because he won a research grant, which had been awarded by the university for an article he wrote examining the word of Jesus in the light of the Aramaic language and post-canonical rabbinical texts.

Moreover, once in Palestine Dalman's work for the *Diwan* was surrounded with interest in local conversions. Even though he gathered material from both Muslims and Christians on the land, he drew fundamentally on guidance from newly grounded Christian organizations, whether the hospital of the Brüdergemeine mission in Jerusalem, other missions, or churches. Furthermore, while he gathered materials (traveling through Constantinople, Ephesus, Athens, Smyrna, Jerusalem, Tiberius, Safed, Aleppo, Antioch, and regions east of the River Jordan to Damascus), he also preached. Staying for seven months in Aleppo at the Scottish Free Church Mission, he gave sermons every Sunday, usually to Germans (and one Jew), but on occasion to an Arab congregation through an interpreter (Männchen 1987, 60). Bearing all of this in mind, then, it is time to turn to my final context for the *Diwan.*

The Missionary Diwan

Palästinischer Diwan can also be viewed in the context of mission, in which Dalman was steeped until the age of about forty-seven. He had attended a missionary school as a child—namely, the Herrnhuter Brüdergemeine (Moravian Church of Herrnhut)—which also ran the theological seminary where he was a student and then teacher (1874–1877 and 1881–1887, respectively). Founded in 1722, the pietistic Brüdergemeine was the oldest missionary establishment in Germany and led the way with work on Jewish conversion. In this respect it intersected closely with Dalman's other primary institutional affiliation, the Institutum Judaicum in Leipzig, where he taught from 1887 until 1891 and was director from 1893 to 1902. Founded in 1886 by his teacher and later employer, Franz Delitzsch, the Institutum Judaicum was intended to prepare theology students to work as missionaries.

Dalman was one of the first Protestant scholars of Palestine to know Hebrew and study the Talmud (another was Delitzsch). He supported Jewish emancipation and published protests about anti-Semitism, and the fact that he specialized in rabbinical sources probably compromised his academic career.[4] His concern for Jews and Judaism was split two ways, however. His first stance was putatively benevolent, following a Christian duty to comfort Jews (Paul had said that God blessed everybody, *especially* Jews), because Christians should be grateful to Jews for their own existence. Dalman regarded Jews as in need of forgiveness for their original human sinfulness and wished to lead them to Jesus to enable them to transcend this problem. The second strand in his thinking was sharply critical. While he contested racial anti-Semitism, he regarded the Jews' denial of the Second Temple as a fundamental problem; indeed he saw this denial as having led to their persecution. His arguments at times elaborated classic anti-Semitic tropes: Jews were fickle and might convert to Christianity for material reasons, for they had a profiteering nature.[5] Plainly his interest in Hebrew and Judaism was there primarily to serve his interest in conversion and to be disseminated to trainee missionaries. As he himself put it, "If the missionary is to follow modern Jews in their philosophical lines of thought, the Talmudists in their legal quibbling and dodging, and the Cabbalists in their mystical speculations, in order to entice them from there into the 'healthy lesson' of the Gospel, then he must know at least the principles of these fields of Jewish knowledge and thought."[6] All this provides a crucial context to two songbooks that I suggest are miniature precursors to the *Diwan*—namely, Yiddish poetry and song compilations from the Jewish communities of Galicia and Russia (Dalman 1888 and 1893). These are based primarily on scattered textual sources and strive to contribute to a potential library of Yiddish material that would be of both linguistic and ethnological value. Yiddish poetry, Dalman claimed, was one of the few sources of Jews' "*natürliches Empfinden*" (natural sentience), and could thus be a means through which Germans could come to understand Jews. The content of the two compilations overlaps in part, but the later book presents the poems as songs with musical notation, attempting to grasp only their "basic character," stating that their tuning and melodic details were not "fully known." Some of these originally unaccompanied songs appear with harmonic accompaniments.

Dalman's missionary impulse is crystal clear here. Let us not forget that he argued that missionaries should get to know Judaism in order to be equipped to move Jews "beyond" it. In his introduction to the first Yiddish collection, he criticized anti-Semites for drawing exclusively on *old* Jewish songs for their source material. His own purpose, he wrote, was to make *contemporary* Jewish material better known. His collections were there to serve missionaries, then, their user-friendly presentation a pragmatic means to create a usable resource.

They were also there to "serve" Jews, who, he argued, would value a Yiddish "library" greatly. In this light it is striking that the last poem of the first volume, "Israel und sein Maschiach" (Israel and its Messiah) by Mark Löw (presumably a baptized Jew), celebrates the coming of Jesus and that it received special attention from Dalman in his introduction: "Obviously it remains true that only the songs at the end of the collection really solve the riddle of Israel's past, present and future, and *explain clearly what these people need.* The key that the poets of these songs know is Jesus of Nazareth, the 'covenant of the people and the light of the peoples,' in whom all the entwined threads of the world's and the peoples' life are so wonderfully disentangled" (Dalman 1888, vii, my emphasis). His citation is a reworking of Isaiah 42:6, an Old Testament source that Christians such as Dalman read as prophetic of Jesus's coming. Jesus was the covenant that the Lord had promised: "I the LORD have called thee in righteousness, and will hold thine hand and will keep thee, and give thee for a covenant of the people, for a light of the Gentiles" (King James Bible). Dalman was thus providing both a song through which Jews themselves should learn their future, and simultaneously (re-) interpreting a text recognized by Jews, specifically to make it affirm the truth of the future that he envisaged.

Even while *Palästinischer Diwan* offers a great deal more than these little collections, I contend that it has a strong link. First, it reveals the hierarchy within Dalman's thinking that we have already encountered. A development from land to Jesus is reflected in the placing of the Christian songs at the culmination of part 1, which starts with the cultivation of the land and moves to pilgrimage. The two Christian songs that close part 1, each collected from schoolboys in Aleppo, are thus in the very center of the volume.

Second, each of these indicates Dalman's core beliefs. One, associated with St. Barbara's Day (the closest, apparently, that Dalman could get to a Christmas song), mentions a ribbon connected to baptism, while the other, associated with Easter, affirms Dalman's interest yet more transparently, as it addresses Jesus and the conflict between Christians and Jews. The Jews' unhappiness here is set into relief with the happiness of the Christians, as if it is a message from Dalman for Jews to change (see figure 1.3):

> The feast came, we celebrated it.
> We visited the grave of our lord:
> Our Lord is our patron,
> Through his blood he gained us,
> And the Jews are sad,
> But the Christians are happy,
> Your eyes were bursting, oh Jew!
> (Dalman 1901, 161)

The *Diwan* could not present such a clear-cut case of missionary zeal as the Yiddish collections, because the appropriate context—and material—was lacking. Whereas the Yiddish collections emerged from Germany in an environment in which Jews and their conversion was a widespread concern, in Palestine the Ottoman law forbade proselytizing to the majority population, Muslims. Thus Dalman would not have found a Muslim equivalent to "Israel und sein Maschiach" (Israel and its Messiah) in Palestine (and even conceiving such an equivalent is difficult, given that Islam already recognized Jesus; the song would have to renounce Mohammed and go "back"). Additionally, the songs Dalman found could not fit into the sectarian groups that structured his thinking. The texts of only five songs of the several hundred that he included were specifically religious—namely, those in his section "Auf dem Pilgerfahrt" (Making a pilgrimage), three of which were Muslim and two Christian (Dalman 1901, 158–62).

1. Um Ostern.

In Aleppo. Mitgeteilt von christlichen Knaben.

Auwal aḥad — mäsch mäsch
  ṯāni aḥad — tāli mäsch
ṯaliṯ aḥad — tenfaṣṣil elʾoḳmāsch
  rābiʿ aḥad — tanchaijeṭ elʿoḳmäsch
chāmis aḥad — schaʿanīni
  sädis aḥad — nislaḳ bēḍa weniṭlaʿ ʿalbesatīni
aġa-lʿīd ʿaijedna
  zirna ʿala ḳabr saijidna
saijidna maulāna
  bidammu ischtarāna
wiljahūd ḥazāna
  wannaṣāra farḥāna
ṭaḳḳet ʿēnak jājhūda.

Am ersten Sonntag — nichts, nichts,
  am zweiten Sonntag — wieder nichts.
am dritten Sonntag — schneiden wir den Stoff zu.
  am vierten Sonntag — nähen wir den Stoff.
am fünften Sonntag — Palmzweige.[1]
  am sechsten Sonntag — kochen wir Eier und
      gehen in die Gärten.[2]
Es kam das Fest, wir feierten es.
  wir besuchten das Grab unsers Herrn:
unser Herr ist unser Patron.
  durch sein Blut hat er uns erkauft.
und die Juden sind traurig.
  aber die Christen fröhlich.
es platzte dein Auge, o Jude!

Figure 1.3. Gustaf Dalman's *Palästinischer Diwan* (1901), p. 161.

The parallel with the Yiddish collections is nonetheless unmistakable. We might say that *Palästinischer Diwan* projects a moment in which conversions *would* take place in Palestine. Perhaps Dalman even entertained the thought that in a distant post-Ottoman time his book could be of use in converting. His presentation, foregoing Arabic text and technical discussion, is in line with his "handbook" collections of Yiddish material. Also, he proposed that the *Gesangsleben* (song life) could be the "key" to a study of the Palestinian *Volk*'s "inner essence" (*Erfassung seines inneren Wesens*), which is reminiscent of his interest in the "natural sentience" of Jews (Dalman 1901, vi). Moreover, he wrote that it was intended to be "a reliable aid to study" (*ein zuverlässiges Hilfsmittel zu Studien*) (vii), not only for those interested in Oriental linguistics, the Bible, or theology, perhaps, but also for those who had a mission.

The Diwan under Construction

In his introductory account, Dalman gives a brief overview of his sources and the people who helped him in his work. His respect for individual Palestinians is remarkable for a foreigner of his time. British and American writers tended to generalize and criticize, whereas Dalman includes many names and takes trouble to identify all of those who helped him with expanding, improving, and correcting his transcriptions. As a result, we know that he benefited in Jerusalem from the resources of a carpenter from the Galilee called Daniel Abraham; from patients in the lepers hospital run by the Brüdergemeine; one "Reverend Zeller" (presumably a Lutheran pastor); and also a manuscript from Beschara Kanaan, who was a Protestant vicar in Beit Jala. In other places he had a range of help, whether Bedouins, schoolboys, peasants, fishermen, or the two donkey drivers who accompanied him on his travels. He had the whole manuscript checked by more than one Palestinian advisor, including a teacher in Salt called Farah Tabri and Dahoud Sagan from Mtalleh in Southern Lebanon (Dalman 1901, viii–xi).

Nevertheless, Dalman's explanations are at times too romanticized and in general too minimal to allow us to imagine how his encounters unfolded. Yet we can turn to sources from the next stage of his life to explore that issue a little further. In 1902 the German Evangelical Church founded an Institute for Archaeology of the Holy Land in Jerusalem, where Dalman was director until 1917. This initiative was already mooted at the time of the German emperor's much-celebrated visit in 1898 (Berman 1998, 142; Goren 2003, 347). Dalman was the only employee in permanent residence at the institute (he had to leave because of the war in 1914), but he hosted a group of visiting researchers every year. Thus he generally invited one senior scholar to be with him for nine months, and six less-experienced researchers (often pastors) to visits for periods of three to five months. He created a curriculum and led them on trips through the region, also editing an annual collection of research papers (Goren 2003, 350–51). Ultimately this meant that he disseminated his ideas both in Palestine and in Germany (and probably beyond).

The move to Jerusalem marks a distinct caesura in Dalman's approach in that his main interest was no longer a mission to the Jews but the development of research at the institute (Männchen 1987, 142–43). The key components of this can be found in a short text he published in 1913, in which he stated that it was axiomatic that researchers apprehend Palestine as the location of sacred history and bring with them their entire inner being ("*den Gesamten inneren Menschen*"). This supplied a bedrock, he wrote, to which they should add all means of scientific inquiry. They would be in a position thereby to encounter "the spirit of the *divine revelation*" within the sacred history. This would be the ultimate goal of the research process (Dalman 1913, 4, my emphasis).[7]

This framework shaped the institute's methods of handling music, because the basic task was to bring it into a form in which it could add to an archive of material and enrich Christians' encounter with the Bible (essentially adding to the archive that *Palästinischer Diwan* had launched). And there were four basic reasons why the project could not be very successful.[8] First, none of the writers who attempted the project were trained to generate musical texts. The Reverend Raimund Graf noted that Dalman wanted him to collect songs and also helped and guided his efforts to gather texts and melodies (Graf 1917 and 1918.). It is not entirely clear why Dalman did not use the recording equipment at his disposal during 1912, for even when the collecting work involved sessions arranged specially for local people to come and "deliver" music, Graf was ill-equipped.[9] On one trip in which he tried to amass a collection of ᶜatābā, he could not persuade musicians to repeat themselves, and sometimes they were not in the mood to sing (Graf 1917).[10] He also hoped to be able to rely on a harmonium on one occasion but had to make do without (Graf 1918, 127). As he said blithely, this did have the advantage that his ear wouldn't be influenced by the fixed pitches of the harmonium, but it meant that everyone had to be very patient. He suggested (perhaps rather ungratefully) that one of the informants was not over-endowed with this quality, for he sang for only "a few hours."

From Graf's reports we encounter not only the practical difficulties but a second obstacle too—namely, that musicians themselves could not be expected to serve the primary goal of the institute very well. When he witnessed the prearranged performance of Isid ibn Hasan, Graf was significantly dismayed (1918, 127–29). He had established a fee for the performance before the musician began, after which he had allowed himself to be swept away by his sense that the musician's soul melted into his instrument. Graf perceived that ibn Hasan became increasingly passionate, created a dialogue with music, and varied the tone color and strength. His body was rocked by his passionate expression of love. Yet Graf then learned from the landlord standing by, who was laughing, that the song was actually a direct request to Graf himself. The musician had made an appeal for a new overcoat. Graf was further taken aback when ibn Hasan responded to his attempt to notate the next melody by asking for an increased fee. This action, reported Graf, was repeated after the ensuing song too. On leaving the house, ibn Hasan apparently helped himself to a bag of onions. Graf was startled once again. There was no sight or sound of divine revelation.

Third, writers' own responses to music were outside the framework set out for the institute, because they were highly emotional. Indeed they led on occasion to fantastical entry points into the Bible and a facile style of reportage from which Dalman generally set the institute apart.[11] For example, Baumann wrote of Arabic song that it seemed "to our ears" to be highly monotonous, but the longer one listened to it, the more interesting it became, and the same thing was the case with what he described as the "almost unbearable twanging and screeching" (*Näseln und schreien*) (Baumann 1908, 70). As he sat and watched dancers in the flickering firelight and heard the trilling of women singing the background,

> I gave in entirely to the undeniable poetry of the event. In silent grandeur the starry heaven of Abraham arched over this piece of holy land, intimately closed in by the darkness of night, whose children had amiably set to their unsophisticated festivities without a care, unaware of the doubts and responsibilities of European Culture. (Baumann 1908, 71–72)

Toward the end of an extensive description of dancing, singing groups of men and women, the author remarked, "*So hatten wir das Schauspiel vor uns*" (Thus we had the spectacle before us), comparing the practices to passages from the Bible and moving swiftly into a mode of writing akin to historical fiction. Even though there was little left on the land to show the earlier Christian presence, he said, the promise of the Patriarch and the continuation through father and son was what provides the joy of the peasants. Despite the confusion of peoples over the centuries, he said, a drop of "ancient Israelite blood" has surely remained, a drop of *Lebensfreude* (joie de vivre) that lives in the present, untroubled by past and future (Baumann 1908, 74).[12]

Perhaps the main significance of such emotion is not that it was out of line with the pleasures of song in Palestine, but that it challenged the researchers' adherence to their Protestant ethos. Dalman realized that he himself, on experiencing a *dhikr* (remembrance/recitation ceremony), found the movements, drumming, and coloratura singing were affecting and went on to explain that during the ceremony "the barriers between man and God are to be broken through in unmediated experience" (Dalman 1917b, 27). He also stated that this overflowed true Islam, demonstrating the need to come closer to God. This willingness to give full consideration to local quests for the divine is remarkable for Europeans of the time.

Yet Dalman closed his reflection with a key theological concern—namely, that whether God really began where human consciousness ended was a separate question. While music was an important enhancement of an experience of Palestine and the Bible, and was something of which he acknowledged emotional impact, Dalman did not trust it. He separated his theological reflections and his quest to grasp the revelation of Jesus on the land from such directly emotional impressions.

If this returns us to my underlying thesis, that the search for revelation was too proscriptive to allow for a very rich musical discovery, it also brings me to my fourth point in this section, that of theological competition with Islam. Dalman found the massed gathering of Muslims to prayer affecting, yet said that it recalled the "discipline with which Islam holds its adherents to violence, which led it once to armed battle against paganism, Synagogue and Church" (Dalman 1917b, 26–27). He also noted that Muslims were "still" hostile toward Christianity. The solution he recommended was to exemplify another way of persuasion, which was precisely the sort of work that his institute led. He and his visitors traveled through the land accompanied by Muslims, he said, and despite the differences between them, they worked together. The future of the Holy Land should be like that, he said; it would be peaceful coexistence between Christianity and Islam. "Then it will become apparent," he wrote, "who the greater Muslim, meaning devout, is—the prophet of Mecca or the crucified Nazarene" (34). Through collaborative research of his theology, then, the superiority of life with Jesus might become apparent of its own accord. Wherever he traveled Dalman did indeed strive to leave evidence that he and his companions were God-fearing and laid trust in their Savior. The activity, he explained, was connected to the institute's position within the German evangelical colony (Dalman 1913, 4; 1917a, 4–5).

It is unlikely that Dalman's Muslim companions and helpers would have escaped his singing, because his education in the Brüdergemeine entailed an intense and highly developed musical practice. Music was certainly a component of social meetings in his Jerusalem home, which had a piano and which his wife used for choir rehearsals (Männchen 1993, 57).[13] Moreover, given that he and his visiting scholars prayed together morning and night when on field trips, they most probably sang together too.[14] They certainly sang as they walked and at particular points on their journeys. One mentioned in his report that the bright tenor voice of one member of the party had kept them in good spirits even when they got drenched by rain, for instance, and it seems unlikely that this "Colleague Schmalz" was the only one to sing (Graf 1917, 129). The same writer remarked that as they walked, "*Großer Gott, wir loben dich*" (Holy God, We praise Thy Name) rang out over the land of the Jordan. His historical interest in pilgrimage song is also suggestive; within his description of a very cold night close to the town of Quneitra, he included the text of a song about the cold that had been sung by a pilgrim there in 1690 (Graf 1917, 137–38, 123). And on at least one occasion the researchers exchanged songs with Bedouins from whom they received hospitality (Gustavs 1913, 166). All in all, then, the institute was part of a rather complex exchange process, projecting itself not only physically, but also through music, into the environment that it sought to discover.

One final strand in Dalman's writings requires exposure here—namely, his position with respect to modernization and settlement in Palestine and his concerns about Christian and Jewish settlement. From these we can trace his resistance to Zionism in its secularized variants, which he saw as displacing the development of Palestine with culture from Europe. His arguments took a strongly preservationist attitude, arguing that the country was very small and that its "grace" was only a product of its history. That history—indeed that revelation—was what really mattered (Dalman 1917c, 48).

Dalman proposed therefore that the function of Palestine and its people was to be the *Denkmal* (Memorial), *Zeuge* (Witness), and *Erklärer* (Clarifier) of the history. We might well understand this proposal as one for a museum. It seems to deny Palestine a living political existence, which is a problem that remains pressing today. In his most pointed statement, Dalman remarked that if Jerusalem became another Berlin or Vienna, if the country gave more space to plants imported from Australia and California than to indigenous ones, if Zionists replaced the melancholy ditty of the shepherd's pipe with their Polish compositions, then Palestine would cease to offer the world anything (Dalman 1917c, 49).

Several Arab writers took up the thread of Dalman's work and published in the British-sponsored *Journal of the Palestine Oriental Society.* Developing an authenticist discourse about indigenous customs in rural populations, like Dalman they identified parallels between biblical narratives and ways of life in rural Palestine of the day. Two of Stephan H. Stephan's articles are particularly telling. In one he identified resemblances between the Song of Songs and seventy-seven songs from Palestinian folklore (thus following up on Dalman's inquiry of 1899 directly) (Stephan 1922). In the other he presented local nursery rhymes and songs as historical materials whose artlessness was to be cherished. They represented ideas "whose origin may sometimes be traced to ancient antiquity" and that "reveal the thought of the people to a greater extent than do the songs, of which it can sometimes be said that they are composed chiefly for the sake of the rhyme" (Stephan 1932, 62). Stephan's interest here, too, was in line with Dalman's as expressed in *Palästinischer Diwan.*

What such writers also took from Dalman—and from other Europeans of the time—was an interest in the Palestinian peasant, whose life radiated an "uncontaminated patriarchal Palestinian atmosphere," which was "fading away" with Westernization.[15] Their perspective involved a clear binary construction between the (scientific) writers themselves on the one hand, and the (natural) peasants on the other, in tandem with the attitude of Europeans. The most prolific of the writers was Protestant physician Tawfiq Canaan, who distanced himself from his subject quite emphatically, stating that it was not easy "to gain the confidence of the *fallaḥ* to such a degree that he will speak freely and with detail" (Canaan 1927, v). And essentially the function of the peasants in Canaan's work was the same as in colonial missionary accounts: to justify the presence of people on the land through their relationship to ancient texts.

But here his angle is significant, for he embraced not only traces of the Judaic and Christian Bibles but also the presence of the Qurʾān and Islamic practices; he sought legitimation, then, for Muslims and the practice of Islam on the land. His main contribution was indeed a monograph with the title *Mohammedan Saints and Sanctuaries in Palestine.* The title radiates the separatist vocabulary of the "master code" ("Mohammedanism" being a common misnomer for Islam)—and thus speaks in the language of colonial law—and yet also makes maximally visible the majority population. The book contains detailed ethnographic discussion and a large range of song texts, along with descriptions of singing in ceremonies. This lends the Muslim population texture and audibility that it lacks in other sources. Alongside references to the Christian Bible, the book includes quotations from the Qurʾān.

Canaan's decision to publish in English (and that he and the writers with whom he associated presented their work in foreign journals), indicates his concern to present a case to the colonial forces who were deciding the fortunes of the region. Salim Tamari describes the movement with which he was associated as an attempt to "establish sources of legitimation for Palestinian cultural patrimony (and *implicitly* for a Palestinian national identity that began to distance itself from greater Syria and Arab frameworks)" (Tamari 2009, 95, my emphasis). Yet we do well to pay attention to the very complex—and by no means entirely comfortable—heritage of such thinking in European philology, theology, Jewish mission, and the preservation of Palestine as a site of "revelation." And we do well to consider the difficulty that the "biblical" identity for Palestine presents for political agency today.

Notes

1. Material from this chapter has been previously published in Rachel Beckles Willson's *Orientalism and Music Mission: Palestine and the West.*

2. This paragraph is indebted to my discussions with two Palestinian musicians, Issa Boulos and Nizar Rohana. The discussions were completely independent, starting with a request that they each tell me how they understood the melodies. Each musician interpreted Dalman's notations in the same way. I am particularly grateful to Issa Boulos, who went through all Dalman's songs with me (Jericho, January 2012) and subsequently sent me several of his own reconstructions of some of them as mp3 files.

3. This is a reference to the Gospels that relate Jesus's explaining that the candle of faith should not be hidden, but placed in a candlestick in order to bring light to the house. See Matthew 4:20–22, Mark 4:20–24, and Luke 8:15–18 and 11:32–34.

4. It precluded his being considered for a full professorship at a German university, for instance (he worked as an extraordinary professor at the Theological Faculty of Leipzig University from 1885 onward, gaining a teaching assignment for Hebrew and Aramaic grammar). See Männchen 1987, 60–62. For detailed discussion of the broader situation regarding the research of Judaism of Germany, see Wassermann 2002.

5. At base this reveals a social anxiety about the rise of the bourgeois Jewish community and the threat it could pose to the educated Protestants of Germany (Männchen 1987, 87–88).

6. Dalman, *Kurzgefaßtes Handbuch der Mission unter Israel,* 46, quoted in Männchen 1987, 82.

7. It is by no means easy to grasp quite what he meant. He understood the spirit of historical revelation he sought as distinct from its "outer facts" (*äußerliche Tatsachen*) or "conditions" (*Bedingnisse*). He identified a resultant paradox in the working process—namely, that one had to engage with the "external conditions" of the history in order to encounter its spirit. These external conditions were not only archaeological remains but all aspects of the land and its people. His account must also be understood in the context of his belief in the ways that the spirit of God worked through human beings. See Männchen 1987, 67–68.

8. Kahle's work also fits into this mold by reproducing song texts. Articles by several other writers do too. See Baumann 1908, Graf 1917 and 1918, and Rothstein 1910.

9. Correspondence between Dalman, Erich von Hornbostel (founder of the Phonogramm-Archiv in Berlin), and the cantor Abraham Zvi Idelsohn reveals that Dalman agreed to make recordings for Hornbostel but then passed the equipment to Idelsohn because he had had no time to undertake the work. Correspondence stored in the Idelsohn collection at the Berliner Phonogramm-Archiv (Abteilung Musikethnologie, Medien Technik). Thanks to Susanne Ziegler for her help with the collection.

10. This article contains descriptions of difficulties with notation and Dalman's help therewith. See Graf 1917, 118–19 and 130–31.

11. He stated that the institute's role was not to gain experiences that were only "*phantasie- and gefühlsmäßig.*" Dalman 1913, 4.

12. Dalman's apologia for Baumann's illustrative (and fantastical) writing can be traced in his introduction to the volume in which this appeared. Reflecting on the many travelogues appearing in Europe that were "empty if not misleading," he stated that those appearing in the *Palästinajahrbuch* could be corrective because they would be properly researched. Dalman 1908, 1.

13. Männchen refers to *Hausmusik* and Dalman playing the piano. Dalman's wife expanded a male quartet into a choir, which sang at missionary evenings and gave concerts connected to the Swedish mission.

14. One traveler's diary included a list of biblical texts used as the basis of prayer for every morning and evening. See Siegesmund 1911.

15. Canaan opens "Light and Darkness in Palestine Folklore" (1931a) by referring to "the present inhabitants of Palestine (who are in many respects as primitive as their ancestors of two thousand years ago)." Elsewhere he writes, "Immutability is the most striking characteristic of eastern life, and the inhabitants of the Near East may not and dare not deviate from the traditional path of their ancestors." Canaan 1931b.

References

Baumann, Eberhard. 1908. "Zur Hochzeit geladen: Bilder von einer ländlichen moslemischen Hochzeitsfeier. Palästinajahrbuch, no. 4, 67–76.

Beckles Willson, Rachel. 2013. Orientalism and Music Mission: Palestine and the West. Cambridge, UK: Cambridge University Press.

Ben-Arieh,Yehoshua. 1986. *Jerusalem in the 19th Century: Emergence of the New City.* New York: St. Martin's Press.

Berman, Nina. 1998. "K. u. K. Colonialism: Hofmannsthal in North Africa." New German Critique 75 (Autumn): 3–27.

———. 2004. *Impossible Missions? German Economic, Military, and Humanitarian Efforts in Africa.* Lincoln: University of Nebraska Press.

Canaan, Tawfiq. 1922. "Haunted Springs and Water Demons in Palestine." *Journal of the Palestine Oriental Society,* no. 2, x–xx.

———. 1927. *Mohammedan Saints and Sanctuaries in Palestine.* Jerusalem, Palestine: Syrian Orphanage Press.

———. 1931a. "Light and Darkness in Palestine Folklore." *Journal of the Palestine Oriental Society,* no. 11, 15–36.

———. 1931b. "Unwritten Laws Affecting the Arab Women of Palestine." *Journal of the Palestine Oriental Society,* no. 11, 172–203.

Dalman, Gustaf, ed. 1888. *Jüdischdeutsche Volkslieder aus Galitzien und Russland* (Schriften des Institutum Judaicum in Leipzig 20/21). Leipzig, Germany: Centralbureau der Inst. Judaica (W. Faber).

———, ed. 1893. *Jüdische Melodien aus Galizien und Rußland. Zum ersten Male aufgezeichnet und unter Mitwirking von Halfden Jebe aus Drontheim herasugegeben.* (Schriften des Institutum Judaicum in Berlin 17). Leipzig, Germany: H. Reuther.

———. 1900. "Auf alten Pfaden." *Saat auf Hoffnung*37 (2): 82–99, 173–75, 216–24.

———. 1901. *Palästinischer Diwan. Als Beitrag zur Volkskunde Palästinas.* Leipzig, Germany: J. C. Hinrichs'sche Buchhandlung.

———. 1908. "Jahresbericht des Institutes für das Arbeitsjahr 1907/08." (mit Karte) *Palästinajahrbuch,* no. 4, 1–20.

———. 1913. "Das religiöse Ziel unserer Arbeit." *Palästinajahrbuch,* no. 9, 3–5.

———. 1917a. "Jahresbericht des Institutes für as Arbeitsjahr 1916/17." *Palästinajahrbuch* no. 13, 3–15.

———. 1917b. "Arbeit aus dem Institut." *Palästinajahrbuch* no. 13, 15–52.

———. 1917c. "Die Juden in Palästina und die Zukunft des Landes." *Palästinajahrbuch* no. 13, 35–52.

Goren, Haim. 2003. *"Zieht hin und erforscht das Land." Die deutsche Palästinaforschung im 19. Jahrhundert.* Translated from Hebrew by Antje Clara Naujoks, with a foreword by Mosche Zuckerman. Göttingen, Germany: Wallstein Verlag.

Graf, Raimund. 1917. "Durch das Heilie Land westlich und östlich des Jordans im Jahre 1911." *Palästinajahrbuch,*no. 13, 3–138.

———. 1918. "Ostertage auf dem Gebirge Ephraim." *Palästinajahrbuch,*no. 14, 111–34.

Gustavs, Arnold. 1913. "Am Jarmuk bei Beduinen zu Gast," *Palastinajahrbuch,* no. 9, 157–68.

Kiesewetter, R. G. 1842. *Die Musik der Araber.* Wiesbaden, Germany: Liepzig, Breitkopf und Härtel.

Kirchhoff, Markus. 2005. *Text zu Land. Palästina im wissenschaftlichen Diskurs, 1865–1920.* (Schriften des Simon-Dubnow-Instituts Herzaugegeben von Dan Diner 5). Göttingen, Germany: Vandenhoeck and Ruprecht.

Löffler, Roland. 2008. *Protestanten in Palästina. Religionspolitik, Sozialer Protestantismus und Mission in den deutschen evangelischen und anglekanischen Institutionen des Heiligen Landes, 1917–1939.* Stuttgart, Germany: Kohlhammer.

Männchen, Julia. 1987. *Gustav Dalmans Leben und Wirkung in der Brüdergemeinde, für die Judenmission und an der Universität Leipzig, 1855–1902.* (Abhandlungen des Deutschen Palästinavereins). Wiesbaden: Harrassowitz.

———. 1993. *Gustaf Dalman als Palastinawissenschaftler in Jerusalem und Greifswald, 1902–1941.* (Abhandlungen des Deutschen Palastinavereins). Wiesbaden: Harrassowitz.

Marchand, Suzanne L. 2009. *German Orientalism in the Age of Empire: Religion, Race, and Scholarship* (Publications of the German Historical Institute). Cambridge, UK: Cambridge University Press.

Marcus, Scott L. 1993. "The Interface between Theory and Practice: Intonation in Arab Music." *Asian Music* 24 (2): 39–58.

———. 1992. "Modulation in Arab Music: Documenting Oral Concepts, Performance Rules, and Strategies." *Ethnomusicology* 36 (2): 171–95.

Nassar, Issam. 1997. Photographing Jerusalem. The Image of the City in Nineteenth-Century Photography. Boulder, CO: East European Monographs/Columbia University Press.

Rothstein, Gustav, ed. 1910. "Moslemische Hochzeitsgebräuche in Lifta bei Jerusalem. Arabischer Text mit Übersetzung." Palästinajahrbuch 6, 102–36.

Schölch, Alexander. 1986. *Palästina im Umbruch. Untersuchung zur wirtschaftlichen und sozio-politischen Entwicklung.* (Berliner Islamstudien). Stuttgart, Germany: Franz Steiner Verlag.

Siegesmund, Reverend. 1911. "Ein Frühlingsritt am 'äußersten Meer.'" Palästinajahrbuch, 123–54.

Socin, Albert. 1900. *Diwan aus Centralarabien.* Collected, translated, and commented on by Socin, edited by H. Stumme. Leipzig, Germany: B. G. Teubner.

Stephan, Stephan Hanna. 1922. "Modern Palestinian Parallels to the Song of Songs." *Journal of the Palestine Oriental Society* 2 (4): 199–278.

———. 1932. "Palestinian Nursery Rhymes and Songs." *Journal of the Palestine Oriental Society,* no. 12, 62–85.

Tamari, Salim 2009. Mountains against the Sea: Essays on Palestinian Society and Culture. Berkeley: University of California Press.

Tobler, Titus. 1868. *Nazareth in Palästina. Nebst Anhang der vierten Wanderung.* Berlin: G. Reimer.

Vreté, Mayir. 1972. "The Restoration of the Jews in English Protestant Thought, 1790–1840." *Middle Eastern Studies* 8 (1): 3–50.

Wassermann, Henry. 2002. "The *Wissenschaft des Judentums* and Protestant Theology: A Review Essay." *Modern Judaism,* no. 22, 83–98.

Wetzstein, Johann Gottfried. 1873. "Die Syrische Dreschtafel." *Zeitschrift für Ethnologie,* no. 5, 270–302.

2

A Musical Catastrophe: The Direct Impact of the Nakba on Palestinian Musicians and Musical Life

Nader Jalal and Issa Boulos interviewed by Heather Bursheh

Along with having worked at the Palestinian Ministry of Culture and more recently founding and running Nawa, the Palestinian Association for Cultural Development, Nader Jalal has spent most of his adult life interviewing and collecting stories from Palestinian musicians and their families and colleagues, amassing an enormous archive of previously unrecorded information about musicians who were active before and after the *Nakba* (catastrophe) of 1948. Issa Boulos is a Palestinian musician, composer, and scholar from Ramallah, now head of the Arab Music department at the Qatar Music Academy. Nader Jalal and Issa Boulos were interviewed in April 2012.

The discussion centers on the music scene in Palestine before the Nakba and focuses to some extent on two major British-owned radio stations: Idhāᶜat al-Quds (Jerusalem Radio) and Idhāᶜat al-Sharq al-ᵓAdná (Near East Radio). The Nakba, and its catastrophic effect on the radio stations, musical life in Palestine, and the musicians who created it, is then described.

Heather Bursheh: Let's talk first about the music scene in Palestine before 1948. Can you describe broadly what it comprised?

Nader Jalal: We have little information about the music scene before 1900, and we don't seem to have a lot of information on the period between 1900 and 1936 in all sectors, but there is information about some of the fields related to music, especially in the context of folklore and heritage material. What I want to do is investigate the music scene before 1948 and track how it was dispersed after 1948, and then try to follow the musicians who were involved in the scene and highlight their productions. In this context we talk about music not only in general terms, classical, folk, or the genres involved; we are in fact talking about a musical life that goes beyond music itself. Folkloric elements in music might not reflect professionalism at the musical level, but it is the musical expressions of the people that make music part of the larger social picture. The broadcasting industry started in Palestine after 1936, and the music practitioners attached to it were described as professional. However, people of course listened to music before 1936, but through different ways and via diverse means, including Radio Cairo or London. There was a musical life in Palestine before 1936, and Palestinians used music to express what they went through, including the national issues that often had priority after World War I, as a result of the Palestinians fearing for the loss of their homeland. And therefore the subjects in the foreground for Palestinian singers, popular or professional, in the city or the countryside, became nationalistic subjects first and foremost.

Issa Boulos: When we talk about music in general, around 1900 there was not much difference between the musical models and forms used in Greater Syria in general. You would find *mayjanā* and *ʿatābā,* and *zajal* [forms of various folk songs] anywhere in the region; music was happening everywhere. If the setting is urban or rural, it did not matter; music happened where there were events such as weddings, deaths, circumcisions, engagements, harvest seasons, planting seasons, festivals, and hunting. It all has repertoire associated with it, and the lyrics change with time. The lyrics were what made people differentiate between one song and another, although the melody might have resembled many other popular melodies. There's something important related to dance and music: what we now call folklore was material not only practiced in the villages. It was also practiced in the cities and urban centers, and we have evidence that people in the cities had models which we would now consider folkloric musical material. At the same time, there were people interested in different types of music—there were families who played organ in churches, or piano at home, especially with the strong presence of different ethnic groups such as the Armenians, particularly in Jerusalem. It must be noted that the first official Armenian presence in Jerusalem was in the third century. So the Armenians did not only appear in Jerusalem after the Armenian genocide [by the Ottomans after World War I], but well before that. And this is only an example: there are plenty of other ethnic groups that passed through or sustained a presence in Palestine that contributed to the music scene enormously, including some that sustained consistent involvement in music. So there was always something new coming from European or other societies to the area here, as the minorities moved around, whether they were Greeks or Armenians, Turks or Russians. And there was also classical Arab music. Thomson, in one of his books written in the second half of the nineteenth century [Thomson 1859], describes a trip he made to Jerusalem, and a visit to one of the coffee shops, and he describes the instruments of the Arabic *takht* [ensemble], playing what seem to have been the Ottoman and Arab classical forms such as *samāʿī, longa* and *muwashshaḥ,* and so on.

NJ: Folklore is the widest pool of material used by the people, and its accessibility allows people to participate in it. Folkloric tunes are often composed in a communal way, and because the melody is simple, it is easy for it to move around, and easy to add to it, so the *dalʿūnā* [a folk song form], for example, becomes hundreds of thousands of verses, not a song in four sections. And this is the case for all the songs we know. And all ages and both genders were participating in them. The songs were living amongst the people. Mothers would sing their babies to sleep: this practice has a song genre attached to it. The children who play in the neighborhood had their own specific songs for catching birds and setting traps; they sang to the bird to entertain themselves and to bring the bird down from its nest. So all the age groups have their own means of expression through song, and they are divided according to the occasion: there are songs for fun, songs for games, songs for work, songs for occasions, songs for festivals, et cetera. Now, in order to understand the scene well, there are issues that we have to conceptualize in the same way they were understood back at that time, not necessarily the way we understand them now. Nowadays, for instance, when we attempt to put on a festival, it serves a certain purpose. Back then a festival would have more of a social purpose, such as the festivities associated with the Nabī Mūsā and the Nabī Ṣāliḥ seasons [the prophets Moses and Saleh]. Magicians, clowns, musicians, and ordinary people used to take part of the festivities. The *dabke* [folk dance] groups were not rehearsed especially for the event or organized as part of the programming, because the whole town practiced dabke, and the idea of having such a practice canonized or staged wasn't in their minds. So you had, for example, the guys from ʿIsawīyah with the guys from al-Ramleh and so on, and they would compete. So maybe the group from Dayr Ṭarīf had a great *mijwiz* [single-reed woodwind folk instrument] player, so they would compete without there being prizes. But everyone in the festival would know, for example, "the group from Bayt Dajjan taught us a lesson." "They taught us a lesson," or just "got served," was like taking the first prize in our modern understanding. So "public music," if we can call it that, or the expression of the people through music and song, was present. I also read about a festival in 1904 which took place in Haifa. It was for folk poetry mainly, for zajal, and people came from as far as Saudi Arabia, Syria, and Lebanon to participate in it, singers and poets. We also didn't mention that Um Kulthoum sang in Haifa, and the person that coined the term *"kawkab al-sharq"* [the star of the east] for her was a Palestinian woman from Haifa.

IB: Now, music within urban circles: it's true that the economy of the country was to an extent dependent on farming. But after the First World War, the British started building roads, building railways, building large service buildings and factories, and a need grew for people to make furniture, and metalworkers, so manufacturers began to appear. These kinds of new activities changed the economic structure that people were used to, and therefore all the signs of a middle class started to emerge. The middle class and aristocracy began to grow, quite differently to the feudal class which was prevalent at that time. All the landowners from the plains, from the most spacious areas for farming, had been feudal landowners, five or six families maybe controlled the plains. Now, in city centers, people started working in, for example, gold manufacturing. People were working in dried foods—Jerusalemites were famous for that—and perfume, this kind of thing. Now, Arab classical music, from its earliest days in this area, always had ties to the aristocratic class. Inasmuch as it was played in the coffee shops, you would also find it in the homes of the rich. [Wasif] Al-Jawhariyyah in his memoirs describes Ottoman Jerusalem and what kind of music was there, what kind of repertoire was being performed [Tamari and Nassar 2003]. During that period the country was not isolated from what was happening in Egypt, or Syria and Iraq and what was happening in other areas, and the area was still open to more influences. So for them, the person who went from Jerusalem to Beirut was just like someone going from Ramallah to Jerusalem today. They were all present in the same area and dealt with it as such. Going to Beirut was just going to another city, where the accent is just a little different.

NJ: As we said, music was living everywhere in Palestine, in the cities and the countryside. I think there is more than one pattern relating to *how* music was living. Prior to 1936 in Palestine, there are limited musical productions that were present at the time and they were primarily carried by amateurs—music lovers and enthusiasts—not by professional musicians. There were *ʿūd* [short-necked lute] players, *qānūn* [zither] players, and *sanṭūr* [dulcimer] and violin players, and there is evidence of exchanges of experiences with other visiting musicians that used to come to Palestine for work. There were many musicians working in Palestine; those include Sami al-Shawwa, Ibrahim Abd al-Al, many of the Egyptian musicians, Mohammad Hasanain, Sayyid al-Safti, Um Kulthoum, Mohammad Abd al-Wahab, and that was all before 1936.

IB: I would argue that there were some local experts or professionals as well. We can indeed claim that Wasif Jawhariyyah was an expert as a professional musician, although he made his living otherwise.

NJ: This is what I mean about the definition of professionalism. Professionalism doesn't mean that it was his main job and he had a studio and an agent—this is a modern concept. Wasif Jawhariyyah was an excellent ʿūd player and was, if you like, more like culturally active, musically active. He hosted players; he made sure to bring musicians through his contacts, and they would play in his coffee shop. Or he would market their concerts for somebody else, in the Maʿārif coffee shop or in a particular hotel, or in the house of one of the rich. And it's not necessarily true that because the music was for the elite, the musicians were also from the elite. Yahya al-Saudi, a great musician at the time, was a shoemaker and was poor. So we can say that musicians marketed their music to the elite, who would offer them a place, a stage, maybe dinner. I think Palestine was a musical platform, in some way or another. Because it was economically active, and economic activity contributed to attracting artists from Egypt, Iraq, and Syria. Because, for example, there was a theater in Jaffa, there was a cinema, and there were three or four cinemas in Jerusalem and in Haifa—this essentially helped to bring Um Kulthoum, Abd al-Wahab, Mohammad Abd al-Muttalib, Mohammad al-Ashiq, Sayyid al-Safti, Abd al-Hayy Hilmi. Palestine was a showcase for great artists. Some of them would visit for short periods, and would mix with the local musicians like Tawfiq Jawhariyyah, the nāy [reed flute] player Wasif Jawhariyyah, and Jalil Rukab. There were short visits: Um Kulthoum visited Palestine in 1927 and again in the '30s; Mohammad Abd al-Wahab in 1927 and in the '30s; and there were people that would come here and stay for tens of years. There were singers and musicians: Mohammad Hasanain, for example, came once, then twice, and then stayed in Palestine. He left in 1948. He was singing *tawashīḥ* and then started singing *muwashshaḥāt* [forms of Arab song] and so on. So there was the appearance and involvement of classical music as well. But Arab music, the classical music, called for certain set of skills and professionalism. Professional in the sense of the study of music, for example, the use of new instruments, different from the folkloric instruments, in addition to the ʿūd. For example, one Armenian from Jerusalem, called Artin, was an excellent sanṭūr player, and he became part of the team in Radio Jerusalem.

IB: The Armenians were very close to Ottoman culture, so many were ʿūd players. Several ʿūd makers in Jerusalem were Armenians.

NJ: And the person who made instruments might also work as a carpenter, because if he wanted to sell one or two ʿūds, he wouldn't make enough of a living for the whole year.

HB: Tell me more now about the radio stations: Idhāʿat al-Quds (Jerusalem Radio) and Idhāʿat al-Sharq al-ʾAdná (Near East Radio). When were they established, why, by whom, and so on?

NJ: Jerusalem Radio was established in 1936. Of course, some of the sources say that the mandate government established it in order to publicize its policies.

IB: The British said that they were doing it as a gesture of good intention. Because after the lack of confidence that ensued in the area after the 1936 strike, which went on for six months, the British tried to say to the Arabs and the locals here, "Let's work together and try to do something good, et cetera, and we are ready to open it for you, and you can do whatever you like."

HB: So this was a British-run radio but broadcasting only in Arabic? Or also in Hebrew and in English?

IB: All three. The daily programming was divided into three periods. There was the Arabic section of the radio, and it had its center and its building and its team. And they were monitored by the British official bodies. The first director was Ibrahim Touqan; he was a poet, one of the most important poets of Palestine at the time. The British were constantly after him, until they finally fired him, because he was single-minded about the question of Palestinian affairs. And this was all before 1948, because all these plots against Palestinians were increasing at that time, from land confiscation to Jewish immigration to the area and so on. There were sometimes skirmishes—people from the Hebrew section would come and protest to the mandate and tell them "those people are using the word 'Palestine' without saying anything else." So one side was calling it Palestine, and the other side was calling it something else. So there was a unique experience where a radio station was broadcasting certain hours in the day, certain hours for the Arabic section, which had its own characteristics and politics, and the next had certain politics, and the other had certain politics, and each one was broadcasting its own politics on the same radio station. When Ibrahim Touqan came, people came and applied from Lebanon, from Syria to join the music ensemble.

HB: Was this an Arab music ensemble?

IB: They had an Arab music ensemble and a Western orchestra. The Arab music ensemble included permanent singers, and players of ʿūd, qānūn, nāy and *buzuq,* [long-necked lute] and composers. In the memoirs of one of the radio managers, in its final days, Ajjaj Nuwaihid [1981] wrote that when he first came and saw the musicians, he brought [Yousef] Batroni, who was present from before, to them to teach them how to read music, as some of them did not know how.

HB: Where did Batroni learn?

IB: He studied abroad, in Italy. And there was also Salvador Arnita, and the Lama family, who had several musicians among them. And the Armenians, of course; in the churches there were a lot of players. On both levels Armenians have always been known for playing Western music and Eastern music. And there were female Armenian singers who used to sing in Turkish—even although the massacres had happened and so on—but they sang in Turkish on the radio nonetheless, because they considered themselves part of that heritage.

NJ: So that was a period which had its particularities, from 1936 to 1948, and then from 1948 onwards has its own particularities, which was the influence of the Nakba on musical life. Now we have arrived approximately at 1936. Jerusalem Radio was established first and foremost in the context of the major strike in Palestine in 1936. Even Ajjaj Nuwaihid in his memoirs [1981] says that at the opening of the radio, which was in Ramallah, there was not such a big reaction to it, because the mood of the people was going in the direction of the strike and resistance and all of those issues.

IB: When the British Mandate came and proposed the idea of the radio, the Arabs refused it three or four times, until Khalil Sakakini [a prominent educator and public figure] got involved, and they promised him that there would be complete independence for the Arabic section in the radio. They even asked him to be the first manager for it, but he refused. [Nasri] al-Jozi mentions in his memoirs [2010] that in the end, the position went to Ibrahim Touqan. Ibrahim Touqan had guarantees that he would have an independent policy, but they also made problems for him, and in the end they got rid of him.

NJ: I think he left in 1940, and then in his place came Ajjaj Nuwaihid. Just to complete the picture, the radio had varied programming; there were three sections and broadcasts in three languages, and each section had its own administration. We are talking about 1936 here, and the importance of the strike in 1936 was that it made the Palestinians more confident to stick to their conditions. But there was also a mix of a certain kind. The [Western] orchestra that we talked about, which had seventy players in it, serviced all the sections of the radio, and it had different roles. Yousef Batroni conducted it once a week when it had a concert for the Arab section.

HB: But the orchestra had in it Jews and Arabs?

NJ: Yes.

HB: Now what about the other radio station?

NJ: The other radio station was Near East Radio. Jerusalem Radio was under the auspices of the Department of Post, Telegraph, and Telephone, apart from the news section. The news section was under the auspices of the Department of Publications, so that it could be monitored. In 1940 the mandate administration established Near East Radio, but not through the Department of Post, Telegraph, and Telephone; this time it was the British Foreign Ministry. And just as the justification for the establishment of Radio Jerusalem was what we mentioned earlier [the strike of 1936], the justification for the establishment of Near East Radio was the start of the

Second World War. That's why it was under the Foreign Ministry. In 1940 it opened in Jenin, and a year later it moved to Jaffa. It lasted longer than Radio Jerusalem. Radio Jerusalem closed down in 1948 with the occupation of Palestine. It seems that Near East Radio had a bigger budget, and the evidence is that Near East Radio started producing. For example, Abd al-Wahab composed *kulli dah kān lay* [All of this for what!] with the financial backing of Near East Radio in Jaffa. The radio produced the song and the work and the record.

IB: According to al-Jozi, the Near East Radio salaries were also higher than those of Jerusalem Radio.

NJ: Now, there's something important we have to talk about in relation to the two radio stations. In the shadow of the competition between Jerusalem Radio and Near East Radio, there was a need for more innovation, a need for professional equality for the musicians. This helped the musicians later. Yousef Batroni started to teach music reading to the musicians of Jerusalem Radio. In 1941 an internal rule in the radio was that all the musicians must have studied music reading. Ajjaj Nuwaihid mentions in his memoirs [1982] that everyone was forced to learn to read music, and the rule was that anyone who did not learn to read music would be fired. So Mohammad Abd al-Karim was fired!

IB: But then he went and studied, in France.

NJ: But Nuwaihid said that he later regretted firing Mohammad Abd al-Karim, because he was of course a unique musician and an amazing buzuq player; he was known as the prince of the buzuq. It turned out that he didn't know how to read and write music, and Nuwaihid was put in an embarrassing position and felt he had to fire him. Abd al-Karim hadn't told him before that he didn't know how to read and write; Nuwaihid discovered after employing him. Also Nuwaihid talks about the period also after 1948; he talks about Radio Beirut and Radio Baghdad and Radio Damascus mainly. He says that the rules which were in place in Near East Radio and the developments that were happening in Palestine in both the radio stations were what revitalized the radio stations in the rest of the Arab world, because the crew that went to them [from Palestine after 1948] were skilled. They had practical experience, they were musically skilled, they were able to read and write music.

IB: One of the examples of this is that Halim al-Rumi moved with Near East Radio to Cyprus, and once he was on a flying visit to Lebanon. The Lebanese ministry called him and said, "We want you to stay longer; we don't want you to go back to your job in the Near East Radio." He told them, "Sorry, I want to go back to my job in Cyprus." So the person from the ministry went and got a Lebanese governmental decree, ordering him to stay in Lebanon. He asked permission from the Near East Radio in Cyprus. His main job was to redesign the musical structure and all the music departments in Ṣawt Lubnān (The Voice of Lebanon). So as soon as they brought him, he ordered that all the musicians of the radio should be sacked, and then he gradually reemployed people based on the new administration. Al-Rumi separated the musicians into two ensembles, as some repertoire (folk, traditional, *ṭarab, shᶜabī,* et cetera) was better suited to the musicians who didn't read music, and the trained musicians, on the other hand, were able to do other things, more contemporary styles that were emerging at the time and more complex material [Al-Rumi 1992]. Al-Rumi was pragmatic enough to keep both in order for the music program to be diverse and appealing to a wide audience. So the culture that [promoted the idea that] reading music was a great asset started at Jerusalem Radio and moved from there to the neighboring countries.

HB: Tell me about how Near East Radio moved to Cyprus and when.

NJ: In 1948 they moved to Cyprus, and then after a short period the studios moved to Beirut and the offices remained in Cyprus.

HB: So when they moved to Cyprus, did all the musicians move with them?

IB: Most of them, yes, according to Michel Mirhij [pers. comm. August 2010].

NJ: The fact that the station continued with a full team until 1956 suggests that the main structure of the musicians was there.

HB: So before we start talking in more detail about 1948 and what happened in 1948, is there anything else or anyone else you would like to talk about? An important musician? Someone whose role you can talk about in more details?

NJ: Oh, yes, there are a lot. When we go into details, there are a number of musicians who excelled and had an influence even after 1948. There is Yahya al-Saudi, Riyad al-Bandak, Yahya al-Lababidi, Mohammad Ghazi, Salam Rifqi, Rawhi al-Khammash. There are many.

IB: Halim al-Rumi, Ramez al-Zaghah. We continued to see them until the 1990s. The main music that made George Wassouf famous is by Riyad al-Bandak. The most beautiful songs written for Wadih el-Safi were by Riyad al-Bandak.

NJ: Like "Yā ᶜaynī ᶜal-ṣabr" [Oh Patience].

NJ: There are a number of musicians who had an influence. There is a very clear recognition about the role of Rawhi al-Khammash in the musical scene in Iraq. He was qualified when he went, and worked both in broadcast arts—he established a number of the ensembles in Iraq—and in the music conservatory, where he established the muwashshaḥāt department. Also, some musicians that we still don't know a lot about who left from Gaza—I mean we usually talk about the central areas of Palestine, because they are closer to us, but there is a group of musicians like Majdi Sirdan who left from Gaza to Egypt and lived there and contributed hundreds of songs.

HB: Let's move on to 1948 and the consequences of that.

NJ: After 1948, if we want to talk about the Palestinians, they were no longer in their land; therefore, they carried with them their projects, in one way or another. A part of the Palestinian population remained in Palestine, and another part was made refugees within Palestine, and this naturally would have an effect on careers, tools, and interests. Some musicians stopped playing. For example, I've never heard of Milad Farah singing after 1948, and I know that he used to sing before. But after that, what happened to him, I don't know. We can't really choose another title for after 1948, except for the influence of the Nakba on music. There is no other title, as it was a huge event that caused a general instability in the infrastructure, interests, perspectives, membership of political parties, and everything.

IB: The other problem in the research is—keep in mind that live music led directly to having very few recordings. I mean, until now I personally have not received any recording that is confirmed to be from Jerusalem Radio. In general they did not record everything. This was ongoing not only in Palestine but also in other places, even in Egypt. There was an Israeli guy, in the Israeli Radio station after 1948, who used to go to a higher-ground area with good reception, and record music that the Egyptian radio was broadcasting live. This resulted in Israel having copies of particular live performances and Egypt not having any. That is why if you listen to Israeli Radio, after 9:00 PM, some of these recordings are rare recordings that were broadcast at that time, and the Egyptians either didn't record it or the recordings were lost or ruined at some point later. When 1948 happened the first thing the Israelis did was go in the direction of the radio. And at that time just a few individuals, employees at the radio, managed to take a few machines and smuggle them to Ramallah, to Irsāl Street. The rest was all confiscated. It's all at the Hebrew University, as far as I know.

HB: Now, in 1948 Jerusalem Radio shut down?

NJ: Yes, it shut down and Near East Radio moved.

HB: Near East Radio moved to Cyprus. So can we say that for music in Palestine the year 1948 was a major turning point, and it did not happen gradually?

NJ: To be accurate, the broadcast art stopped, but not all the music stopped. This is another issue. Because as we said, some musicians left Palestine, and others stayed. In the memoirs of ᶜIsam Hammad, after 1948, when Jordan became in charge of the [Jerusalem] radio station, he mentions that he used to always make a mistake and say, "This is Jerusalem," instead of saying, "This is Jordan" [Hammad 1952].

HB: Oh, so Jerusalem radio actually remained but was moved to the authority of Jordan?

NJ: Yes, it was moved to Ramallah, and it was under the authority of Jordan, the Hashemite Kingdom of Jordan's radio station. Music continued there, but in a different way. The musicians from Lebanon, for example, were not a part of the Jordanian radio; they went back to their country. The Syrian musicians, such as Sami al-Shawwa, went back to their country. The Egyptian musicians went back to their country, to Egypt. They did not stay in Jordan's radio station.

IB: Now, as Nader mentioned, the music did not stop after that, but what happened is that the subject matter of the music changed. Those who used to sing patriotic songs, and remained in the country, started singing songs within the political framework of the Hashemite Kingdom of Jordan. Although the Palestinian issue was perceived as an Arab issue, the particularity of the Palestinian narrative was moving gradually in the other direction, in the songs that we see. And gradually the Palestinian ceased to talk about himself—he stopped being the one singing about Palestine—and the nationalists, who were supported by Egypt or the political nationalistic movement that was common at the time, were the ones talking about this issue. So regarding the identity, on the eve of 1948 individuals who thought of themselves as existing within Greater Syria understood that they were in the only area in Greater Syria that was targeted by Jewish immigration; therefore, it was politically unique. But on the other hand, this political uniqueness influenced its culture, because it felt that it was under attack and under threats on a daily basis. So when 1948 happened, and *al-hijrah* [the expulsion/emigration] happened, these people moved to other areas. What we saw—for example, in Riyad al-Bandak—was someone who, in the prime of Arab nationalism, was visited by Gamal Abdel Nasser, who told him that "One of your songs, Riyad, is equivalent to all the Arab armies," or something along these lines. So Riyad al-Bandak continued to have this passion to write and talk at that time, but even Riyad al-Bandak wrote about this cause in a Pan-Arab context. After the defeat of 1967, Arab nationalist thought weakened across the Arab world. The ramifications were seen across all levels and layers of the social and political lives of Arabs. We heard very little in the way of nationalist songs from Riyad al-Bandak thereafter.

IB: The people that went to Lebanon and Syria are known. Interestingly enough, those we know the least about are those who went to Jordan, and those who stayed. Because, at the time when Jordan imposed its authority on the West Bank, in the Jericho conference in 1949, the musicians almost instantly became part of this new program which King Hussein supported. So the musicians that, like Jamil al-As, went to work in Jordan—his center became Jordan, since he had become part of the Hashemite Kingdom of Jordan—they had a program to encourage Bedouin music. So you would see Bedouin programs, and Bedouin songs started to appear. So there was a character which was desired to exist in Radio Jordan, which the Palestinians became a part of in the West Bank. So the Palestinians went through a process of "Jordanization" in the period between 1949 and 1967, and that continued to have an impact for years afterwards. Musical pockets of different kinds started to appear after 1967. Mustafa al-Kurd, and Emile Ashrawi, and Balaleen, and George Qirmiz, and those groups which started trying to say something different through songs, they appeared after the Jordanian period. If we look at the material that was present during the Jordanian period, including the Festival of 1965, there were nationalistic things, like "*Barūdaih ʿal-Barūdaih*" [The Rifle]. But they were always written in the Jordanian context of, this land is Arab, and Jordan is its guardian, so therefore it is natural to sing for Palestine.

IB: Post-1948 the regional features of song were clarified—in other words, there were specific musical qualities that a particular geographical area in the Arab world specialized in, like the Gulf songs, Kuwaiti songs, Saudi Arabian songs, Syrian songs, Lebanese songs, Iraqi songs, Egyptian songs. So when the Palestinians left in 1948, they went to countries which had become separate states several years previously. Lebanon started behaving as a sovereign country with a national project. The really good Palestinian musicians who left Palestine after 1948 found themselves in this atmosphere. So, as Nader said, the natural stream of music, if music in Palestine had continued as it had been from 1948 until now, we would have had a kind of music, or a musical atmosphere very different to the one we have now. We would have accumulated particular qualities. This was a situation of interruption, and a complete void opened up in the area. The Jordanians came and put a different kind of music here and said, "Hush, *this* is what you're going to do." We went to Lebanon and they said, "Hush, *this* is what you're going to do. You shouldn't be doing something else." And in reality, when Halim al-Rumi came [to Lebanon], he filtered everything, he changed everything around. He started to go along with the situation. Halim al-Rumi stayed until 1978 in this state, and he witnessed the whole development of the Lebanese song as we know it now. So therefore there was a state of interruption in music, and we inside Palestine feel that in 1948 that we lost the connection with its path towards progress. The musical material that a musician uses to express himself, a large part of this was lost. Because the situation of half the people leaving and going to other places, when half the people leave, their songs leave with them. All those songs are gone; all those words are gone. There used to be thousands of verses, and now there are no more thousands of verses.

IB: There is another important point also, which is the fact that art on the radio was broadcast live; they were performing to a live audience, so the accountability was there for making a mistake in front of the audience. Therefore, through these two radios and through having art that was presented live, it created strong musicians, who, when they went to work in other places, carried this method with them, and there was a clear difference between them and the people who were in that country, especially regarding the ability to read music. This was even to the degree that, one of the directors of the radio station in Lebanon said—and this story is according to what Mansour al-Rahbani had said—that when Assi [al-Rahbani, Mansour's brother] went to work in Radio Lebanon as a musician who reads notes, as a violinist, and a composer, he was the worst performer among the musicians. And at that time the musicians who were in the station were people like Hanna al-Salfiti, and Farid al-Salfiti, and so on, all of whom had come from Jerusalem Radio.

HB: What about those people who stayed in 1948 Palestine? Not under the Jordanian government. What happened to them? What happened to their music?

IB: After 1948, when Israeli Radio was established—I heard this from Emile Ashrawi, who remembers it from his mother—they made a program with 1948 Arab musicians, and they used to gather and sing traditional songs from throughout Greater Syria. They brought together the musicians in the studios, and they used to do it live. And this heritage continued: I remember that period, Bassam and Farhoud Bishara broadcasting six days per week in the period of the '70s and '80s.

NJ: It was called Studio Number One.

IB: Studio Number One. They would go and do *mawawīl, qaṣā'id,* and do *bastāt* and *ṭaqaṭīq,* and *qudūd ḥalabīyyah* from Aleppo and *muwashshaḥāt* [various Arab musical forms]. It continued not less than thirty years on Radio Israel.

NJ: Look, 1948 had more than one effect. For example there were very important Jewish musicians that used to work in Radio Baghdad. Now, the response of the Arabs to the occupation of Palestine was to deport the Jews from their countries, and they came to Palestine. There were [Jewish] musicians in Radio Israel, and they formed an Arabic takht. So they had a department in the 1950s; it was as if they took from the experience of Jerusalem Radio—I mean the Arabic section and the Jewish section—so they formed takhts. And some of the Jewish musicians were geniuses of Arabic music. So the Arabs of 1948, where would they go? Many of the Palestinians of 1948 were singing in the Israeli Radio. Yousef Matar, for example, from the 1950s, sang in the [Israeli] radio, I mean, a Palestinian composed for him, and the only platform where he could perform those songs was on Radio Israel.

IB: I know that when the Jewish immigration to Palestine was happening at the end of the nineteenth century and the beginning of the twentieth century, some of them were musicians. One was a singer who came from Iraq, and he kept working as a singer in the families of Nashashibi and Husseini in Jerusalem, because he was an expert singer. And this kind of thing remained the case. Abraham Salman in 1967, he did a concert in Tel Aviv on the qānūn, and when he was playing and modulating into another *maqām* [mode], the people in the hall were calling out, "*Allāh,* the maqām *bayāt!*" They were pointing out the specific maqāms. So it wasn't strange after 1948 that they attracted a specific portion of the Palestinian residents of 1948 and employed them in the radio stations, because there was a demand for this.

NJ: Personally I have not seen any written documents about music in 1948 Palestine between 1948 and 1967, and I admit that between 1948 and 1967 it is a bit of a foggy area. As a researcher I have found more outside. Maybe I have not looked here enough, or maybe one is complacent; one is always afraid that the diaspora will be lost, so one goes to the diaspora to find what's there and does not focus on here. But there are fragments. I know, for example, that Abu Saud al-Asadi was very active; someone named al-Rinnawi was very active in the area of popular zajal and took the genre closer to song. I remember in the 1970s there were audio cassettes which were not through Israeli Radio. There was someone called Atallah Shoufani; he had a takht and sang, and he made cassettes.

HB: If we go back to the folklore, what happened to those festivals you talked about earlier—Nabī Mūsá, Nabī Ṣāliḥ, for example?

NJ: They stopped in 1948. Of course, they stopped.

IB: But what we know is that in general, inside 1948 Palestine there remained instrument makers, there remained musical heritage. Simon Shaheen, for example, learned because his father was making music; he had many ensembles. And Bassam Bishara and Farhoud Bishara. Now, I remember in the 1970s when the borders opened—because they were closed between 1948 and 1967—when people wanted to listen to Arabic and Oriental songs and muwashshaḥs and so on, they would say, "We will bring an ensemble from 1948 Palestine." So it seems—and until today it's still true to a large extent—it seems that the heritage of the Golden Age, of Asmahan, Um Kulthoum, Abd al-Wahab, Karem Mahmoud and Zakariyya Ahmad, was not interrupted in the inside [1948 Palestine]. Kamilya [Jubran], for example, was coming from the heritage of those people; she was brought up listening to Zakariyya Ahmad. On the other hand, we [in the West Bank] in the 1970s, when I talk to Emile Ashrawi, he tells me that there was something like a general directive to the people that Um Kulthoum's music was like heroin and you shouldn't be consuming it, because it keeps you lying down for hours and hours without being active or doing anything. It seems that this idea remained until the 1980s, when Radio Israel used to put on the classical Arabic music of the Golden Age from 9:00 PM until 1:00 AM. In my generation we used to say the same thing—Abd al-Wahab and Um

Kulthoum and all those; you can listen to them when you're relaxed, but you have to be careful, because if you listen to too much of that, you will be passive, and you'll be on the road to heroin! It keeps you numb, it doesn't encourage you to be critical.

HB: Who spread this idea?

IB: Every time we go through a particular national period and the question of art for art is raised, the first person to be mentioned is the artist himself. So people start saying, "You as an artist should be making music in order that people will go out on demonstrations"; "You as an artist should be painting so that people can see what you're saying about the cause." Some people even take it further. Um Kulthoum used to sing and people would be calling out "Allāh!" And by the time they leave her performance, they feel good about themselves and so on, and they're relaxed—no, no, that wasn't something that the PLO [Palestine Liberation Organization] wanted, or even that the advocates of Arab nationalism wanted. The Palestinians of 1948, for whatever reason, retained their connection to the heritage of the Golden Age, from Abd al-Wahab to Um Kulthoum to Asmahan to Layla Murad, much more than we did.

NJ: After 1967 it's a different story and it needs more research and scrutiny. Nothing comes from a vacuum. The Palestinian musicians from 1948 Palestine are good, they are strong, and therefore they consider their heritage as their point of reference. And this comes cumulatively, not overnight, not without foundations.

Afterword

It is vital to point out that this interview does not provide a comprehensive overview of the music scene in Palestine before and after 1948. In particular the two interviewees freely admitted that they are not experts on what happened inside 1948 Palestine and Gaza. These are large and significant areas to investigate more fully, and we hope they will be studied in future research. The gaps in the knowledge of these two highly experienced people in the field of music in Palestinian society also remind us of the ongoing separation of the Palestinian people from each other. The fact the both of my interviewees carry West Bank identity cards means they cannot visit 1948 Palestine without a special permit from Israel, thus rendering the organic interaction between Palestinian musicians and cultural figures from the whole of historic Palestine that would otherwise occur much diminished and lacking in spontaneity.

Nevertheless, the interview covers many fundamental angles and areas. We discover that Palestine before 1948 was a vibrant center of musical activity on all levels. From folklore to festivals, household gatherings to major stars performing at large venues, Palestine before the Nakba was clearly on par musically and culturally with its neighbors and perhaps surpassed some of them in terms of its cosmopolitanism. Particularly from 1936 onward, with the advent of Palestinian broadcasting, the music scene was evidently lively and progressive. The events of 1948, the resulting mass exodus of Palestinian refugees to neighboring countries, and the partitioning of Palestine created an immediate chasm in musical life on all levels, whether in the professional music scene, which lost many of its finest musicians, or in the folkloric repertoire, which was quickly depleted or transplanted into refugee camps outside Palestine. However, one of the more intriguing results of the Nakba was the significant influence that Palestinian professional musicians and musical thought went on to have in the host countries after 1948—an influence that changed and enriched the musical landscape of those countries appreciably.

References

Al-Jozi, Nasri. 2010. *Tarīkh al-Idhāʿah al-Filasṭīnīyyah Huna al-Quds 1936–1948* [The History of Palestinian Radio in Jerusalem]. Damascus, Syria: Al-Hayʾa al-Sūrīyyah al-ʿĀma li al-Kitāb, Silsilat Āfāq Thaqafīyyah.

Al-Rumi, Ḥalīm. 1992. *Mudhakkarāt Ḥalīm al-Rūmī* [Memoirs of Halim al-Rumi]. Beirut: Riyāḍ al-Rayyis li al-Kutub wa al-Nashr.

Hammad, Isam. 1952. *al-Idhāʿah li al-Jamīʿ* [The Radio Is for Everyone]. Damascus, Syria: Dār al-Sharq.

Nuwaihid, Ajjaj. 1981. *Rijāl min Filasṭīn* [Man from Palestine]. Beirut: Manshūrāt Filasṭīn al-Muḥtallah.

Tamari, Salim, and Issam Nassar. 2003. *Al-Quds al-Uthmanīyyah fi al-mudhakkirāt al-Jawharīyyah: al-Kitāb al-ʾawwal min mudhakkirāt al-musīqī Wāṣif Jawharīyyah, 1904–1917.* [Ottoman Jerusalem in the Memoirs of al-Jawhariyyah: Book One from the Music Recollections of Wasif Jawhariyyah]. Beirut: Muʿassasat al-Dirasāt al-Falasṭīnīyyah.

Thomson, William McClure. 1859. *The Land and the Book.* New York: Harper and Brothers.

3

Negotiating the Elements: Palestinian Freedom Songs from 1967 to 1987

Issa Boulos

The study of Palestinian music making during the second half of the twentieth century poses various challenges due to the complex ramifications of *al-Nakba* (the catastrophe) of 1948. Aside from the natural changes that occur in any given musical culture over time, abrupt political and social transformations such as this have been a driving force of change in Palestinian musical culture. In this chapter I examine the predominant social and cultural forces that have influenced Palestinian musicians active between 1967 and 1987. In this endeavor I track myriad musical choices and artistic processes and investigate how their musical performances or productions were initiated, approached, and achieved. The collective processes of making music were intrinsically tied to how these artists conceptualized art, themselves, and their role in society. Building from various case studies I speak to how musicians achieved their art while navigating the politics of tradition and innovation, Western classical and popular musical forms, and indigenous Palestinian folk material.[1] I focus this discussion on four highly influential musicians and ensembles active between 1967 and 1987: Mustafa al-Kurd, a songwriter from Jerusalem; al-Baraem and Sabreen, two Jerusalemite musical groups; and Firqat Aghāni al-ᶜAshiqeen, or simply Al-ᶜAshiqeen, a Palestinian protest ensemble operating from Syria. My analysis focuses on Palestinian musicians who stayed in historic Palestine after al-Nakba of 1948,[2] including Hussain Nazek of Al-ᶜAshiqeen, who left Jerusalem after 1967, and interrogates many of the political, social, and cultural factors that influenced their music-making decisions.

During the first half of the twentieth century a lively debate was well under way among Arab musicians as to the nature of art in contemporary society. This debate centered on two conflicting discourses: *al-fann li al-fann* (art for the sake of art) and *al-fann li al-nās* (art for the people). Among Palestinian musicians this debate became a cultural magnet that connected northern urban centers such as Istanbul, Beirut, Aleppo, and Damascus with the southern regions of Egypt and northern Africa. However, following 1948 these discussions were marginalized as remaining Palestinian musicians were displaced throughout the Arab world, Israel, and in the refugee camps of Gaza and the West Bank. Due to the traumas of 1948, the entertainment-oriented repertoire associated with Arab classical art music (*ʿAṣr al-Nahḍa*) became of less importance to a community that was struggling to recover from forced displacement. Philosophical discussions of modernization, interpretation, and authenticity, common among Palestinian musicians before 1948, took an entirely different route. In the post-1948 era of pan-Arabism, Palestine became central to the struggle against colonialism and foreign occupation. Many of the region's great musicians and composers, such as Um Kulthoum, Asmahan, Layla Murad, Zakariyya Ahmad, Riyad al-Sunbati, and Mohammad Abd al-Wahab, gladly worked for the promotion of this wider nationalist agenda. Larger political discourses of pan-Arabism directly affected the ways music was composed and performed. In addition, musicians were challenged by the predominant idea that the majority of secular art songs associated with ʿAṣr al-Nahḍa seemed irrelevant to the Palestinian struggle. Among Palestinian musicians the vast repertoire of secular art music gradually disappeared due to the dual pressures of pan-Arab nationalism and the traumas of al-Nakba. Within these discussions the Palestinian issue became a powerful rallying point for advocates of pan-Arabism, which directly influenced music-making practices leading to the 1967 war. Music of this period (1948–1967) was interpreted through the political and artistic lenses of pan-Arabism and al-fann li al-nās. Later, a Palestinian-specific nationalist agenda emerged during the mid-1960s and was firmly institutionalized by the 1970s and early 1980s. Palestinian music making gradually transformed as a result of these political forces in profound ways, branching out into several aesthetic directions. The repertoire of Palestinian music associated with this period (1967–1987) therefore incorporated indigenous Palestinian folklore, tales, lyrics, tunes, and dances, while simultaneously negotiating the aesthetics of Arab classical *maqām* (modes) and Western musical traditions. Each of these repertories was then employed within a larger political discourse of popular mobilization and propaganda. Meanwhile, in the West Bank, the issue of al-fann li al-fann versus al-fann li al-nās took an interesting turn.

During the 1950s and 1960s, towns of the West Bank, particularly Jerusalem, Bethlehem, and Ramallah, were booming with the sounds of the growing Latin vogue that was generally of interest to the younger urban generation. Introduced into Arab popular music and cinema, jazz and rock became accessible forms of aesthetic innovation. The feel of rumba rhythms and melodies soon appeared in the work of the Rahbani brothers, Abd al-Wahab, and Abd al-Halim, encouraging the younger generation of the1960s to pick up so-called Western instruments.[3] While the urban lifestyle associated with new musical trends of the time was typically embraced by the elite long before, this time around Western popular music styles came into vogue among the emerging middle class of the 1950s and '60s. After the 1967 war, most of the professional musicians operating in and around the Jerusalem municipality permanently settled in Jordan and essentially never returned. Among those musicians who left for Amman was Hussain Nazek,[4] who played in the Jordanian army's band at the time. It was left to the remaining musicians in Palestine, amateurs and enthusiasts, to figure out what to do next (al-Kurd, interview).

The outcome of the Six-Day War of 1967 damaged the credibility of pan-Arab ideology and weakened Gamal Abdel Nasser's influence. The war also radicalized Palestinians and opened the way for the ascension and expansion of the Jordan-based Palestinian Liberation Organization (PLO). The West Bank was going through yet another wave of migration and displacement following the war, and its laws and educational infrastructure were entirely dependent on Jordan. In addition, it was also subjected to further restrictions by the new Israeli military occupation administration. In contrast to the pre–1967 era, access to 78 rpm records, compact cassettes, books, art material, and related instruments and equipment became entirely controlled by Israel. Arab recording companies and dealers were unable to bring their products into the West Bank while Israel and Jordan became the only available media outlets. The main repertoire broadcast by Jordanian radio and television, for example, was primarily Bedouin-themed folk songs popularized by the Jordanian government (al-Kurd, interview).

The early 1970s witnessed a political-cultural revival in the West Bank, where a growing interest in music making formed among young urban enthusiasts. As a result new types of music began to emerge. Some were influenced by the 1967 war and the expansion of the Israeli occupation, while others were influenced by the 1960s and 1970s era of activism and free expression. In many ways this atmosphere set the foundation for an alternative aesthetic movement dedicated to the creation and performance of meaningful and cause-committed art. This *fann multazim* (cause-committed art) was contrasted with *fann ghayr multazim* (non-cause-committed art) and presented specific political messages. Among the fann multazim emerging from Jerusalem during this period, Mustafa al-Kurd is routinely cited as a forebearer of music focused more on personalized narratives of Palestinian history and experience.

Mustafa al-Kurd

Born in 1945 in the old city of Jerusalem, Mustafa al-Kurd grew up in a diverse musical environment. From an early age, he was exposed to ʿAṣr al-Nahḍa classics, Sufi and Byzantine chants, European organ music, Armenian ballads, Turkish and

Greek classics, and Palestinian traditional music. It was shortly after the Israeli occupation of East Jerusalem in 1967 that he started composing music with lyrics of various renowned Palestinian poets such as Mahmoud Darwish, Rashid Hussain, Tawfiq Zayyad, Fadwa Tuqan, and Zakariyya Shaheen. Al-Kurd remembers al-Muṣrārah neighborhood in East Jerusalem days after the 1967 war when he witnessed Israeli-organized bus caravans transferring Palestinians to other neighboring countries through the border with Jordan. "It was happening again!" he said, referring to al-Nakba of 1948. Al-Kurd wasn't involved in politics per se during that time, but this incident, as he recalls, prompted his interest in speaking out through song. When I asked him about the main force that promoted his involvement in the arts, al-Kurd remembers that his interest in making music has always fallen under his commitment to telling the truth.

During this early phase al-Kurd would mostly accompany himself on the *ʿūd* (lute), and for a short period of time in the early 1970s his appearances took place with other musicians, as he was collaborating with Balaleen,[5] an experimental theater group where Mustafa worked as an actor. This imagery of a songwriter accompanying himself on the ʿūd was becoming commonplace in the 1970s and a symbol of the protest-song movement. Despite minimal orchestration and simplicity, al-Kurd's songs were heard all over the Occupied Territories and were viewed as entirely political in nature. His influence is still seen today in terms of singer/ʿūd imagery, simplicity and accessibility of lyrics, and straightforward familiar melodic structures. One of his most iconic songs, "Hāt al-Sikkaih" (Give me the plow), became an instant hit at the time and was transformed into an anthem against the occupation. Although both the melody and rhythm are consistent with what was commonly used in the earlier nationalist and protest genres, most of the early songs that Mustafa wrote were set in a distinct Jerusalemite colloquial dialect. Mustafa said he wanted to establish a more personalized narrative through his songs, one that chronicles life in Jerusalem under occupation from the perspective of someone who is actually going through it. This explains the idiomatic Jerusalemite colloquial dialect as well as his emphasis on personalized messages and experiences. Because of his strong urban dialect, some of his songs did not resonate among Palestinians in rural areas or other urban centers. However, collectively, Mustafa al-Kurd's performances, charisma, and unique stage presence made him one of the most influential songwriters of his generation, with influences that go beyond the simplicity of his songs.

Throughout his repertoire al-Kurd insisted on simplicity in the way he performed his songs, including their instrumentation, arrangement, and melody. He sang in a direct way, using his own most comfortable native dialect. His convictions were strong on matters of aesthetics and performance practice, as he recalls resisting the incorporation of a simple harmony to the vocal line in "Hāt al-Sikkaih."[6] He remembers how discussions of instrumentation used to emerge among those involved in music making during his tenure with Balaleen. It was during that time when elements of Palestinian folk song were incorporated into the newly emerging protest-song genres.

Mustafa al-Kurd's works fall into a category that is distant from the national liberation themes popular at the time, in many ways establishing his own localized sense of meaning. His local songs addressed issues that were politically and socially relevant, clearly defined by his personal experiences under Israeli occupation with added folkloric elements. His impact and popularity were far-reaching, eliciting the attention of the Israeli military, which arrested him on several occasions throughout the 1970s and essentially placed him under administrative detention and subsequently forcibly deported him in 1976. He spent the following nine years in involuntary exile in Europe.

Al-Baraem

Many Palestinian musicians of the 1960s and 1970s played Western instruments. Under the Israeli occupation, Western instruments were available to purchase, attainable to learn at the missionary schools, popular, desired, and easily accessible. By contrast, Arab traditional instruments were difficult to find, with only a handful of musicians teaching them. In 1966 a group of young enthusiasts established the group Sec. Cit. Por. & Per, playing only Western pop and rock music. Emile, Samir, and Ibrahim Ashrawi started off with one acoustic guitar and percussion, played pop and rock music, and sang in English. They changed the name of the group to the Tigers Five to reflect the expanding number of members in the group. They followed the basic Western pop/rock setup—an electric lead, rhythm and bass guitars, in addition to a drum set—and soon changed their name to the Blooms as the group continued to expand. The group later incorporated keyboards, a violin, and Arab percussion. As a reaction to the Black September events of 1970, where the Hashemite monarchy forcibly evicted the PLO from Jordan, resulting in the deaths of thousands, the group began singing in Arabic, translating its name into al-Barāᶜim, or simply al-Baraem. Emile recalls that, in the years following the Six-Day War (1967) and Black September (1970), there was a pervasive sentiment of disappointment in the great Arab singers, including Um Kulthoum. He remembers that the repertoire associated with these icons was viewed as contributing to the defeat of the Arab armies against Israel in 1967, based on its propagandist exaggerations of Arab power (Ashrawi, interview).

Throughout this period, many of al-Baraem's songs were written by the Rahbani brothers, including "Sanarjiᶜu Yawman, Baᶜdanā" (We shall return one day, after we leave; originally released in 1972), and "Baldatī Ghābatun Jamīlah" (My town is a beautiful forest; originally released in 1957). Despite adapting Rahbani brothers' songs, al-Baraem maintained its pop/rock set while performing, believing that this was in line with their larger artistic vision. They also believed it was crucial to maintain their artistic integrity as far as lyrics, musical arrangements, and compositions. This was the main reason for selecting the Rahbani brothers' repertoire, as it was carefully crafted in terms of lyrics, composition, and performance. While also under Balaleen, al-Baraem collaborated with Mustafa al-Kurd on various occasions, including his most famous song, "Hāt al-Sikkaih." In fact, it was al-Baraem that added important harmony to the vocal line and added guitar to its most popular live recorded performance (Ashrawi, interview). Although al-Baraem embraced the ideals that Mustafa presented, particularly at the level of lyrics, they openly disagreed with him regarding the quality of his musical presentation and believed that, musically, more could be done to enhance the quality of his work. As Emile remembers, they also appreciated the power of Mustafa's performances; often after his performances the audience would demonstrate against the Israeli occupation.

During this period, and immediately after their first debut as a group singing in Arabic, al-Baraem realized that it was not enough to just perform songs written by others, so they began composing their own pieces. They took up a different type of political song, however, critically focused on posing provocative questions rather than falling into the general themes of the day: resistance, endurance, and emigration. I asked Emile about the group's reasons for taking this path. He responded, "To provoke questions and create a community around it." While he remembers how PLO factions were coming down hard on them for what they viewed as Westernization and nonproductive criticism of the PLO, I asked him about whether or not there were any discussions or debates surrounding their choices.

> Yes, of course there was, especially after we started singing in Arabic. The discussion got heated up and became a controversy that spread to the newspapers as we injected Palestinian political and social topics in original works delivered in Western rock style.[7] The question was whether resistance songs and music must be played and delivered on traditional instruments or the message is the key regardless of the medium. Our inability as individuals to play traditional instruments caused a dilemma. Should we stop singing in Arabic because of that, or just deliver our message with the medium we best know how to use? The latter argument won.

One of al-Baraem's most popular songs within the community was written in Jerusalemite colloquial and criticized the corruption and self-appointed symbols of authority.

Oh no people,	*laʾ yā nās mish hayk*
Don't call him Master	*tnādū hādā yā bayk*
It's just an old title	*hāy ʿanāwīn ʾadīmaih*
That lost its power	*baṭṭal ilha ʾīmaih*
Car, a villa and image	*siyyārah w villah w ʾāmaih*

A suit, and fat belly	*badlaih maᶜ karsh kbīr*
A thief, his job is	*lakin bishtighil ḥarāmī*
And steals the poor's money	*w byusruʾ taᶜab il-faʾīr*
Your wish is my command!	*shubbaik lubbaik*
We're slaves in your hands!	*ᶜabīdak bain idaik*
He calls upon us!	*huwwaih ynādīnā*
Oh no people	*laʾ yā nās*
We have a response	*wiḥna binrud ᶜalaih*
And it's not like this!	*mish haik*
We're becoming like machines	*ṣirna zay il-ʾālaih*
He turns us on whenever he pleases	*bidawwirna bain idaih*
Your wish is not my command	*shubbaik lubbaik*
We're not under your hand!	*wish shaᶜb mish rādid ᶜalaik*

The group disbanded in 1976, and to my knowledge there is only one surviving recording of its songs. Among the members of al-Baraem were George Qirmiz, a songwriter whose influence is yet to be examined, and William Voskarjian, who later worked as a music teacher and writer. Their influence can be tracked through al-Baraem II, Sabreen, and al-Rahallah. In the same year, Marcel Khalife released his influential album *Wuᶜūd min al-ᶜĀṣifah,* (Promises of the storm), which consisted of the songwriter accompanying himself on the ᶜūd.[8] Marcel's performance and delivery of the vocal line, his accompaniment on the ᶜūd, and the compositions were perceived to be of high artistic quality, and it sent a strong message to musicians, singers, lyricists, poets, and songwriters working within the protest-song genre that achieving a balance of political, aesthetic, and traditional terrains is possible. By this, Marcel seems to have offered a subtle and more conceptual view of fann multazim versus fann ghayr multazim, one that favored enhancing the artistic presentation in the service of the message rather than focusing on the possibility of conflicting ingredients. Although Marcel himself is Lebanese, the main impact of his album was that it offered hope to the minority of Palestinian artists who advocated for a more artistic and alternative approach to music making and a substitute to the widespread use of direct rhetoric, mediocre performance quality, and what they viewed as simplistic musical expressions. It encouraged many young artists to focus on becoming better musicians and maintain high artistic standards in their works, and to pursue an alternative route to artistic expression. Among those was Said Murad of Sabreen.

Al-ᶜAshiqeen

In 1977 the PLO's Media and National Guidance Committee produced a TV soap opera called *Bi Ummī ᶜAynī* (With my own eyes) to be broadcast on Syrian TV. The songs of the show spoke directly of the core issues of the struggle and articulated how Palestinians viewed their path to liberty. The songs seemed to have linked Palestinians to their collective memory of the past, connecting them to their present and future. One of the best examples of this was "Wallah la-ʾAzraʿak bi-al-Dār." The song was set in colloquial urban Palestinian, performed by a group of female and male vocalists, and became an instant marker of the Palestinian struggle as it articulated core principles, bringing all Palestinians under one flag. The song was based on traditional folk poetry (Arnita 1968), and was reinvented by Palestinian poet Ahmad Dahbour and set to music by Hussain Nazek.

The success of the TV show was noted by Abdullah al-Hourani, the head of the Media and National Guidance Committee. He then facilitated the establishment of the musical group Aghānī al-ʿĀshiqīn (Al-ʿAshiqeen), made up of Palestinians living in Syria, with Hussain Nazek as principal composer. The group incorporated a wide selection of Western and traditional instruments as needed and appeared on stage while standing, an act that symbolized commitment, awareness, and resistance. They used primarily Palestinian folk materials and expanded short melodic forms into songs suitable for staging and choreography. The trend initiated a new era of cultural activity that systematically targeted folk materials for the purpose of the public stage. This movement went beyond the mere politicization of lyrics to include the addition of instrumental accompaniment, changes in rhythms, maqāms, and some standardization of diverse folk tunes. There are several interesting examples of how Al-ʿAshiqeen managed to achieve sustainability through rough political climates and emerging modern musical trends. "Wallah la-ʾAzraʿak bi-al-Dār" (I vow to plant almonds in the home) was one of the songs that was based on folk material. It is referenced in Yusra Arnita's 1968 *Al-funūn al-shaʿbīyyah fī Falasṭīn* (Traditional arts in Palestine), and appears in the book in maqām bayāt, and in 5/4 meter, whereas in Al-ʿAshiqeen's version it is changed to the more Western-friendly maqām *ḥijāz* and in 4/4 meter. Both of these changes drastically altered the interpretation of the piece, adopting a more cosmopolitan/urban melodic and rhythmic framework. In my interview with Nazek back in 2007, I asked him about these changes and reinventions. He said that many of the folk melodies that Al-ʿAshiqeen presented were modified for the purpose of becoming viable songs suitable for stage productions and performance. They had to be catchy, and they had to appeal. Their status as short folk melodies just didn't fulfill the purpose, he said (Nazek, interview).

The PLO gained substantial strength during the 1970s and managed to facilitate its activities through its wide base. It utilized a large body of poets, journalists, lyricists, writers, artists, educators, college graduates, and students in leading the efforts of mobilization and expansion. In the West Bank, activists and PLO affiliates who were in line with PLO ideals started to influence music making. Some active musicians of the period were aware of the ramifications of PLO influence and were critical of its impact and outcome. They often described the repertoire associated with this movement as artistically limited in scope or politicized (Ashrawi, interview).

By the end of 1970s, musicians were having difficulties navigating the intensely politicized scene in the West Bank. While attempting to achieve a reasonable sense of artistry, identity, and relevance, the near-absence of Palestinian intellectualism in music and the continuous marginalization of many alternative ventures further deepened the authoritarian principles of the PLO's cultural policy. The pressures increased, and the gap between what was considered fann multazim versus fann ghayr multazim became wider and more hostile. This was an era where Palestinian cultural ventures in the West Bank were being defined based on new parameters.

Sabreen

The early 1980s witnessed the development of other contrasting musical ventures where the arts were employed as a vehicle for creativity, free expression, and alternative politics. Propaganda and mass mobilization were not necessarily the main motivations behind the work of some of the most influential artists of the era. Instead, musicians attempted to add a different expressive or symbolic dimension to their work. So instead of engaging in an organized political movement, which was often seen as a restrictive approach to making art, many groups used the politically charged situation as an opportunity for experimentation and learning.

In 1982 singer and musician Kamilya Jubran joined the musical group Sabreen. The group was established earlier in 1980 by a group of young musicians in Jerusalem who released an album using the basic Western pop/rock setup similar to the one used a few years before by al-Baraem, but with the addition of clarinet and ᶜūd.[9] The album was not a commercial success. However, shortly after Kamilya joined the group, they decided to adopt acoustic instruments. Unlike their first album, which followed the generic electric-pop band structure, the second album presented a rich tapestry of Western and Arab instruments. With the release of *Dukhān al-Barākīn* (Smoke of the volcanoes) in 1984, the group quickly transformed itself into the most influential ensemble in Palestine. With Kamilya as lead vocalist and *qānūn* (zither) player, Sabreen had declared itself as a rising star in Palestinian music. This reputation was solidified in their primary connection with the Arab classical music past as well as their experimentation in and development of Western idioms.

Kamilya comes from a family with a sustained musical background, and her initial musical training was given to her by her father and through the classics of ᶜAṣr al-Nahḍa. She seems to have convinced the group to adopt acoustic instruments, including the ᶜūd, *buzuq* (long-necked lute), and qānūn, thus transforming the group musically into something completely different. After *Dukhān al-Barākīn* Sabreen positioned itself at the frontier of the Arab classical revivalist movement in the West Bank. The group was well received by Palestinians, and an enthusiastic and a dedicated following started to emerge. "We were very conscious of our words, but music always played a role as important as our identity. We tried to combine the two, presenting a modern identity and culture with a new musical point of view," Kamilya says (Snaije 2004).

There are several terrains that Sabreen successfully navigated. Their lyrics were either based on folk themes or structured in established folk poetic meters. Their use of traditional and Western instruments dovetailed with experimental arrangements and the use of diverse rhythmic and performance styles. One of the most interesting examples of the negotiation of folk, classical, and Western repertoires is a song that they based on a Palestinian folktale of Jbaineh, included on their album *Dukhān al-Barākīn.* The story is about a young woman named Jbaineh who is mistakenly forced into slavery. One day her master hears her singing and realizes that she isn't a slave after all, essentially setting her free. A version of the original lyrics was borrowed and modified by poet Hussain al-Barghouti, who also added a second section that contained a set of symbolic elements and hidden political messages. The lyrics of the new song were then set by Sabreen to a new melody vaguely based on traditional folk songs. One of most significant modifications to the lyrics comes in the first section, where Hussain al-Barghouti replaced the main character Jbaineh with the city of Jerusalem, thus allowing the city to tell its own story while referencing the original Jbaineh as part of the city's cultural and historical memory and narrative. In other words, Jerusalem becomes a living character in the song, and Jbaineh is mentioned just to highlight the parallelism between the two. Another interesting play on the words appears in the second section, "Māl al-ṣumūd w mālnā bidnā nᶜayyish ᶜiyālnā." *Māl al-ṣumūd,* or the steadfastness fund, is a term describing the fund that was allocated to supporting Palestinians under Israeli occupation in the West Bank and Gaza. In this song the lyrics "māl al-ṣumūd w mālnā bidnā nᶜayyish ᶜiyālnā" may have more than one meaning. First, the line can be translated as "the steadfastness fund is ours; we just need to support our families." Or, alternatively, the line can be translated as "we don't buy into steadfastness [possibly referring to PLO's version of resistance]; we just need to support our families." In either case the wording offers harsh criticism of the way this fund was handled by the PLO and sheds new light on how the local resistance became dependent on funds regardless of how effective it was at fulfilling its intended purpose. The song brought Jerusalem to the forefront of the struggle against occupation as the narrator and enforced its role as a primary symbol of resistance. It also offered hope and insight into the role of the people as the main source for change rather than those who claim legal representation of the struggle. The song continues, "mālikum w mālha fālha ᶜa ḥālha ṣāmdaih w law ᶜāryaih," (leave her [Jerusalem] alone, she can handle her own destiny and will endure even when naked, or stripped of everything).

ya ṭyūrin ṭāyiraih ^{c}ajbāl al-^{c}āliyaih
gūlī lammi wa buyaih al-Quds rā^{c}iyaih
tir^{c}a waz w timshi ghaz witnam taḥt il-dāliyaih

māl al-ṣumūd w mālnā bidnā n^{c}ayyish ^{c}iyālnā
willi bā^c ḥālū w bā^{c}hā willi jā^c ma^{c}hā dhrā^{c}hā
mālikum w mālha fālha ^{c}a ḥālha ṣāmdaih w law ^{c}āryaih
ya ṭyūrin ṭāyiraih ^{c}ajbāl al-^{c}āliyaih
guli lammi wa buyaih Jbaineh sāḥiyaih
tākul lūz w bid'ha jūz kullu saḥḥah w ^{c}āfiyaih

qāymaih nāymaih sāḥyaih ḥāfyaih
taḥt al-qamar bayn al-shajar ^{c}ain al-ḍabi^c fuq al-nabi^c
māl al-dabi^c w mālha fālha ^{c}a ḥalha
ma^{c}lish shu ṣār al-ḥurra shu^{c}lit thār
ma^{c}lish mish ^{c}aib ^{c}adhra janb al-dhib
mīn baddū ysīb ḥurra janb al-sāqīyaih

English translation:

Oh flying birds over high mountains
Let my mother and father know
that Jerusalem is a shepherd.
She takes care of geese and walks on her toes
and sleeps under grape trees.

We don't buy into steadfastness
we just need to support our families
Some people sold themselves and the struggle
And some starved but never gave up
Leave her (Jerusalem) alone, she prevails, and will endure even when stripped of everything.

Oh flying birds over high mountains
Let my mother and father know
Jbaineh is awake.
She eats almonds and is craving walnuts
all for good health.

She is always attentive although barefooted
under the moon, around trees and springs she wanders in hyena territory.
Whatever hyenas seek from her, she'll prevail.
Never mind what goes on, the free-spirited lady (Jerusalem) is full of revolution

and it's not a shame for the virgin to be near wolves,
no one will ever be able to touch her free spirit as long as she is a
waterwheel.

The lyrics were set in a colloquial Palestinian dialect distinct from the urban colloquial used by Mustafa al-Kurd and al-Baraem. This was one of the core cultural elements Sabreen was navigating at the time. As the 1980s brought many political activists and intellectuals from rural areas to the urban political and artistic forefront, most of these activists were also trying to literally invent a new political dialect that captured the politicized rhetoric of the street and employ it in new emerging song genres. The idea was to unify speech in a way that communicated a common ground between all Palestinian dialects, one that could speak to both urban and rural communities and be accepted by all. This trend was promoted by intellectuals, political activists, artists, actors, and others. It is documented through the lyrics of several poets and lyricists of the time, including Hussain al-Barghouti, Wasim al-Kurdi, Yaqub Ismail, and Subhi al-Zubaidi. Although Sabreen members came from urban backgrounds and primarily spoke urban dialects, their colloquial songs featured on *Dukhān al-Barākīn* followed closely the dialect patterns of the lyricists. This approach was based on the authority of the poet in Arab culture and the mastery and power of words in a politically charged environment. It wasn't until their 1987 album, *Death of the Prophet,* when lyricist Subhi al-Zubaidi wrote several songs in Palestinian urban colloquial dialect, that the group performed in this linguistic register. In the patriotic songs "Khayyāl al-Muzaghritāt" (Knight of the yodelers) and "ᶜĪsh Yā Kdīsh" (Long live the plowing horse), Sabreen's aesthetic navigations came through in subtle ways. With this recording the group utilized Arab classical elements in the use of traditional instruments, maqām structure, and, most importantly, vocal style. Kamilya adopted this vocal style throughout her tenure with the group and ultimately positioned Sabreen in line with the great classics of the past. In these compositions Sabreen embraced the maqām musical traditions and encouraged others to study them.

Despite all of their initial fame, Sabreen maintained a low profile, appearing only a few times live as a group. One of their most memorable performances took place in the West Bank at Birzeit University in 1984. The rest of their performances took place outside of Palestine. Essentially these two albums became iconic in their influence of subsequent generations of lyricists and composers. Traces of these influences are profound and can still be found in the works of the many contemporary groups active in the West Bank and abroad.

The innovation that characterized most of the 1970s and extended up to the late 1980s had a great impact over the music scenes in the West Bank. Although most of these committed musicians avoided formal political recruitment into one of the PLO factions, the majority were considered leftists. With a wider and more flexible view of culture and politics, many of these Palestinian musicians believed that through their songs they could function as political mediators. Through their work they attempted to align the politics of the PLO and its factions into a consolidated platform whereby the PLO could play the role of beneficiary rather than the stakeholder of the nationalist movement. In other words, these artists were encouraging the PLO factions to play a passive role, where they would potentially benefit from the music without influencing its creation, a compromise that has resulted in benefits to both sides. This relationship brought some of the most powerful and rich examples of Palestinian culture and revealed how the arts often struggled to establish an intellectually independent space in response to the politically charged transformations of the 1970s and 1980s. Collectively, musicians attempted to navigate the contested fields of traditional folk material, contemporary politics, and Western and maqām traditions. They used indigenous language dialects in an attempt to distance themselves from the emerging regional dialects of Lebanon, Syria, and Jordan, establishing a political voice of their own. While many of these musicians attempted to distinguish their songs through lyrics, some also attempted to achieve balance through mixed instrumentation and arrangements. A common denominator among these groups, however, is that they all made political statements. Some managed to find balance between these elements, but the widespread belief was that the quality of the political or social message was more important than the artistic quality of the song. By the beginning of the first *Intifada* (uprising), in 1987, Palestinian song narrative was driven mostly by politics, and art songs were becoming more of a luxury. Nevertheless, the current generation of performers, lyricists, and composers has been greatly influenced by Mustafa al-Kurd, al-Baraem, Al-ᶜAshiqeen, and Sabreen.

Notes

1. Traditional music in this context refers to music of *ᶜAṣr al-Nahḍa,* or the Arab Renaissance or Golden Age, which is the repertoire produced in Egypt, Lebanon, and Syria during the period from 1920 to the 1950s. The repertoire consists of various secular vocal and instrumental genres. These traditions are often called *maqām* traditions. See Racy, *Making Music in the Arab World.*

2. By this I mean Palestinians within Israel, the West Bank, and Gaza.

3. See *Ghīb Ya Qamar* (Oh moon, fade out) by the Rahbani brothers, with Fairuz and Hanan as a duet.

4. Of al-ᶜAshiqeen group.

5. Balaleen was established by François Abu Salem in 1970 as an experimental theater group.

6. The available recording of "Hāt al-Sikkaih" goes back to one of the live performances of 1972–1973; the harmony appears in the recording. You can also hear his *dabke* (dance) group stomping on stage, the same group that he carried along to Balaleen.

7. Some of these discussions took place in newspapers, primarily between Adil Samara and Salim Tamari (Ashrawi, interview).

8. Marcel Khalife is a Lebanese singer and songwriter who worked closely with the late Palestinian poet Mahmoud Darwish.

9. Electric guitar, drum set, electric bass, and keyboards.

Interviews

Mustafa Al-Kurd, April 8, 2012. Jerusalem, Palestine
Emile Ashrawi, April 11, 2012. Ramallah, Palestine
Hussain Nazek, February 18, 2008. Telephone interview Chicago/Damascus

References

Arnita, Yusra Jawhariyah. 1968. *Al-funūn al-shaʿbīyyah fī Falasṭīn* [Popular Arts in Palestine]. Beirut, Lebanon: Palestine Research Center.

Racy, Ali Jihad. 2003. *Making Music in the Arab World: The Culture and Artistry of Tarab.* Cambridge, UK: Cambridge University Press.

Snaije, Olivia. 2004. "Finishing a Musical Odyssey Alone." *Daily Star,* June 23, 2004.

Part 2

Identity

4

Identity, Diaspora, and Resistance in Palestinian Hip-Hop

Randa Safieh

The Inception of Palestinian Hip-Hop

Since the late 1990s Palestinian hip-hop has developed as a national and cultural phenomenon. Politically charged hip-hop, with its spirit of resistance, has become the soundtrack for pro-democracy movements around the Arab world, from the streets of Palestine and Tunisia to Cairo. Palestinian hip-hop artists today are recounting the Palestinian cause and struggle via their art, telling the story of a people whose existence and history has long been denied and neglected. Many Palestinian artists today are creating politically charged music as a significant factor in the construction, preservation, and assertion of their identity and as a tool for resistance against Israeli oppression, while also paying respect to, and drawing upon, traditional Palestinian musical influences. This essay investigates the role of hip-hop in the assertion of a Palestinian cultural identity among artists within Palestine and the diaspora, through a study of their themes and messages emerging in their music.[1]

The Development of Palestinian Hip-Hop: From the Bronx to the West Bank and Back Again

The hip-hop scene in Palestine is primarily divided into three locations: Gaza; the West Bank, including Jerusalem; and the area that became Israel after 1948. DAM, a three-piece collective from al-Lid (Lydda) in pre-1948 Palestine, are pioneers of the Palestinian hip-hop movement, beginning in 1998. The movement did not emerge without struggle: economic limitation, travel restrictions, and even opposition from Islamic groups have all posed obstacles for hip-hop artists. Palestinian sound artist and hip-hop producer Basel Abbas describes the Arab hip-hop scene as being as "diversified (or fragmented) as Arabs themselves are. It expresses as much frustration, polarization and diversity as Arabs themselves enjoy and suffer" (2005, 42).

The Palestinian American hip-hop artists discussed in this essay are Will Youmans, who performed as a hip-hop artist between 2000 and 2006 under the stage name the Iron Sheik; Excentrik, a hip-hop producer/composer; the Philistines, a three-piece collective consisting of two Palestinian American brothers, Ragtop and B-Dub, along with Cookie Jar, who is of Filipino origin; Fredwreck, who has obtained huge commercial success as a hip-hop producer, having worked with artists such as Xzibit, Snoop Doggy Dog, and Mack 10; and one non-Palestinian outfit, the NOMADS. The NOMADS started their hip-hop career as a Syrian-Sudanese duo (Omar Offendum and Mr. Tibbz) and have collaborated with Palestinian hip-hop artists expressing a trend within Arab American society to identify with the Palestinian cause as the root of America's collision course with the Arab world.[2]

As a result of the *Nakba* (catastrophe) of 1948, approximately eight hundred thousand Palestinians were expelled from their homes and have formed a global diaspora. Part of those relocated to America, which is now home to a large Palestinian community of more than three hundred thousand spread across the nation.[3] Approximately half of the Palestinian population in the United States arrived in the late 1960s after the 1967 Israeli occupation of the West Bank, Gaza, and East Jerusalem.

Ideologically, Palestinian hip-hop, both in Palestine and in diaspora discuss many of the same subjects. Arab Americans (Arabs who were born or raised in America and usually have obtained American citizenship) convey their identity as Arab Americans and also as minorities through their artistic names, music, symbols, and political activism (Youmans 2007, 1). What distinguishes Arab American hip-hop from other genres of hip-hop is that it blends hip-hop culture with Arab American identity. There is, however, an important distinction between Arab American hip-hop and Palestinian Americans in hip-hop. Arab American hip-hop refers to hip-hop created by Arab Americans who express their identity as Arab Americans through the use of the Arabic language, symbols, images, and Arabic musical influences (4). Palestinian American hip-hop emerged as a conscious way of establishing an alternative identity formation. Young Palestinians living in America are also "faced with two Americas, white and black, many young Palestinians now identify more with the latter" (Weir 2004).

Hip-Hop and "Glocalization"

Hip-hop has been appropriated in different contexts to represent the causes adopted by ethnic minorities. It has also been employed as a tool for youth protest and to make statements about sociopolitical concerns. Sociologist Roland Robertson uses the term "glocal," a combination of "global" and "local," to describe the ways these two entities interconnect (Mitchell 2001, 11). The terms "glocal" and "glocalization" are eminently applicable to the Palestinian hip-hop movement, in which its artists have created their own local versions of hip-hop, drawing on influences from urban American hip-hop as a result of globalization. It may seem a little ironic that Palestinian youths resort to a transatlantic cultural phenomenon for this purpose, and the accusation of Americanization has sometimes been leveled against them from more traditional schools of thought. In fact, globalization and the global distribution of hip-hop are part of the reason why Arab youth have chosen hip-hop as an outlet for their self-expression. "Black culture" has now become a "global culture" by different communities appropriating and responding to its style, music, and image (Bennett 2000, 137). Palestinian youth have modified and adapted African American hip-hop to express their own disillusion with the social and political climate in which they live. Hip-hop, as a culturally mobile genre of music, is constantly being redefined and reinterpreted as it is appropriated by various different ethnicities and nationalities around the world. It has become evident that while hip-hop is a form of cultural expression for youth of African descent, it is also applicable and transferable to various marginalized and oppressed cultures and ethnicities who relate to the issues of African American hip-hop. Palestinian and Palestinian American hip-hop artists have not only made use of African American hip-hop imagery but have also adapted it to express their own concerns, frustrations, and specific localities. Tamer Nafar of DAM asserts: "We are political, social and anti-commercial—it basically boils down to 'protest rap.' But our songs also have philosophical, poetic and even ironic overtones. In addition to being influenced by hip-hop, we've learned from Arab poets how to use metaphors. Instead of stealing them from books, we develop our own images using our street slang" (Franzen 2007).

Hybridized Identity in Palestinian American Hip-Hop

The desire of a minority community to redefine itself can lead to the construction of hyphenated identities. The term "hyphenated identities" was developed as a way to describe "the construction of cultural authority within conditions of political antagonism or inequity" (Bhabha 1997, 58). Palestinians of the diaspora have a constant reminder that they are separated from their homeland and that they are a minority in their host country. Perhaps this explains why many minority youths use their status as ethnic minorities in a positive manner by celebrating their culture. Ethnomusicologist Martin Stokes addresses it thus:

> The emergence of "hyphenated identities" has been hailed as a force undermining the oppressive identity-producing apparatus of the nation-state, and putting into play new, inclusive, and open-ended notions of belonging. No

longer can one safely assume that globalization produces cultural homogenization or acquiescence to the political status quo, as proponents of the cultural imperialism hypothesis once argued. (2003, 303)

Hyphenated identities are a form of hybridity, a subject much researched by postcolonial studies, that deals with cultural exchanges between race, ethnicity, gender, and class (Beard and Gloag 2005, 84). Through the formulation of hyphenated identities, minority communities are resisting being defined by others. Hybrid cultural forms can strengthen the sentiment of national belonging and can signal "empowerment and cosmopolitanism" (Stokes 2003, 306). Hybridized identities are often the consequence of cross-cultural exchanges and cultural appropriations between different groups resulting in a third culture. This creates a third idea or space that bears "something different, something new and unrecognizable, a new area of negotiation of meaning and representation" (Bhabha, quoted in Beard and Gloag 2005, 84–85). Ragtop relates this philosophy to his own condition: "I can't separate the two. I'm Arab American, influenced by 'both' cultures. A line [in the Philistines and NOMADS song "Hala"] like 'See us in bars and sheesha parlors mūsīqá al-Intifāḍa' is actually about how the two are intertwined, how we flow easily between so-called Western and Middle Eastern cultures" (Ragtop interview with author, 2007). Sociomusicologist Simon Frith's hypothesis on the link between music and identity is very much aligned with Ragtop's view: "What makes music special—what makes it special for identity—is that it defines a space without boundaries. Music is thus the cultural form best able both to cross borders . . . and to define spaces" (Frith 1997, 125).

For Palestinian Americans, the appropriation of "American" as part of their identity is a way to reconcile their attachment to their homeland with integration into their host countries. However, since the events of 9/11 they often find it difficult to live their Palestinian American identity amid the surveillance of the American war on terror.

The Question of Identity: Redefinition and Representation of the Self

Palestinian and Palestinian American hip-hop artists have resisted the existing constructions of an imposed identity and challenged the negative profiling of their identity by reformulating it as positive, still bearing the original aspects of their identities. Through performance, participants can construct notions of "self" that challenge and refashion hegemonic organization, and through performance and music participants can offer an alternative notion of power and resistance in Palestine and across the Atlantic (McDonald 2005, 5).

Youmans's artistic name, for example, the Iron Sheik, is an attempt to reverse, redefine, and challenge Arab misrepresentation. The original Iron Sheik is an Iranian wrestler who epitomizes, for some, negative stereotypes of Middle Eastern people.[4] Ragtop (which is also a derogatory term for an Arab), like Youmans, reclaimed disparaging Arabic terms in a way to reverse stereotypes and transform negative terms into positive ones. When asked about the connotations and meaning of the name "The Philistines," Ragtop answered, "The definition of a 'philistine' is taken directly from the Webster's dictionary . . . a philistine is 'an enemy of Israel' [*sic*]. We chose the name to reclaim it, as we believe the dictionary definition [coincidentally?] fits stereotypes of modern-day Palestinians. Our first album is called *Self Defined,* because we reject that definition" (Ragtop, interview with author, 2007). Ragtop refuses to be defined only in terms of Israel without an independent identity.

Self-definition is a recurrent theme in Palestinian hip-hop and expresses the refusal of an imposed Arab identity. The Philistines, in their song "Self Defined," narrate their frustration of confinement to such an imposed identity:

> Since the very first time, I find my rhymes
> To be labeled as malignant, never once benign
> Inspirations divine, intelligent in design
> But I find myself confined, in between these lines
> Self Defined means I'm unchained / From your
> Name brand narrow way of thinking / Your wack ship is sinking
> Your practice is bringing mad stresses to your life
> But you can / Open your eyes son the P have arrived

Hip-hop communities in Palestine and the diaspora are actively employing hip-hop simultaneously as a vehicle for asserting their "otherness" as Palestinians and also as a common form of cultural expression of identity: "otherness" to distinguish themselves from the Israeli population of Palestine and from American society. One inherent similarity between Palestinian and Palestinian American hip-hop is their efforts to make a distinction between "self" and "other." Again, Frith's theoretical framework can be very closely aligned with the issue of a Palestinian American cultural identity. What Frith suggests is not that "social groups agree on values, which are then expressed in their cultural activities[,] but that they only get to know themselves as groups (as a particular organization of individual and social interests, of sameness and difference) through cultural activity" (1997, 111).

Hip-Hop in Palestine and the Diaspora: The West Bank to the West Side

Popular culture is engaged in a constant interplay with political, economic, and social factors. This reasoning explains the differences in the output of Palestinian and Palestinian American hip-hop. One of the most distinctive differences between both musical groups is the issue of diaspora, which plays a central role in Palestinian American hip-hop artists' creative production. On being a Palestinian of the diaspora, Excentrik says, "Palestine is like a phantom for me; I know who I am, I know where I am from, and I know where I am going, but the future is always so random and seemingly bleak at times, I'm sure every diaspora cat can feel me" (interview with author, 2007).

Ethnomusicologist Mark Slobin's diaspora theory advocates, "through songs, each locale and each generation . . . finds ways to connect to actual or imagined *pasts,* not *presents*" (2003, 289). This is generally true of American hip-hop artists in the Palestinian diaspora. It appears that many Palestinian American hip-hop artists are fulfilling Slobin's proposition that "many people themselves think they are living away from a homeland, and respond nostalgically or angrily, actively or apathetically to the fact of separation or to the outsider's view that they are potential terrorists" (285).

There have been many studies conducted on the Palestinian population living within Palestine and in the refugee camps. Academic literature shows that although it is common for second-generation immigrants to have a reduced sense of "political consciousness and ethnic pride," this is not the case for Palestinians of the diaspora (Christison 1989, 19). Palestinians of the diaspora have at times adopted dual national identities and have succeeded in merging both cultures and to formulate dual perspectives and attitudes.

The late Palestinian literary theorist Edward Said regarded authorities as having frequently implemented the invention of tradition as a means to rule mass societies when small communities and social units were disbanding and disintegrating. Authorities used the invention of tradition as a means of linking large groups of people to one another (Said 2000, 259). Although Palestinian hip-hop artists are not seen as authority figures, in Palestine and in the diaspora they follow a similar path to forge a sense of unity, especially among the artists themselves, in the form of musical collaborations. This has been conveyed with musical collaborations such as the Lyrical Alliance collective, explained later in this essay. Said further argues that people prefer to rewrite memory to provide themselves with an identity, a national narrative, and a status. Mahmoud Jreri of DAM describes his role in this common endeavor: "As young people in schools we wasn't [*sic*] aware to our culture. We knew that we are Palestinian, but in schools they teach us about Zionist 'heroes,' the same heroes who killed and transferred most of our people. We don't learn about Mahmoud Darwish. You have to figure it out along, and we did figure it out" (interview with author, 2007).

Speaking from another angle, Palestinian American hip-hop artist Excentrik elucidates on the idea that artists can create, and to a certain extent control, a status for themselves, through their musical output.

> [Music] humanizes who we are. When people see us on stage they are like, "What? They ain't terrorists." If all I rapped about were political stuff, no one would hear it. People use Fox News and the Bible for analysis these days,

> and to that majority we are merely blood-sucking anti-Christs. That is obviously the furthest from the truth, so doing what I'm doing—I should say what *we* [Palestinian hip-hop artists] are doing—makes a huge difference in the pictures of us the majority of Americans have painted in their minds. We are no longer boxed in, we can be human, artistically important humans; they cannot demonize an artist like they can demonize falsified imagery. (interview with author, 2007)

Ethnomusicologist Bruno Nettl describes how the music of immigrant groups is affected, including the size and selection of the group, reasons for immigration, and the contact upheld with their home country; the "degree of physical, cultural, linguistic isolation and cohesion of immigrants in the host country, the cultural and musical differences and compatibilities of an immigrant culture in its relationship to the host culture, the attitudes of such a group toward diversity and change—all these obviously play a part" (1983, 227). While each of these issues plays a part, the reasons for immigration dominate all others in Palestinian American society, many members of which come from families who were forced to leave Palestine.

Nettl poses certain questions about immigrant musical culture within their host countries: whether maintaining immigrant musical tradition supports the preservation of the cultural tradition as a whole, whether musical change conveys the acceptance of their host culture, and whether music acts as a reminder of the group's heritage while other behaviors of the group assimilate. Some immigrant groups integrate into the conventional behavior of their host country while remaining faithful to their traditional music, performing it at special occasions as a reminder of their home country. Parallels can be drawn between the musical behavior of indigenous minority groups and immigrant minority groups, and it is their minority status that allows for comparisons and similarities within their musical behaviors (227–28).

A common theme that exists in Palestinian American hip-hop is politically charged lyrics recounting the Palestinian struggle fused with traditional Palestinian musical influences and hip-hop culture. Youmans upholds this idea: "I use American instruments more, but some Arabic samples. The beats are hip-hop beats. The politics, though, are purely Palestinian. The content is very Palestinian—more so than it is Western hip-hop. My words are political translations" (interview with author, 2007). While Western influences are prevalent in Palestinian American hip-hop, Ragtop, of the Philistines, explains that much of the essence of Palestinian tradition is still drawn upon in their music: "There's a long poetic tradition in the Arab world that is similar in many respects to hip-hop: we have 'battle' rhymes and love poems, we have poems about our homes and traditions, and we have poems that basically serve as boasts on behalf of the poet or his sponsors. All of this is reflected in Palestinian American hip-hop" (interview with author,

2007). Jreri describes DAM's music as "60 percent hip-hop and 40 percent Arabic/Palestinian music" and interprets a correlation between Palestinian culture and hip-hop culture: "breakdance: *dabke* [Palestinian folk dance]; graffiti: *shiʿārāt* [political slogans]; freestyle: *zajal* [Arabic oral tradition of poetry]" (interview with author, 2007).

Say What? The Language Barrier

Palestinian hip-hop in the United States is a direct blend of urban American hip-hop and Palestinian musical influences. Palestinian hip-hop bands often rap in English as well as Arabic. According to Stormtrap of Ramallah Underground, "Through English I can make the same message understandable to wider audiences around the world" (interview with author, 2007). Mr. Tibbz, one half of Sudanese/Syrian, US-based rapping duo the NOMADS, agrees that "part of the effect of rapping in English is putting the Arab experience in English terms, making it pertinent to an audience that would most probably never have understood what Arabs live through and deal with" (interview with author, 2007). The Hebrew lyrics appear to have a similar purpose: to reach a society that is increasingly uncomfortable with the "Palestine under Israel issue," the continued presence within Israel of the indigenous population of Palestinians. Palestinian hip-hop in Hebrew is an eye-opener to remind the Israelis that the ostrich policy of hiding their heads in the sand—in this case behind walls—is not a solution, and that the issues of occupation of the West Bank and Gaza and the rights of those Palestinians with Israeli passports need to be addressed. Jreri explains his usage of Hebrew in his music as being a message specifically directed at the Israeli occupation: "We also did it [rap] in Hebrew. It's the second language that we learn in schools, and we had a lot of anger. They [Israelis] don't live the life that we are living, but they know about it. It's important for me to say that I know that you know about it and you choose not to do anything" (interview with author, 2007).

Palestinian American hip-hop artists have made a deliberate choice to rap in English so as to remain accessible to non-Arabs as well as Palestinian Americans of the diaspora, for whom Arabic may not be spoken. Ragtop explains this in his experience: "I actually try to avoid excessive use of Arabic or references to Middle Eastern history or culture that may be obscure even to an Arab American who hasn't extensively studied the region, because it makes the music inaccessible to the majority of listeners. I do not think my purpose is solely to create music that Arabs or Arab Americans can relate to—in fact quite the opposite, hence this creative choice" (interview with author, 2007). Ragtop's choice is also upheld by Youmans: "I see it [rapping in English] as a way to communicate with the American public. Also, my use of English tells Arab Americans that while Arabic is the language of their ancestors, we can command the tools here to speak for us" (interview with author, 2007).

Palestinian and Palestinian American hip-hop artists, through their music, are communicating to several demographic audiences: native Palestinians within the homeland, Palestinians of the diaspora, as well as non-Palestinian audiences globally. The choice of language in Palestinian and Palestinian American hip-hop is a very conscious and intentional decision in the targeting of specific audiences to hear their message and has performed a vital function in positioning artists and their audiences within a larger communities of practice.

Comparison of Themes

Palestinian and Palestinian American hip-hop artists cover many of the same themes and topics, such as identity, Middle Eastern politics, U.S. foreign policy, racism, discrimination, gender issues, and pride of their heritage. Palestinian hip-hop artists, both those based in Palestine and those within the diaspora, endeavor to preserve traditional values to narrate their own history and resist oppression. Jreri insists that they are advocating a "message of change also, and to change you have to get up and do it in your hands, because no one will do it for you" (interview with author, 2006). This is most movingly expressed in the lyrics of the chorus of DAM's "Ng'ayer Bukra," meaning "change tomorrow": "We want education, we want improvement / To have the ability to change tomorrow." Youmans speaks in similar terms: "Change comes from collective movement, not individual aspiration" (interview with author, 2006). Mr. Tibbz also draws attention to the wider ramifications of the unresolved Palestinian issue:

> I want to convey that the Palestinian situation is a major problem for the world and must be dealt with immediately. I want the audience to realize that Palestinians are victimized human beings living in one of the most deplorable humanitarian and political situations. Until we see the Palestinians as what they are—innocent, honest people forced into one of the shitiest [*sic*] situations on the planet—we can never truly understand the mentality of the Palestinians let alone address their needs." (interview with author, 2006)

When I asked Jreri about the ideological differences between Palestinian hip-hop artists based in Palestine and those of the diaspora, he answered, "In our daily life everyone faces different problems, so we sing about different subjects." Stormtrap, however, reminds us that the life of a Palestinian today is not normal: "Being Palestinian you don't really get a chance to live a normal life in your home. I will always be wishing for what have been and are denied, and those thoughts always seem to find their way into my music" (interview with author, 2006). Youmans also sees the differences between artists within Palestine and the diaspora as linked to their immediate life experiences: "The difference between me and Palestinian groups is they live the oppression. I live under a much softer system than they do. Discrimination happens, but it is nowhere as bad as Israel's policies. I can only be a solidarity rapper. They have the authentic voices" (interview with author, 2006). Excentrik agrees: "The oppression we feel here is but a fraction of the shit they gotta go through—and that really makes a difference in how you approach your sound" (interview with author, 2007). However, Ahmed Jay, a Palestinian-Jordanian hip-hop artist, considers that all Palestinian hip-hop artists, whether based in Palestine or the diaspora, "hold the same message" (interview with author, 2006).

Peaceful resistance to the Israeli occupation of Palestine is evident in the lyrics of DAM, as in their song "Mali Huriye," meaning "I don't have freedom": "You won't limit my hope by a wall of separation / And if this barrier comes between me and my land / I'll still be connected to Palestine."[5] The "wall of separation" mentioned in the lyrics refers to the Israeli-built separation wall that cuts through the West Bank, surrounding villages and separating and dividing Palestinians from their land.

The two approaches to celebrating and conveying national identity among Palestinian and Palestinian American hip-hop artists are very different, given their cultural, social, and political contexts and subjectivities. Palestinian Americans have appropriated hip-hop as a channel for the recreation and reformulation of their migrant or refugee identity; in Palestine it is part of a struggle against the occupation.

The Future of Palestinian Hip-Hop

For many people internationally, the Palestinian struggle for freedom has been shaped by popular uprisings—images of youth confronting tanks with stones on the streets of occupied Palestine etched into our consciousness—but seldom is the role of the arts or poetry in the Palestinian struggle highlighted in mainstream media headlines. Palestinian hip-hop artists contribute to promoting and advancing a distinct Palestinian identity, beyond the boundaries of the Palestinian communities themselves, by way of culture and music rather than political discourse, although the latter is part and parcel of Palestinian hip-hop. The emergence of Palestinian and Palestinian American hip-hop illustrates the fact that colonized, oppressed, and marginalized peoples will always find a means to express themselves and narrate their own history, and that music continues to be a tool in that struggle. Hip-hop has achieved a counter-hegemonic status with many Palestinian youths, with the intention of empowering a generation of youths who relate to the way in which Palestinian hip-hop artists help to change the stereotyped perceptions of Palestinians. Hip-hop is giving a voice to those who might otherwise not have been heard. It is doing so in a manner not significantly different from any other cultural revival, building upon the essence of Palestinian musical tradition.

As a movement with rising momentum it appeals to many young Palestinians, across national boundaries, bridging the distance between a segment of young

Palestinians living within Palestine, and those within the diaspora, whose paths might otherwise not have crossed. There have been multiple musical collaborations between Palestinian and Palestinian American hip-hop artists, as well as between Palestinian hip-hop artists and others from the Arab world, launching Palestinian hip-hop into the international arena. A glowing example of these musical collaborations is the Lyrical Alliance collective fronted by DAM's Tamer Nafar. Lyrical Alliance, which comprises some of the most prominent Arab hip-hop heavyweights, crossed many linguistic and cultural boundaries. Among the Arab hip-hop artists in the collective was Brooklyn emcee Talib Kweli, whose social and political awareness places him in a league of his own. The Arab artists came from an array of countries around the Arab world, from Algeria to Amman, from the West Bank to West London. Among them were London-based rapper/singer Shadia Mansour; Rabah Ourrad, the controversial Algerian rapper notorious for his courageous and witty political critique of the Algerian reality; Lebanese bilingual rapper Rayess Bek; Samm, ambassador of Jordanian hip-hop and winner of the Jordanian "Beit El Hip-Hop" talent show; and video jockey Jana Saleh from Lebanon. Despite the geographical dispersion of the Arabs, their music still has the ability to unite them in their continuous attempt to define their culture and identity. Nafar, who primarily rapped in Arabic, thought that the Lyrical Alliance experience would lead to "more collaborations in the Arab world and more hip-hop unity" and hopes this collaboration will have attracted more hip-hop fans outside of the Arab audience: "We know all about the African Americans through hip-hop; now we can exchange cultures and more work with the world's artists, such as Talib Kweli."

Most recently, hip-hop played a role in the Arab Spring. Many hip-hop artists reverted to hip-hop's origins and used it as a form of political commentary and as a way to unite communities from the streets of Tunisia to Cairo. Hip-hop also carved a space for itself within the academic sphere when on June 26, 2012, a group of well-known hip-hop artists, critics, and intellectuals came together at the Barbican in London to address the question, "Does rap enhance or degrade society?" Among the participants were rapper KRS-One; Victorian literature expert John Sutherland; David Cameron's youth advisor, Shaun Bailey; and African American civil rights activist Jesse Jackson. The questions that they addressed include themes such as whether hip-hop is the "authentic voice of the oppressed that turns anger into poetry and political action, or a glorification of all that holds back oppressed minorities and hinders them from mainstream assimilation" (Toppin 2012). Often a cultural movement precedes political change, maybe because artists often reflect what a society is thinking and feeling long before laws are changed. Artists often do more than merely reflect circumstances, sometimes assisting in the generation of cultural practices and ways of thinking about political circumstances. It was also at the height of the anti-Arab furor, in the aftermath of 9/11, that Arab American comedians such as Maysoun Zayed and Dean Obeidallah, first made a breakthrough and together co-founded the New York Arab-American Comedy Festival in 2003 and are often featured on mainstream American television channels.

Sales of Palestinian hip-hop music in the Arab world would be an indication of the success that the movement has achieved thus far. The applause that Palestinian hip-hop artists receive at pro-Palestinian demonstrations, which often dwarfs the applause of the speeches, is another indication of its popularity. As for Palestinians, hip-hop has helped to provide the younger generation with a new tool—an innovative approach to self-expression and identification—as much as a therapeutic and creative outlet for their frustration.

"Someday I hope for us to make more songs celebrating than politicizing" (Fredwreck, interview with author, 2006). This aspiration also represents that of the general Palestinian hip-hop movement. The late Yasser Arafat used to say, "The Palestinian National Movement is not only the gun of the freedom fighter but mainly the pen of the writer, the brush of the painter, the words of the poet.[6] Now that the Palestinian side has abandoned the dialogue by arms and resorts to the arms of dialogue, the Palestinians' cry for freedom will express itself more and more through the poets, the composers, and the musicians." Until then, where many Palestinians are concerned, a song will never be only a song, but an act of resistance.

Notes

1. Research was undertaken between September 2006 and July 2012. This essay is based on empirical data and research conducted by the author. Ethnographic research methods such as observational and participatory fieldwork were used, with regular contact with the artists in question. The primary research tool employed is qualitative interviews conducted via face-to-face meetings, telephone exchanges, as well as direct email correspondence with the hip-hop artists. The initial interviews were followed by exchanges of continuous correspondence with the artists. My recourse to ethnographic research methods through interviews allowed my informants to self-define and self-represent.

2. Omar Offendum and Mr. Tibbz have since embarked on solo performing careers.

3. No precise records exist of this figure because of the absence in American census forms of any Arab category.

4. Hossein Khosrow Ali Vaziri, aka the Iron Sheik.

5. Translation taken from DAM's official website: http://www.damrap.com/lyrics/english/ihda2/Mali_Huriye.html.

6. Yasser Arafat quoted by Afif Safieh, February 15, 2006, Georgetown University's Intercultural Center, Washington, DC.

References

Abbas, Basel. 2005. "An Analysis of Arabic Hip Hop." Bachelor's dissertation, SAE Institute, London.

Beard, David, and Kenneth Gloag. 2005. *Musicology: Key Concepts.* Oxon: Routledge.

Bennett, Andy. 2000. *Popular Music and Youth Culture: Music, Identity, and Place.* Basingstoke: Palgrave.

Bhabha, Homi. 1997. "Culture's In-Between." In *Questions of Cultural Identity,* edited by Stuart Hall and Paul Du Gay. Oxford: Berg.

Christison, Kathleen. 1989. "The American Experience: Palestinians in the U.S." *Journal of Palestine Studies*18 (4): 19.

Franzen, Stefan. 2007. "We Are the Sugar Hill Gang of Palestine." *Qantara.* http://en.qantara.de/wcsite.php?wc_c=8803.

Frith, Simon. 1997. "Music and Identity." In *Questions of Cultural Identity,* edited by Stuart Hall and Paul Du Gay. Oxford: Berg.

McDonald, David A. 2005. "Performing Palestine: Resisting the Occupation and Reviving Jerusalem's Social and Cultural Identity through Music and the Arts." *Jerusalem Quarterly* 25, 5–18.

Mitchell, Tony. 2001. *Global Noise: Rap and Hip Hop Outside the USA.* Middletown, CT: Wesleyan University Press.

Nettl, Bruno. 1983. "The Singing Map." In *The Study of Ethnomusicology,* ed. Bruno Nettl. Chicago: University of Illinois Press.

Said, Edward W. 2000. "Invention, Memory, and Place." *Critical Inquiry* (Winter).

Slobin, Mark. 2003. "The Destiny of 'Diaspora' in Ethnomusicology." In *The Cultural Study of Music: A Critical Introduction,* edited by Martin Clayton, Trevor Herbert, and Richard Middleton. London: Routledge.

Stokes, Martin. 2003. "Globalisation and the Politics of World Music." In *The Cultural Study of Music: A Critical Introduction,* edited by Martin Clayton, Trevor Herbert, and Richard Middleton. London: Routledge.

Toppin, Alexandra. 2012. "Hip-Hop's BBC Showcase Raises the Gangster Dilemma." *Guardian,* June 25, 2012.

Weir, Laila. 2004. "The Iron Sheik Rapper Will Youmans Taps into the American Minority Experience to Address the Palestinian-Israeli Conflict." *San Francisco Chronicle Magazine.* August 22. http://www.sfgate.com/magazine/article/The-Iron-Sheik-Rapper-Will-Youmans-taps-into-2700122.php.

Youmans, Will. 2007. "Arab-American Hip Hop." In *Etching Our Own Image: Voices from within the Arab American Art Movement,* edited by Anan Ameri and Holly Arida. Cambridge, UK: Cambridge Scholars Press.

5

Transgressing Borders with Palestinian Hip-Hop

Janne Louise Andersen

As fifteen-year-old rapper Hussam Ikbarey enters the studio Taht al-Ard (Underground) in Nazareth, he looks all teenager—tall, skinny, and shy. "Hussam, spit the Tech N9ne [pronounced Tech Nine] track you memorized," his producer, Anan Kseem, says, referring to the American rapper from Kansas City—one of Hussam's favorites.

Hussam's blue eyes focus and he starts rapping. There are no pauses, no hesitation; he knows the lyrics by heart—or he has memorized the sound of the words, because Hussam's English is very limited, and in reality most of it is gibberish to him. But his flow and delivery are incredibly tight. Anan watches his novice with eyes full of acknowledgment and affection. "There are twenty guys like Hussam, but none as dedicated," he says.

Hussam's journey into hip-hop brings Anan back to his own when he was Hussam's age. More specifically, it brings him back to a mild October night in 2001 in downtown Nazareth. The hip-hop group DAM is performing its first show on an outdoor stage in the city center—and the place is packed.

The crowd in front of the stage is mostly young, and among them are Anan and his friend Ala Bishara, both sixteen and full of expectations. They are about to see their first hip-hop concert performed in Arabic, and as the three rappers start rapping and the audience absorbs their vigor, it's as if a beam of light from the sky hits Anan and Ala.

"Hip-hop—*ʿarabī* [Arabic hip-hop]," Tamer calls out. "Hip-hop," he repeats and points his microphone toward the crowd—"*ʿarabī*!" Anan and Ala scream back with the rest of the audience.

Figure 5.1. DAM performing at The Shrine, Harlem, New York City, as part of a US tour in 2011. Photo by Janne Louise Andersen.

And just like that, in that one concert Anan's life changed. From that day on, Anan had DAM's music on repeat on his stereo along with 2Pac, Public Enemy, and Notorious BIG. In school in Nazareth, Anan scratched DAM's lyrics into a wooden table with a ruler. And as he changed classrooms, he insisted on bringing that same table with him. The words kept flowing out of his pen; he was determined to be a mic controller, an MC.

So together with Ala and Adi Krayem, who had also been at the concert, they joined We7—Wlad el 7ara (Boys from the Hood, pronounced *walād al-ḥārah*)—and five weeks after DAM's concert, We7 had their first show. "Our generation, we were in need," Anan explained to me in an interview in February 2012. "We needed something new to be someone special."

The Music of Movement

Ten years later, Anan, now twenty-seven, is still a member of We7, a music producer, and the founder of the music label Taht al-Ard. I hadn't seen Anan in more than three years, when he took part in a hip-hop project I managed at the Sabreen Association for Artistic Development in 2008–2009. He and We7 performed along with other Palestinian hip-hop artists on tours we organized around the West Bank. Anan and his counterparts Saz (aka Sameh Zakout, from al-Ramleh, the first Palestinian rapper to produce an album) and the Danish Egyptian rapper

Zaki taught interested teenagers in the West Bank the basics of hip-hop: writing lyrics and practicing flow, delivery, and performance.

The summer program stretched over five weeks and took place in Shoufat Camp in Jerusalem, Dheisheh Camp in Bethlehem, Jenin Camp in Jenin, and Balata and Askar Camps in Nablus. During that time, Anan and Saz had to return to their hometowns every now and then, and for every camp they had to plan a new route using new means of transportation.

To get to Jenin and Nablus, Anan could use the checkpoint by Tulkarem, which is situated on the Green Line in the middle of the West Bank. From here he had to take a taxi to Jenin or Nablus. But to reach the southern camps, he had to take two buses to get from Nazareth to East Jerusalem—a two-hour drive—change to a Palestinian shuttle bus to go to Shoufat Camp, cross the checkpoint, and enter the camp. And to go to Bethlehem he had to take another bus from Jerusalem, cross the checkpoint on foot, and get a taxi to the camp. Altogether it was a three- to four-hour journey, depending on the line at the checkpoints.

Anan and Saz, twenty-three years old at the time, had never moved around the West Bank before. In fact, because they are Israeli citizens it is illegal for them under Israeli law to enter Palestinian Authority–controlled areas (Area A as defined by the Oslo Accords), and they risk arrest and fines for staying in these areas if checked by Israeli soldiers. However, many Israeli citizens move around the West Bank daily to get to and from the Israeli settlements, and Palestinians with Israeli ID can also enter and leave the West Bank on the infrastructure designated for the settlers and their colonies. So, technically, Anan and Saz can be deported from the West Bank only if they are stopped and checked by Israeli soldiers inside Area A.

And they were. During the last week of the summer program, we all went on a bus from Jenin in the north to Bethlehem in the south for a final week of training and performances. As we reached the "Container" checkpoint between Ramallah and Bethlehem—both in Area A—Saz and Anan and a couple of other artists were forced off the bus by Israeli soldiers who saw their blue ID cards and Israeli citizenship. They were denied entry and had to walk to the nearest main street, catch a cab to Jerusalem, and drive around Bethlehem to enter the city from another checkpoint, which settlers also use to enter the southern part of the West Bank. They arrived at Ibdaa Center in Dheisheh Camp in the evening, exhausted and visibly upset.

"It was like, phew . . . ," Anan said thinking back on that summer from his studio in Nazareth. The fact of the matter was that he and Saz and the rest of the artists in the project were dedicated to connecting with youth in the Occupied Territories and sharing their passion for hip-hop.

The Segregation of Palestinian Hip-Hop Artists

At the risk of being fined if caught, at least Anan can enter the West Bank. Since the second *Intifada* (uprising), very few rappers based in the Occupied Territories have been able to cross the checkpoints and leave the West Bank to go anywhere other than Jordan—a border that is also controlled by Israel.

The physical fragmentation of the Palestinian hip-hop scene, particularly for the West Bank and Gaza-based hip-hop artists, is close to absolute. Of all the artists whom I became aware of during and after the project, very few Gazan hip-hop artists have ever received a permit to visit the West Bank, and none have been inside Israel. A small number of West Bank–based hip-hop artists have visited Israel or East Jerusalem with a permit, but to my knowledge, none have ever been allowed access to enter the Gaza Strip. The same holds true for the Palestinian citizens of Israel. Moreover, none of the artists we got to know during the project have ever met any of their counterparts from the refugee camps in Syria and Lebanon, except from encounters on tours in third-party countries. For the artists in Jordan and Egypt and the rest of the Palestinian diaspora—largely Europe and U.S.-based—the difficulty of entering the Israeli-controlled borders and the possibility of being deported upon arrival is sometimes enough to keep them from visiting. During the course of the project, the Palestinian rappers Ledr P from Sweden and Marwan and Sha D from Denmark were denied entry by Israeli authorities, and most of the other artists of Arab descent were allowed in only after a full day of interrogation.

Defying Physical Borders

The Palestinian hip-hop scene is with all likeliness the most segregated in the world. Still, the words and music of the hip-hop artists transgress those physical borders that separate them from one another. Long before the project started, groups and solo artists had been collaborating across the board.

American filmmaker Jackie Salloum's 2008 documentary, *Slingshot Hip-Hop,* shows the history and development of Palestinian hip-hop inside Israel and in the Occupied West Bank and Gaza Strip. The film was screened at the 2008 Sundance Film Festival and features DAM and Abeer Zinaty, aka Sabreena da Witch, from al-Lid (Lydda); the then Gaza-based Palestinian Rapperz (known as PR); and Arapeyat and Mahmoud Shalabi from the city of Akka.

Salloum and her crew toured the whole country and screened the film, an event that further sparked international interest in Palestinian hip-hop, especially in the Occupied Territories. The film shows the failed attempt of PR, the first hip-hop group to emerge in Gaza, to leave the Gaza Strip and enter the West Bank to perform in a concert with DAM and other Palestinian rappers at the Cultural Palace in Ramallah.

Today everyone in the group has left Gaza except for the rapper Ayman Mghamis, who later founded Palestinian Unit, a group that includes Black Unit and Watan Band. Ayman finally met Tamer Nafar of DAM in Ramallah in 2008, when he received a permit to visit. So far that has been their only personal encounter, and at the time they both had no idea what destiny would later befall Ayman.

During Israel's invasion of Gaza in December 2008-January 2009, Tamer phoned Gaza City from his house in al-Lid. He was calling Ayman to check up on him. With simple recording equipment, Tamer recorded the conversation and a verse that Ayman started rhyming on the phone.

> *Tamer:* Salam alaykum.
> *Ayman:* Yes, my friend?
> *Tamer:* How are you, Ayman?
> *Ayman:* All right, thanks God.
> *Tamer:* Tell me, how are you doing, how is your family?
> *Ayman:* So far it's okay. Now the Israelis separated the north from the south, they are entering [Gaza City]. By now there's more than twenty martyrs, and on the radio they keep telling us to leave our houses.
> *Tamer:* When they tell you to leave the house, how much time do they give you for that?
> *Ayman:* Look, Tamer, you spent your life building your house, you worked your whole life for it, you have no other home. They transferred us in 1948, and now they want you to get out of your home so they can bomb it? That's the idea, now where do they want me to go? If I had kids, for example, where should I take them to? My family? They want me to sleep in the streets?[1]

Only a few days after the phone call, a bomb hit Ayman's family home, killing his father and destroying the house. Following his father's death, Ayman sat down and wrote the song "Madinati" (My city), and he asked Palestinian rapper Shadia Mansour in London to feature on it. She recorded a chorus and verse and sent it to Ayman's sound technician to mix.

> [Ayman Mghamis]
> This is my story
> It's a story of people deprived of their rights on their own land
> Their right of living freely in their country that has been taken from them
> And they have been deprived of their mothers.
> With expectations of what happened and what is going to happen
> You can see tears are being shed for more than a thousand martyrs
> And today another one was martyred, but in front of me
> I held him with my own arms
> His last words followed by his last breath
> Asking my mother to take care of her children
> It was me who wiped her tears
> I gathered my wounds of sadness and enshrouded them; then I buried them in my heart
> Now January 16th has turned to be my funeral instead of my birthday

Today the one who's asking for peace is abandoning his life
They advised me to be patient but I have been more than that
Now I have no other choice but rejecting truce
[Shadia Mansour]
This is my message for the people of Gaza,
For the children of the camps,
For every mother and father, for all martyrs who rest in heaven
Maybe I'm far away but my heart is with Gaza
I'm not living the situation but I can feel your wounds inside, all over my own body
Once a six- or seven-year-old child saw what is happening to Gaza's children in the news and asked me:
Why?
Why are those kids not living the way I do?
Why are they suffering?
Why don't they have homes like me?
I feel like crying
I told him not to cry, I know their path is long, tough and hard
But tomorrow we are going to get Gaza back
We will get it back with victory and pride
And I will sing again

This song and the recording with Tamer and Ayman were created by three Palestinian artists in three cities—Gaza City, al-Lid, and London—all wanting to address the Israeli invasion of Gaza but unable to meet in person. Their second-best option became online collaboration.

Today musical collaboration between hip-hop artists is a common concept. But it became popular in Palestinian hip-hop before it did on the Western commercial hip-hop scene—simply out of necessity. The Internet is obviously the superglue of the segregated Palestinian hip-hop scene. Palrap.com (managed by Ibrahim Bassa, from Shoufat Camp) and mmdrap.com (managed by Rami Mansour, from Jenin) were two significant Palestinian websites that for years distributed and promoted hip-hop by Arab artists. Since neither Bassa nor Mansour have been able to find a way to make the sites profitable, they were closed down in 2011. However, Palrap continues to post new music and videos to YouTube, where, at the time of this writing, it has 441 subscribers and 289,000 video views.

Most recently Tamer Nafar started his own weekly two-hour radio show, *Ras Bras,* on Ashams Radio, where he invites rappers on the air to freestyle. The shows are also uploaded on YouTube.[2]

Other main vehicles for distribution are the many social networking websites: Facebook, Myspace, Google +, Twitter, LinkedIn; large-file-sharing software; live streaming and online radios; music-sharing sites like Spotify, Soundcloud, and Soundreverb.com; and video-conference technology, such as HipHopKom.

HipHopKom: Breaking Down Borders

When the Los Angeles–based Palestinian producer Fredwreck (who has produced music for artists like Snoop Dog, Dr. Dre, and Britney Spears) hosted a show on MTV Arabia in Dubai in 2007 called *HipHopNa,* many Palestinian artists criticized the fact that there were no Palestinian artists represented. That spurred the idea to organize Palestine's first national rap competition.

So as part of the project, Sabreen Association held HipHopKom (Your Hip-Hop) in June 2009, under the slogan "*Bi-kalimatikum al-ḥawājiz kassirū*" (Break down the barriers with your words), which was transmitted between the West Bank and Gaza by means of a satellite video uplink. On the day of the audition, young hip-hop enthusiasts poured in from all corners of the West Bank and the Gaza Strip, from cities, small towns, and refugee camps, to the audition venues in Ramallah and Gaza City. In Ramallah the jury had watched performances by West Bank–based rappers all morning. By the afternoon it was time to assess the contestants in Gaza. Since Israel had denied all the jury members permission to enter the Gaza Strip, however, these auditions took place in front of a camera in Gaza City and were transmitted to Ramallah via a satellite uplink.

The very last group from the Gaza batch was Darg Team. As they began their a cappella performance, the weary jury members started leaning forward in their seats. "It's them. They are the winners. We don't have to continue the competition," joked Suhell Nafar of DAM. The other four jury members—Mahmood Jreri, also of DAM; Palestinian British rapper Shadia Mansour; Iranian American rapper and dancer Mazzi; and Egyptian Danish rapper Zaki—all agreed.

"They have so much energy, man. It's by far the best we've seen today," Zaki said, clearly excited about the four Gazan rappers who had all but broken through the wide screen in Ramallah while performing their song.

Yet it was not an inevitable victory for Darg Team. There were fifteen finalists, and Darg Team was up against both skilled and ambitious rappers, all eager to prove their abilities and to win the prize: a concert tour of Denmark and attendance at the World Music Expo. Being able to enjoy the prize, however, would be more difficult than winning the competition—for this, not only the artists but also the organizers of HipHopKom faced another, more intransigent obstacle: getting permission for the group to leave the Israeli-controlled borders of the Occupied Territories. Transgressing borders with words is one thing; doing it physically is another.

Up until the day of the last HipHopKom show, the finalists and trainers had been working hard. Every group or solo artist had written and rehearsed his or her own track. Despite the competitive nature of the event, young aspiring MCs from Nablus, Qalqiliya, Tulkarem, Jerusalem, Ramallah, and Hebron quickly developed strong bonds with one another.

On Friday evening al-Kasaba Theater in Ramallah and the Palestinian Red Crescent Theater in Gaza filled up with fans, friends, and family, anxiously await-

Figure 5.2. Sarouna Mushasha performing at the HipHopKom rap contest in Ramallah, Palestine. Jury in the background; (front left) Mazzi (US), Zaki (Denmark), Shadia Mansour (UK), Suhell Nafar and Mahmood Jreri from DAM. Photo courtesy of Hussein Zuhour. 2010.

Figure 5.3. Darg Team, Gaza. The winners of HipHopKom contest 2010. Photo courtesy of Darg Team.

ing the evening's stars. In Ramallah a satellite-transmitting TV car was parked in front of the building, streaming the live recording of the show to Gaza and to Palestine TV.

The Ramallah finalists went on stage first, while the audience in Gaza watched on a theater screen. For forty-five minutes fifteen nervous finalists threw hand signs, waved their black-and-white- or red-and-white-checkered *kūfiyyahs*, break-danced, and hurled their words and rhythms to an enthusiastic audience who were rocking to the Arabic-influenced beats and the lyrics calling for change.

A Ramallah-based trio called Enough was particularly well received by the Ramallah-dominated crowd. Talha, a dedicated twenty-five-year-old rapper from the town of Tulkarem, also received serious applause. Four of the semifinalists were female and attracted much attention with their obvious talent, gumption, and attitude, despite the male-dominated culture of hip-hop amplified by the highly patriarchal society of Palestine. The female duo Katia and Majd from East Jerusalem performed break-dance, songs, and rhyming. The jury's female favorite was then fourteen-year-old Sarouna Mushasha, a student at Jerusalem's Lycée Français, a break-dancer and rapper, and a walking hip-hop encyclopedia.

"There's one song I sing about women's rights: how people view women in the society and in general in the world; how we don't have as many rights as men do," Mushasha said in an interview with Media Line before the contest. She also wrote a song about Gaza and several about the Israeli occupation. "I thought we could use hip-hop as a tool to show them the conditions that are actually going on," she said.[3]

After the performance of the last West Bank finalist, a break-dance crew from Askar Camp in Nablus performed with Mazzi. Then the theater screen in Ramallah was rolled down and it was time for the Gaza finalists to perform.

Although the jury could only see the rappers on screen, they were visibly impressed with the Gaza finalists. During the break everyone agreed that the hip-hop scene in Gaza appeared generally more feisty than the one in the West Bank. Zaki suggested that it could be the impact of Gaza's more difficult living conditions that accounted for the difference. No sooner did he finish his sentence than the link to Gaza was cut off. Hamas's intelligence service had arrived at the Red Crescent Theater, and all the rappers quickly scattered, fearful of the consequences of their participation in what Hamas perceives as immoral activity.

Darg Team's first-place win had to be announced via telephone to Ayman Mghamis, the project coordinator in Gaza, who then had to locate the group and convey the happy news to them.

The Long Wait

Darg Team has been making music since 2004 and performed at schools and venues in Gaza when the political situation allowed them to do so. But Israeli military incursions, internal violence, and Gaza's increasing conservatism and religious dogmatism have all frustrated the artists' artistic ambitions.

Before the HipHopKom contest, the group had never visited or performed with other Palestinian hip-hop artists outside the Gaza Strip. Their music had been reserved for their supporters in Gaza and dedicated hip-hop fans elsewhere who downloaded their home-recorded tracks from the Internet. So for them the prize tour in Denmark was a big step in their musical and personal endeavors. Even more exciting was the promise of tickets to WOMEX, the World Music Expo, where Darg Team's manager would meet industry moguls and promote the group to festivals and venues in Europe.

It was clear from the start that the first obstacle would be finding the right strategy to ensure the group's exit from Gaza, but it proved even more difficult than anyone had expected. For three months political-diplomatic efforts took place between the Danish organizers and any authorities capable of influencing access to and from the sealed-off Gaza Strip. After Israel closed the northern Erez border crossing from Gaza to the West Bank (via Israel) in 2006, the only way for Palestinians to leave Gaza was through the Rafah crossing to Egypt, which was subject to arbitrary opening policies and accessible only to people who obtained the proper permissions.

At the time of the competition, Hamas controlled the Gaza side of the Rafah border and Egypt controlled the other side in coordination with Israel. The border openings were therefore contingent upon the political situation of the four parties in play and their quota policies. Few were allowed to travel from Gaza to Egypt, and they had to meet numerous criteria.

The negotiations for Darg Team's exit were taking place in the wake of "Operation Cast Lead," the Israeli invasion of Gaza in December 2008-January 2009 that resulted in a tightening of the closure of the strip that had been in effect since the year 2000. More than fourteen hundred people were killed and thousands severely wounded by bombardments. Therefore, priority for exit permits was given to the sick who needed to leave Gaza for emergency medical treatment. The hip-hop group was not on the priority list of any official parties: Hamas, the Palestinian Authority, Israel, or Egypt.

As the dates of the tour and WOMEX approached, the members of Darg Team were waiting nervously, living with their suitcases packed, ready to leave at any minute. They missed the World Music Expo, but coordination attempts continued for another six months until the borders finally opened and they obtained permission to leave. A year after the competition took place, Darg Team finally performed in Denmark and in several other European cities after featuring in *ʿAisheen* (Still alive in Gaza), a documentary film by Belgian film director Nicolas Wadimoff.

Six months later the adventure ended and the four artists had to return to the besieged Gaza Strip. The traveling gave Sam Bakheet, Bassam, and Mohammad el Masry a thirst for freedom, and they have since found residence in Europe, just like several other Gazan hip-hop artists.

Opposition from Within

Mohammed Antar still lives in Gaza and now makes music on his own or in collaboration with other artists. He also works with youth in the disciplines of the genre while keeping political Islamists at bay. Antar says he has been detained (sometimes heavy-handedly) numerous times by local Hamas intelligence officers who question him about his financial means to pay for studio time and other issues.

It is unclear whether there is a relation between the political affiliations of the rappers, who are predominantly secular or by family affiliated to Fatah, or if it has to do with Hamas's perception of music and dance as un-Islamic. Antar claims it is the latter and points to *dabke* (folk dance) shows and cultural events involving children that are also targeted. It could be both.

In any case, growing opposition against activities that were perceived to be un-Islamic erupted in Gaza on November 30, 2010, leading the local authority to close down the Gaza branch of Sharek, a national youth organization that runs cultural and social activities focused on youth empowerment. Sharek also ran the Social Arts Center, a club that served as a habitat for the local hip-hop artists with a recording studio and video-conference equipment, which was established as part of the project to address the lack of access to and implementation of activities in Gaza.[4]

Following the clamp-down on Sharek, a group of young Gazans connected to the organization formed Gaza Youth Breaking Out (GYBO) in January 2011. The youth then wrote a manifesto articulating their frustration with political organizations that seemingly control their lives instead of supporting their endeavors.

> We are sick of being caught in this political struggle; sick of coal dark nights with airplanes circling above our homes; . . . sick of bearded guys walking around with their guns abusing their power, beating up or incarcerating young people demonstrating for what they believe in; sick of the wall of shame that separates us from the rest of our country and keeps us imprisoned in a stamp-sized piece of land; sick of being portrayed as terrorists, homemade fanatics with explosives in our pockets and evil in our eyes; sick of the indifference we meet from the international community, the so-called experts in expressing concerns and drafting resolutions but cowards in enforcing anything they agree on; we are sick and tired of living a shitty life, being kept in jail by Israel, beaten up by Hamas and completely ignored by the rest of the world.[5]

The Arab Spring and Palestinian Hip-Hop

Although the GYBO statement was written in Gaza in 2010, it reflects many of the young Arab voices who in 2011 called for political reforms and the ouster of repressive regimes in their respective countries across the Middle East and North Africa. During this time there has been an increased focus on rappers in the region who have played a role in "oiling the wheels of the struggle," as Iraqi-British rapper Lowkey defined it in an interview with me in May 2011.

And indeed many Palestinian hip-hop artists, both locally and in the diaspora, have been engaged musically in the Arab uprisings across the region. Numerous collaboration tracks involving Palestinian artists have been uploaded on YouTube and circulated online to support their protesting peers in the region or the homegrown calls for Palestinian unity and political sovereignty.

In ecstasy over the Tunisian people's ousting of ex-president Zine al-Abidine Ben Ali, in February 2011 Mahmood Jreri of DAM, Adi Krayem of We7, and other young Palestinian artists wrote and recorded "Green Tunis: A Dedication from Palestinian Artists to the Tunisian People."

> Out loud, out loud, let it reach most far,
> out loud, a flower blossoming out in the sky.
> Tunisia showed us how it's done,
> to throw out the evil and wear the beauty, most eloquently.[6]

And when Egyptians went demonstrating in the streets, Shadia Mansour was featured on Egyptian Arabian Knightz's "Not Your Prisoner" track,[7] and MC Gaza was featured on their track "Hand in Hand." Palestinian American rapper Patriarch wrote and recorded "Egypt Stand Up" with Egyptian rapper Rajjy Raji,[8] and rapper Boikutt wrote the song "Ignite" from Ramallah:

> From leaders to parliamentarians
> I do not exclude any of you
> But you don't care
> Until chants are directed at you and shake you.
> Let me explain,
> Tyranny leaves the street prepared.[9]

"Before the revolution you wouldn't see hip-hop on major TV channels. Now you do," Jrere said in an interview with me in April 2012. "Hip-hop and rap played a major role in the music of the revolution from Egypt to Libya to Syria to Yemen to Tunisia." Jreri said their second—and highly anticipated—2013 album also reflects on the past year's development in the region. But he also underscored the no-news value of linking music and political change, saying, "For us as DAM, we have been singing about politics and the need for freedom and justice since 2000." Jreri's point of view is echoed by Lebanese composer and ʿūd (lute) player Marcel Khalife. In an interview with me in April 2012, Khalife said there has never been a revolution that was not influenced somehow "by a poem, a word, lyrics, notes." He went on to say, "It was the poetry, the words of so many before me, such as Mahmoud Darwish, who said no to the kind of desperate conditions we have come to." Khalife also emphasized that music and poetry alone cannot make the change. "Politics is involved, so people should be involved. When changes occur on that level then, yes, music pushes forward, definitely. It's something all people relate to, whatever their background. And it doesn't matter whether you know the words or not."

In that process Khalife welcomes all artistic contributions, including hip-hop. "In this world, there are no more boundaries, it's a big village and people are reaching out to each other to try and express what their reality is," he said. "If these young people feel that this will best express the occupation, love, hate, agony, and grief they go through every day, so be it."

He said he occasionally listens to hip-hop: "I will not sit back and say, now I have reached a certain point, and my gray hair has given me a certain position. No, there is a restless child in me that is always looking to experiment with something new." That next "something new" might be featuring on a hip-hop track—an invitation from Mahmood Jreri. "Why not?" said the sixty-two-year-old Arab cultural icon, smiling in his gray beard.

A New Generation of Palestinian Hip-Hop

That Palestinian hip-hop is expanding, more than ten years into the making of the scene, is something Anan can testify to. In a drawer under his mixer are ten years of lyrics and productions that he says he intends to release as a solo project—soon. He says he has a lot of things on his mind that not everyone will be happy to hear about. "After ten years, this is the age of being real. But being real is difficult, because reality is a motherfucker," Anan said grinning. "We should spit things people don't want to listen to." While still rapping about Israeli police brutality and discrimination and the occupation of the territories, Anan says he is ready to lash out at local political dynamics as well by articulating other issues like domestic violence, the infestation of drugs in his community, and political corruption and hypocrisy at large.

Murad Abo Ahmad, thirty-three, who also started rapping at the same time as We7, agrees. "Our generation only talks about politics. Now the scene is switching to put out more personal songs, about the community—the hood," he said. "And there is even a new kind of gangsta rap—from rappers who went to jail."

"There is a new generation now. Every day I meet ten guys just wanting to sit with me," Anan says. He is currently producing a mix tape that features eight new young artists from around Nazareth. It includes tracks with Hussam Ikbarey. At fourteen years old, he is the youngest rapper on the label, and in Anan's words, he is the Eminem of Palestine. "We7 and Murad were influenced by DAM. I can't influence a fifth-grader now," Anan said, "but Hussam can. He sees things I can't see." And according to Anan, Hussam is already a celebrity at his school.

Hussam said that every available minute he has, he writes out rhymes. "I see that my community is in deep, and I don't want to be connected to that. I want to change that," Hussam said. When he is not in school, he is working at a car wash earning money to help support the family. His older brother is involved with drugs. "If Anan wasn't here, I would have given up. He is like a teacher who keeps pushing me," Hussam said before heading to the studio to record a verse for a song by a Lebanese rapper he has never met.

The Palestinian hip-hop scene today is constituted of myriad artists, inside and outside Palestine, not only adding a new genre to the contemporary Palestinian music spectrum but also manifesting a subcultural identity and a connection for new generations of physically segregated Palestinians seeking unity and new sources of representation. This includes Palestinians of non-Arabic countries whose affiliation to the Middle East varies from fluent Arabic speakers to those not speaking a word of it and from those who have visited their parents' country of origin every summer to those who have never been.

Obviously the idea of trying to squeeze all of these artists into a nondescript genre termed "Palestinian hip-hop" is a far leap. However, the cases presented in this chapter show that although the Palestinian hip-hop scene is fragmented and has no stated manifesto or any kind of formal organization, when bricked together the artists, their music, and fans constitute a language and a subculture of a generation that has grown up in segregated societies with an urge for connection. The music-production process of hip-hop and the available means of distribution allow the artists and their fans to defy whatever physical or national borders separate them, utilizing online platforms and alternative means of communication. In the words of H2Z, a Palestinian rapper from Lebanon:

> I'm Jerusalem, Bethlehem, and Jenin refugee camp
> The call to prayer, the bells, the crescent and the cross . . .
> I'm the teacup and the falafel sandwich
> Generosity and greed, morality and farce
> Lies and betrayal and honesty and persistence
> I am Palestinian until I die.[10]

Notes

1. The recording appears on the album *Hip-Hop 4 Gaza,* produced by Sabreen Productions, 2010.

2. *Ras Bras* radio shows: http://www.youtube.com/watch?v=inUtsvSR080.

3. Matthew Kalman, "Hip-Hop, Palestinian Style," *Media Line,* June 17, 2009, www.youtube.com/watch?v=NBOqW8cGUts.

4. The center was funded by the Danish Center for Culture and Development and the Roskilde Music Festival in Denmark.

5. Part of the Gaza Youth Breaks Out manifesto from January 2010. The full text is available at http://gybo.counterorder.com.

6. "Green Tunis: A Dedication from Palestinian Artists to the Tunisian People," verse by Mahmood Jreri. Music video available at www.youtube.com/watch?v=w2RxmGriZlU.

7. Arabian Knightz, featuring Shadia Mansour, "Not Your Prisoner" music video, http://www.youtube.com/watch?v=schIdC3LdLk.

8. Rajjy Rajj, featuring Patriarch, "Egypt Stand Up" (*Om il Dunya*) music video, http://www.youtube.com/watch?v=2mQBbtRdEvc.

9. Lyrics of "Ignite" in *Shahadat,* Exploring Popular Literature Series (Winter ed., January 2012). Special issue on hip-hop, edited by Rayya el-Zein. Published by ArteEast.

10. Lyrics of "I Am Palestinian" in ibid.

6

Performing Self: Between Tradition and Modernity in the West Bank

Sylvia Alajaji

> Freed from its various earlier involvements, consciousness views its own past layers and their content in perspective; it keeps confronting them with another, emancipating them from their exterior temporal continuity as well as from the narrow meanings they seemed to have when they were bound to a particular present.
>
> —Erich Auerbach, *Mimesis: The Representation of Reality in Western Literature*

Upon my return to the United States from the West Bank, friends, family, and colleagues all wanted to know how my research went, but those inquiries were often secondary to the more general (yet quite loaded), "What was it like?" Aside from the realities both they and I expected I would experience (the checkpoints, the soldiers, the wall), the message I wanted to communicate most of all was the awareness with which the Palestinians I encountered navigated, negotiated, and articulated the many layers inherent in their overwhelmingly politicized identities. I was there to study Palestinian music and identity in the refugee camps of the West Bank, specifically as expressed through the well-documented hip-hop scene. But from the first eye rolls I received after my initial inquiry into hip-hop's place in the Palestinian soundscape to the heated debates that would transpire after ostensibly simple questions about the reasons for the preponderance of *fallāḥ* (peasant) characterizations and village folk songs in programs and recitals put on by the children of the camps, it became clear that each musical utterance carries with it the burden of representing "Palestine"—a burden of which my interviewees were well aware. For in their rolled eyes and exasperated sighs were not necessarily judgments on the aesthetic qualities of those musical expressions after which I inquired, but an exasperation with the burden of representation they each must carry and the essentialist narratives they espouse—or, rather, are seen to espouse.

In this essay I examine the ways the Palestinian soundscape becomes implicated in the trappings of identity politics and look at the tensions between tradition and modernity that emerge in the musical expressions and activities of the various cultural centers in Ramallah and refugee camps in the West Bank. At issue here is not whether or not these musics are implicated (clearly, they are), but rather how each genre—from folklore to hip-hop—must answer for, symbolize, and epitomize "Palestine" and how this burden of representation plays out among the different strata and generations of Palestinian society. Each genre potentially represents a different Self, and when considering the immediacy of the identity politics at play, the Selves these disparate genres represent evoke a multiplicity that threatens any purported cultural singularity.

Of the exilic condition, Edward Said once lamented: "There is this tremendous thing about authenticity and ethnic particularity. The politics of identity is the problem: the failure to take account of, and accept, the migratory quality of experience" (2001, 222). He continues: "Instead of seeing it as something beyond the binary opposition, 'us versus them,' and therefore being able to see it in different terms, *there's this obsession about returning to yourself*: only in the community, and the purer form of the community is my salvation—which is, I think, a form of perdition" (221–22; my emphasis). These expressions of, and obsessions with, cultural particularity—this need to assert "authenticity in an environment which has been basically hostile" (221)—must also be seen as something productive, producing the discourse, or narrative, against which alternative expressions of the Self exist. These alternative expressions often evoke a hybridity that fundamentally conflicts with and compromises the essentialized Self that claims a purity—or particularity—under threat. When identity itself operates as a site of contestation, the channels through which it is mediated and negotiated—music, art, dance, literature, poetry, and so on—become spaces in which the Self is imagined and performed into being and thus become sites of contestation themselves.

For the Palestinians, expressions of cultural particularity occur in an especially urgent capacity. As numerous scholars have noted (e.g., Abu-Lughod and Saʾdi 2007a; Said 1979 and 1995; and Swedenburg 1990), the identity construction(s) at play must be seen as occurring against the backdrop of the Palestinian-Israeli conflict, during which Palestinian land and livelihood—their identity—have been (and continue to be) under threat. Golda Meir's comment that "there was no such thing as Palestinians . . . They did not exist" embodies the erasure that Palestinian expressions of the Self resist.[1] These resistant identities mobilize and unify in times of struggle, and, as Ted Swedenburg asserts:

> The Palestinian intellectual's claims regarding the need for preservation is not motivated by naïve romanticism or the desire to restore a pure origin. It is rather part of a communal attempt to "save" by establishing and reasserting an Arab cultural presence, in the face of the challenge of continual colonial effacement. Given the relentless Israeli suppression of all traces of Palestinian identity, it is little wonder that when Palestinian writers and artists mobilize rural signs, they describe this activity not as the production of meaning but as the deployment of signs with natural and authentic relations to their referents. (1990, 21)

Thus, at issue here is representation of Self to an outside world that is watching. The scores of journalists, activists, aid workers, and scholars who have frequented the camps I visited have evoked not only a sort of exasperation among the residents (as one resident told me, "We're happy you come and write about us, but why is nothing changing?") but also a distinct awareness that they are being watched and observed.[2] Their awareness of the gaze has indeed in some ways allowed for its reorientation and refocusing. Although there is an opportunity in this refocusing for a carefully conceived presentation of Self, there also emerges what has been called a "burden of representation." As Ella Shohat notes, "For artists and cultural critics on the margins, speaking, writing, and performing are a constant negotiation of this burden," each "act" ostensibly responsible for "synecdochically summing up a vast and presumably homogenous community" (1995, 169).

As Swedenburg implies, the Palestinian burden rests not only on defining the Self but also in proving that the Self once existed—not just exists, but *existed.* Proving that the Palestinians were there, living in what is no longer Palestine, in what are no longer their houses, dancing on and tending land that is no longer theirs, affirms a past existence that directly counters and resists the narratives that account for the birth (or rebirth) of Israel—narratives embodied in early to mid-twentieth-century Zionist films, songs, and album covers that convey beaming, intrepid young men and women overlooking or encountering an empty land.[3] Countering this narrative means inserting the Palestinian into those "empty" spaces. Thus, there must be a figurative and literal return to that moment of erasure. As long as that Palestinian is kept alive—whether through poetry, art, music, literature, graffiti, or other means—then the struggle is validated. The Palestinian counter-narrative finds life not just in these popular cultural forms but also, to borrow a phrase from Michel de Certeau's seminal work, in the practice of everyday life (1984). These little resistances—wearing the black-and-white-checkered *kūfīyyah* and other traditional dress, referring to Tel Aviv by its Arabic name (Tal al-Rabīᶜ), eating national dishes—establish a public transcript that normalizes this counter-narrative (Scott 1990).

The "authentic" Palestinian located in this public transcript—this "authentic" Self that is being returned to and kept alive—is often embodied in the notion of the Palestinian peasant, or fallāḥ. As Anthony Smith points out, peasants become "quasi-sacred objects of nationalist concern, since they carry many memories and myths (ballads, dances, crafts, customs, social organizations, tales, and dramas) which the nationalist intellectuals [draw] upon for the construction of their ethnic myth of descent" (1999, 85). In addition, as Smith claims, through the "rediscovery, appropriation and politicization" of the peasantry, ethnic groups are able to attain a sense of cultural uniqueness that provides substantiation to claims of nationhood (2001, 115). However, herein lies the significance of this appropriation, which bears repeating: it is this signifier through which nationhood is claimed. Thus, performances of "Palestine" that waver from these traditional representations of Palestinian-ness are often fraught with controversy.

As numerous scholars have noted, fallāḥ characterizations abound throughout Palestine and function, in Swedenburg's words, as a national signifier:

> The symbology associated with the peasantry therefore represents a form of digging in, a response to the deracinating thrust of the Zionist movement . . . In response to the Israeli state's radical, material denial of their existence, Palestinian poets . . . confected an array of symbols—the *fallāḥ,* the *kūfīyya* (Palestinian headcovering), the olive tree, the embroidered dress, the orange tree, and *zaʿatar* (wild thyme)—connected with a rural way of life. These figures were readily understood by readers and listeners as allegories for Palestine, the land, and the people's intention of remaining permanently on that land. (Swedenburg 1990, 20)

Numerous songs echo this romanticization of the peasant. Take, for instance, the following lyrics by the Sharaf al-Tibi troupe:

> O shepherd, O you taking your flock out early in the dewy morning
> How beautiful is your flute letting fall the sweetest melodies,
> the flowers spreading smiles around you
> (Oliver and Steinberg 2002, 638)

Or the following lyrics from the song "Yā Falasṭīnīyyah" (Oh Palestinians), popularized by the Egyptian singer Sheikh Imam (lyrics by the poet Ahmad Fouad Najm):

> O Palestinians, the fusilier has shot you
> With Zionism which kills the doves that live under your protection
> O Palestinians, exile has lasted so long
> That the desert is moaning from the refugees and the victims
> And the land remains nostalgic for its peasants who watered it
> Revolution is the goal, and victory shall be your first step[4]
> (Massad 2003, 30)

And finally, from "Hāt al-Sikkaih" (The plow), by the popular Palestinian revolutionary and singer Mustafa al-Kurd: "Give me the plow and sickle / And I will never leave the land." These songs literally and directly invoke the figure of the fallāḥ (or, in the case of the latter, are symbology directly associated with them) as a site around which to mobilize—both unifying and affirming. However, they also echo a critical point raised by Swedenburg: the peasants and their associated imagery and symbology inhabit a past "which is at the same time continuous with the present" (1990, 21). Thus, the Self that is being saved from erasure—the "authentic" Self, the Self that embodies and validates the counter-narrative—is and must be (for it is in this *must* that the burden arises) ever *present.* Inscribing the past onto the present not only negotiates the two into simultaneity, but it also binds them together: the past dependent on the present, the present on the past.

This simultaneity is often invoked through the use folk imagery as a blank slate onto which present-day needs can be read. Political groups such as Fatah and Hamas insert new lyrics into traditional folk melodies, thus attaching their cause to and making it synonymous with, to use Said's words, the "purer form of the community" (see Massad 2003, 31). This practice also extends into recreational music making in the camps and various performance avenues. For example, two young musicians I interviewed—an *ʿūd* player and a singer (residents of Dheisheh and Aida Camps, respectively, both trained at the Edward Said National Conservatory of Music)—also spoke of composing new lyrics to old folk songs taught to them by their parents and grandparents. In a private performance they gave for me, the singer told the ʿūdist which folk song to play (a song, he told me, "from his grandmother's village") while the singer accompanied him with improvised lyrics about his grandmother and his sadness.

The three songs excerpted above also exemplify this simultaneity of past and present, each bringing the figure of the peasant into present-day struggles. The first song seems, on the surface, to be a simple romanticization of the fallāḥ. However, here the simultaneity of past and present lies not in the lyrics, necessarily, but in external associations. The Sharaf al-Tibi troupe was a *dabke* (dance) group active in the late 1980s through early 1990s and took its name from a young Birzeit University student killed by the Israeli army in 1984 (considered by many the first student martyr). As Nicholas Rowe and Elke Kaschl write in their studies of dance and Palestinian national identity, dabke groups such as Sharaf and El-Funoun (see below) were often targeted by the Israeli military, and many of the dancers were imprisoned at one point or another (see Kaschl 2003 and Rowe 2010). Their performances—which featured folk music, dancing, and dress—thus became inseparable from the struggle. As Rowe writes, "Since the Israeli military often raided performances to try and arrest performers, being a dancer in such a group became perceived as a heroic act of resistance against the occupation" (2010, 151). Thus, songs and dances that evoked the fallāḥ and local cultural traditions became doubly imbued with revolutionary significance—by asserting, on the one hand, connections to those lands that were no longer theirs and, on the other hand, through the immediate risks involved.

In the second and third songs, however, the association is immediate. In "Yā Falasṭīnīyyah" the personified land yearns for those who once tended it—those either killed or now in exile (the song expressly written for and addressed to the latter)—while in "Hāt al-Sikkaih" the Palestinian exile vows to take up the symbols associated with the peasantry.[5]

In many ways these songs and the evocation of fallāḥ characterizations can be seen as a form of what Gayatri Spivak terms "strategic essentialism"—effective at times (within limits) in dismantling or encountering a hegemonic narrative. The role of music and other forms of expressive culture in countering this narrative can be a critical one, reflecting Simon Frith's assertion that music can "put into play a sense of identity that may or may not fit the way we are placed by other social facts" (1987, 149). In this way it functions as a form of resistance, insisting upon a sense of identity that directly counters the narrative that invalidates, for the Palestinians, claims to nationhood. Though the identity put into play by the aforementioned songs and dabke performances is rooted in the past, the simultaneity—and thus inextricability—of past and present that they negotiate into being produces a particularized narrative that strategically asserts Self. As Paul Gilroy writes of the musics of the Black Atlantic, "In the simplest possible terms, by posing the world as it is against the world as the racially subordinated would like it to be, this musical culture supplies a great deal of the courage required to go on living in the present" (1993, 36).

The courage that results from the wielding of this counter-narrative (and, in some ways, the dependence on it) can be seen in the expressive culture of Dheisheh Camp in the West Bank, described below. However, in this and in the examples that follow, the potential consequences of the dependence on this narrative can be seen as well. The burden of representation discussed earlier is multilayered. While on the one hand this counter-narrative must, as Ella Shohat states, "[sum] up a vast" community, it is also entangled with the hegemonic narrative against which it exists (1995, 169). The hegemonic narrative serves, in a sense, as a limiting factor: it produces a mode of resistance that in turn produces the discourse against which alternate expressions of the (Palestinian) Self exist—the resistance, then, becoming its own limiting factor.

Musically and culturally speaking, the consequence has been both internal and external. As Issa Boulos—a renowned scholar and active performer of Palestinian music (and contributor to this volume)—writes, in the 1980s practitioners of traditional music began to find their art compromised, as they were "increasingly categorized and labeled according to their loyalty or faithlessness to the struggle for Palestine" (2006, 12). Although he lauds groups such as Sabreen and al-ʿAshiqeen for their innovation and their knowledge of and preservation of folkloric genres, he laments the consequences of the transference of local, regional forms to the urban stage. While, on the one hand, traditional forms became "canonized" and frozen in time, on the other hand, different traditional forms became indistinguishable when performed on the urban stage (11). Consequently, as Rowe points out:

> The belief in the intransigence of intangible heritage and the rejection of innovation by Palestinian nationalist folklorists could also be seen as serving the Israeli cultural image in the international arena. The presentation of a static cultural past at the expense of a dynamic cultural present and future supported the representation of the indigenous population as backward looking, when compared to a progressive image of Israeli national culture. (2010, 133)

What follows, then, is a brief look at the way cultural expressions in the West Bank embody the burden of representation as a lived reality. I would like to emphasize, though, that rich internal dialogues do take place among Palestinians regarding their expressive culture (as I was privy to not only in my fieldwork but also in the symposia leading up to the publication of this volume), and that no one is more aware of the burdens and consequences of forms of representation than the Palestinians themselves.

Upon my first visit to the Ibdaa Cultural Center in the Dheisheh refugee camp, on the outskirts of the West Bank city of Bethlehem, the concurrence of past and present was immediately evident. Entering Dheisheh, one is immediately greeted by a drawing of the Palestinian flag on one of the many concrete walls that surround the camp. The handprints of the children of the camp can be seen in the red, green, and black color blocks in the flag, below which is signed (in English), "Children of Dheisheh."

Above the flag a profound sentiment reads, "We'll make our history"; a translation from the Arabic saying "*Nabnī tarīkhunā*," numerous layers of meaning emerge when this popular slogan is written in English. Clearly this message is for the many foreigners who frequent Dheisheh; aid workers, journalists, tourists, English teachers, and researchers come through often, with many staying overnight at the guesthouse in Ibdaa. The statement realizes upon the Palestinians their agency over history—a past and future history from which they will not be left out. In addition, that agency is acquired consciously and with awareness—the past consciously interwoven with the present.

Mahmoud, my interviewee, met me at the entrance to Ibdaa. As one of the main teachers at the cultural center (and a resident of the camp himself), he spoke candidly of the consciousness with which he tries to convey Palestinian identity through music and dance. Most importantly, he said, he wants to convey to the children of the camp—these children for whom the occupation is a daily reality and who have been personally touched by it in one way or another—a sense of pride in being Palestinian. Expressions of Palestinian-ness seemed to be of primary concern to the leaders of the cultural centers I visited at the various camps. Kamal, another music and dance teacher with whom I spoke (at the al-Rowwad Cultural Center in the Aida Refugee Camp, also in Bethlehem), told me explicitly that his mission in the performances he puts on is to present an "alternative Palestine." According to both Mahmoud and Kamal, giving the youth an alternative to the "violence and religious fundamentalism" that seem to be on the rise (as Mahmoud said to me, "We have three mosques and no playground"), and, more important, an alternative to the narrative that feeds on the stereotypes of the rock-throwing, suicide-bombing (or completely absent) Palestinian are the primary goals of the programs put on by the children of the camps (interview, June 10, 2010, Bethlehem). Again, however, this "alternative Palestine"—the Palestine in which the children are to take pride and perform into being—is one plainly rooted in the past. And, as the performances demonstrate, this past is interspersed with a present with which the children are all too familiar. The present is not always inscribed directly into these performances of the past. However, too often one cannot help but associate one with the other, as I did during this choreographed dabke, seen in figure 6.1, performed by the children of the al-Rowwad Cultural Center.

Entering Ibdaa, one is immediately greeted by a beautiful, colorful mural that covers every inch of the walls of the main stairwell. Each person who comes to Ibdaa must use these stairs to access the main offices and classrooms, the guesthouse, and the café (which happens to be on the top floor and where, during my visit, World Cup soccer competition matches were screened). Walking up the four flights of stairs, one encounters various images of Palestine past and present. At first the mural seems to progress chronologically. Scenes of village life—of villagers in traditional dress (men in kūfiyyahs and women in brightly embroidered dress), dancing dabke, fetching water from wells, tending to the olive trees—are set against the background of a sweeping, desert landscape not unlike those conveyed in the early Zionist films. This time, however, these landscapes are peopled with Palestinians. Images like these abound in Palestinian art. As Swedenburg notes, "Palestinian artists who employ peasant symbols are naturally engaged in processes of invention, transformation and interpretation. But although the symbolic rural armature they use has a recent history, they routinely describe what they are doing as the 'preservation' of peasant culture" (1990, 20). Certainly this "preservation" takes on a special significance in the camps, whose residents are referred to as "The Palestinians from '48." They are the ones in exile, who claim the land in what is now Israel as their own. These preservations keep alive that to which they hope to return.

As I ascended the staircase, however, the chronology that I assumed was in place (past to present, the latter conveyed by images of the camps over the years and pictures of children in modern dress[6]) gave way to images that instead made past and present contemporaneous. Two village women, both in embroidered gowns and

Figure 6.1. Dabke performance by the children of al-Rowwad refugee camp at the SOS Children's Villages' Graduates Association (June 13, 2010, Bethlehem). Photo by Sylvia Aljajaji.

with heads covered, were placed in scenes directly evocative of the needs, desires, and symbols of the camps. In the first image a sitting woman is shown against a landscape similar to the one conveyed at the bottom of the staircase. However, this time she is flanked on one side by the keys that symbolize the homes lost in 1948, and, farther to her right, by the names of those villages that were depopulated during what Palestinians now refer to as *al-Nakba* (the catastrophe).

In the second image (figure 6.2), a woman is shown with a resolute determination, no tears in sight, with stones in hand, ready to throw them. The background is a barricade of tin drums not unlike the bullet-hole-ridden ones I saw in the embattled city of Hebron, also in the West Bank.[7]

Thus, even before viewing the performances, a distinct "Palestine" was beginning to emerge—one in which the past informs the present, the present informs the past, and both become inextricable. The intertwining of the two is evident from a quick look at the program from the children's most recent performance tour of the United States.[8] Mahmoud explained that most full-length programs follow the same chronology, more or less: the first section, "The Well" (about 40 minutes long), followed by "The Tent" (about 25 minutes), and ending with "The

Figure 6.2. Mural in the Ibdaa Cultural Center. Photo by Sylvia Aljajaji.

Political Prison" (about 20 minutes).[9] Each section features a mix of dancing and acting (typically miming) to a mix of prerecorded and live music (the children do all of their own singing).

Similar to the mural, at first the chronology seems simple enough. As one of the young dancers states in the 2002 documentary *The Children of Ibdaa: To Create Something out of Nothing* (Smith 2002): "When I am dancing, my goal is to deliver my story. Because it represents my story and my grandparents' story from the moment they left Bayt Nattīf until the point I reached the refugee camp."[10] The performance begins, of course, with scenes of village life. Based on the traditional dress, types of dabke performed, and the actions mimed, "The Well" clearly evokes life in pre-1948 Palestine. The dancing is lively and joyous, and the actions convey the simple yet happy life of the villagers. Traditional folk songs such as "Song for the Farmer," "Song for Water," and "Song for Building Houses" are juxtaposed with the traditional dabke of various villages.

This act provides a chance for the children to perform as though they were living in the villages of their grandparents and great-grandparents (children of the camps typically introduce themselves to visitors with their name and the name of the village from which their family originally came). As one young male dancer, approximately fourteen or fifteen years of age, states in the documentary: "I dance with the group about my grandparents and my grand-grandparents. How was their life and how was their work? How was the land there?" One of the young female dancers echoes a similar sentiment: "When I am dancing, I feel that I am expressing the meaning of Palestine. It expresses what it means to be a Palestinian farmer, and what is the Palestinian dress." "Palestine," once again, is inscribed directly onto the Self that emerges in these "returns" to the past.

The following two acts, "The Tent" and "The Political Prison," advance the chronology and shift the setting away from scenes of village life. "The Tent" portrays life in the refugee camps in the years directly following 1948 (an image of which can be seen in the mural at Ibdaa), while "The Political Prisoner" portrays the false imprisonments, incursions, and beatings endured by refugees during and after the first *Intifada* (uprising). The group dances in "The Well" give way to solo portrayals of the post-1948 plight of the villagers and their descendants. Although the dancing becomes more modern, as does the music, the soundscape created is still distinctly Palestinian. Songs such as "Falasṭīn" (Palestine), featured prominently in the film, are sung as offstage solos by female members of the dance troupe.

Although both scenes are effective in and of themselves in portraying post-1948 traumas and difficulties, their message is made even more potent when viewed through the framework established by "The Well." As the very first act, it establishes the foundation for the rest of the performance. Every scene that follows emerges from its images and its characterizations—this is the Palestine we will eventually see destroyed, these are the Palestinians we will see suffer (portrayed on stage by their descendants). Past and present come together when children playing stock characters from village life in "The Well" return in later acts to portray other characters: the child who portrays a farmer later portrays, in scenes that take place decades later, a teenager being beaten by the Israeli Defense Forces. The young village girl fetching water from the well is shown in a later act being dragged across the stage during a portrayal of a military incursion into a camp. Although the scenes have shifted (from a village to a camp to a prison), the familiarity of the faces draws continuity from one scene to the next.

Toward the end of the performance, however, a remarkable juxtaposition of past and present occurs. A young man portraying an Israeli soldier brutally drags a girl in a white silk dress across the stage.[11] He beats her and then she slumps forward, apparently dead. The audience is given a few moments to take in the image of the beautiful young girl (angelic in her white dress) on the stage. Then, the "villagers" from "The Well" quietly come onto the darkened stage, holding candles and looking protectively over the young Palestinian girl. The music is mournful, but it soon becomes triumphant and eventually segues into a joyful dabke that closes the performance.

What emerges from these murals and performances is the dependency on the past by the present: present-day needs are justified by the past. Without the past in full view, present-day claims to injustices committed—to the memories of the Nakba—come into question. As I mentioned above, when I first arrived at Dheisheh,

I wanted to interview hip-hop groups (such as Bad Luck) that are comprised of residents of the camp. However, in a group interview with several young refugees (ranging from fifteen to twenty-two years of age), I realized that views on hip-hop are rather complex. Though enthusiasm for the genre ranged widely (from "Eh, it's okay" to "I love it!" and "I've downloaded every song by Eminem!"), one sentiment was particularly striking: "It's not us." According to Mahmoud, "Hip-hop is not as popular as it seems. It's 'Western' and doesn't represent Palestine. It's good for showing others what is happening in Palestine, but it's ultimately not Palestinian, not Middle Eastern" (pers. comm. June 10, 2010). Clearly these few opinions regarding the popularity and importance of hip-hop are not enough to draw any general, sweeping conclusions. However, the sentiment "It's not us" deserves further interrogation. Hip-hop's past is firmly rooted in the United States—the South Bronx, more specifically. The past that validates the plight of the refugees is nowhere to be found: a "modern" genre, rooted in the past of another, appropriated to express the current plight of the Palestinian.

Many with whom I spoke bemoaned the "burden of the past"—this "obsession" with it, as Said puts it. One man with whom I spoke, a Palestinian writer who splits his time between Berlin and Ramallah (and a close friend of the poet Mahmoud Darwish), became visibly agitated when speaking of this "silliness." With a roll of the eyes and a wave of the hand, the topic was quickly dismissed. His friend, a professor at Birzeit University, expounded just a bit further: "It doesn't allow us to move forward." Clearly there are important demographic differences that cannot be overlooked: the economic and political needs and desires of the (comparatively) more upwardly mobile Ramallah residents are far different from those of people who reside in the camps. However, the emergence of these tensions directly affects the decision-making processes of arts organizations throughout Ramallah.

Before looking at those organizations specifically, however, it is necessary to point out, as many scholars of postcolonialism have, that one of the pathologies of colonialism is the very dependency of the colonial subject on an identity defined by the colonial struggle (Fanon [1952] 1967). Among the Palestinians with whom I spoke, the fear that their identities are rendered immobile by the conflict resonates in Anne Marie Oliver and Paul Steinberg's study of popular music during the first Intifada. They write: "Mythicizing history, Intifada song provided narratives of epic identity. For Palestinian youth, in particular, it helped answer the question, 'What am I?' and it did so, paradoxically, through the negation of that 'I' in the name of the people and on behalf of the eternity of the land" (2002, 639). They cite the following lyrics as an example (*fidāʾī* means revolutionary):

> What am I? What will I be?
> What am I? What will I be? And what will be my words?
> I am a *fidāʾī*, standing at the border

I am a *fidāʾī,* standing at the border.
What am I? I am a *fidāʾī.*
(639)

A similar negation (in addition to an identification with the past) can be seen in the Palestinian national anthem, "Fidāʾī":

My country, my country.
My country, my land, *land of my ancestors.*
Revolutionist, Revolutionist,
Revolutionist, my people, *people of perpetuity.*
With my determination, my fire and the volcano of my revenge,
With the longing in my blood for my land and my home,

Palestine is my home, Palestine is my fire,
Palestine is my revenge and the land of endurance
By the oath under the shade of the flag.
By my land and nation, and the fire of pain
I will live as a Revolutionist, I will remain a Revolutionist,
I will end as a Revolutionist—until my country returns [emphases mine].[12]

In interviews with the leaders of the Popular Arts Center and the First Ramallah Group, it was clear that tensions between modernity and tradition factored strongly into the controversies both groups have endured. A falling out between members of the popular dance troupe El-Funoun, housed at the Popular Arts Center, led to a dramatic restructuring of the group. According to one former dancer with the group, the seeds of this falling out were planted in the late 1980s and early 1990s, during what he called "Phase Two"—the phase in which El-Funoun consciously decided "to no longer be a slave to the political situation." The controversy arose when more of their performances began to feature classical ballet and modern dance and incorporated programming that did not directly refer to the conflict or rely solely on representations of pre-1948 Palestine. This group, which had already faced severe censure from the Israeli government during the years 1975–1985 (many members were arrested and frequently called in for interrogation), during Phase Two began to face censure from various Palestinian groups (including religious groups who objected to the males and females dancing together publicly—a plight faced by the dance troupes of the refugee camps as well).[13] Elke Kaschl, who has written extensively on El-Funoun, notes the many critical reactions that would occur after performances that featured hybridized musics, modern choreography, or modern clothing—moves interpreted as an "abandoning of authenticity" (2003, 133). In Kaschl's account, criticisms of the shifts in El-Funoun's performances seemed to come generally from two directions: from a general public who found the "stylistic experiments" alienating and elitist, and from folklorists who felt that Palestinian heritage was being commercialized and cheapened through misrepresentation.[14] The latter's objections, similar to Boulos's regarding the consequences of the performance of traditional music on the urban stage, speak to the paradox of the counter-narrative. As much as it relies on folklore and traditional expressive forms to counter dominant paradigms, those traditional forms become adapted in a way that best fits contemporary needs.

A similar situation befell the First Ramallah Group for Music and Dabke (now the First Ramallah Group for Music and Dance). As Rowe describes it, the shift from "Music and Dabke" to "Music and Dance" came as a result of a "shift in conceptions of collective cultural identity, from an indigenous culture that only existed within the imagined community of pre-1948 Palestine to an indigenous culture that was dynamic and reflecting a contemporary social experience" (2010, 194). The tension between representing the past versus representing the present eventually resulted in a division within the group, with half the group leaving once the latter was decided upon (194). In an interview with Khaled Elayyan, the choreographer and technical director of the First Ramallah Group for Music and Dance, he bemoaned the people who "smoke Marlboros, drink French wine, but don't want to see anything but dabke in their culture" (pers. comm. June 25, 2010). Swedenburg notes that one of the consequences of the fallāḥ characterizations is their homogenizing effect. Underlying the frustrations of the directors with whom I spoke seemed to be the difficulties endured in pushing representations of Palestinian-ness beyond those determined by the conflict.

Lila Abu-Lughod and Ahmad H. Saʾdi, in their recent edition on memory and the Nakba, reflect on Erich Auerbach's belief that consciousness can view the past in perspective only when it is "freed from its own past layers." But as Abu-Lughod and Saʾdi state:

> When the past is still entrenched in the present existential conditions of the individual, affecting the myriad aspects of her or his life, perhaps he or she cannot secure the conditions to narrate the past. For Palestinians, still living their dispossession, still struggling or hoping for return, many under military occupation, many still immersed in matters of survival, the past is neither distant nor over. (2007b, 10)

Clearly the inextricability of past and present, as seen in the examples from the camps and in the controversies facing El-Funoun, affects the freedom with which Palestinians can navigate the many layers with which they must contend. And with the past and present in question, the need to control the lens through which they are seen becomes urgent, and that lens becomes fraught with the responsibility of representing the Self.

Notes

1. Meir was the fourth prime minister of Israel, from 1969 to 1974, and made her famous remark in the *Sunday Times* of June 15, 1969.

2. This mix of appreciation and exasperation was evident in the more "public" of the camps I visited, such as Dheisheh and Aida, which host visitors and volunteers rather frequently (unlike Bourj al-Barajneh in Beirut, for example, which receives far fewer visitors, given its deplorable conditions and prison-like atmosphere, and which I had a chance to visit shortly after my initial visit to Dheisheh).

3. For a discussion of the role of Israeli cinema in the shaping of a national consciousness, see Shohat [1989] 2010.

4. Although neither Sheikh Imam nor Ahmad Fouad Najm are Palestinian, this song and poem reflect how the symbolism of the Palestinian peasant permeated Arab culture in general.

5. Mustafa al-Kurd was born in 1945 in Jerusalem. His songs about the occupation and Palestinian resistance made him one of the leading Palestinian revolutionary singers but also led to a number of arrests. After being exiled for a number of years, eventually he was permitted to return.

6. In an interesting cross-cultural connection, a poem written for the children of Dheisheh by an African American child from California whose father was killed by the police appears on the wall directly facing the entrance to the café.

7. Palestinians who live in the Old City of Hebron (under Israeli military control) endure frequent attacks by the extremist settlers who wish to claim the Old City as their own. These settlers are allowed to bear arms and live under the constant protection of the Israeli military stationed there.

8. The tour took place in 1999 and consisted of performances in San Francisco, New York, and Washington, DC, among other cities. Mahmoud was very pleased, overall, with the success of this tour and mentioned that they were met with only one protest (in Washington, DC). The main complaint was not with the content of the program but with the fact that the performance was not coupled with a performance by Israeli children.

9. A similar program was viewed and analyzed by David A. McDonald (2009) in an interrogation of the performativity of violence in Israel and Palestine.

10. The documentary was made under the auspices of the Middle East Children's Alliance, an organization that at the time of this writing no longer has ties with Dheisheh or Ibdaa.

11. When I spoke with the members of the dance troupe, many of them told me that no one ever wants to portray the Israeli soldier, and they expressed the pity they feel for whomever is chosen for this role.

12. The national anthem exists in a number of slightly different versions. The lyrics for the original version, above, were written by the Palestinian poet Said al-Mozayyen and the music by the Egyptian composer Ali Ismail. According to Salim Tamari (1995), the period from September 1993 (the signing of the Oslo Accords) to the summer of 1994 saw three different national anthems: "On the eve of the establishment of autonomy, the natural

selection was 'Biladi' as rendered from the Fatah militarist hymn of the 1960s (originally 'Fida'i'). This version soon proved unsuitable for the peaceful character of the transitional authority, and the more melodic rendition of Sayyid Darwish's 'Biladi,' with a Palestinian script, was adopted. When public schools opened last September the students were mandated to sing a third anthem, 'Mawtani,' a nationalist ballad from the 1950s."

13. Khaled Elayyan, now choreographer and technical director of the First Ramallah Group for Music and Dance but formerly with El-Funoun, explains Phase One as the period when El-Funoun was primarily concerned with "gathering and presenting information about Palestine—largely a response to Golda Meir" (pers. comm. June 25, 2010).

14. These criticisms came from leading Palestinian folklorists, most notably those at Birzeit University. As Rowe states, Birzeit "became the central forum for experimentation and debates over cultural interventions in the West Bank" (2010, 134). See, in particular, Sharif Kanaana's (1994) work on the misrepresentation of indigenous cultural forms.

References

Abu-Lughod, Lila, and Ahmad H. Sa'di, eds. 2007a. *Nakba: Palestine, 1948, and the Claims of Memory.* New York: Columbia University Press.

———. 2007b. "Introduction: The Claims of Memory." In *Nakba: Palestine, 1948, and the Claims of Memory,* edited by Lila Abu-Lughod and Ahmad H. Sa'di, 1–26. New York: Columbia University Press.

Boulos, Issa. 2006. "The Past and the Current in the Palestinian Music Scene: A Personal Perspective." Paper presented at "Diwan: A Forum for the Arts, March 30-April 2." Accessed June 2, 2012. www.issaboulos.com/General-Document-Linked-to/Palestinian-Music-2007.pdf.

de Certeau, Michel. 1984. *The Practice of Everyday Life.* Berkeley: University of California Press.

Fanon, Frantz. (1952) 1967. *Black Skin, White Masks.* Translated by Constance Farrington. New York: Grove Press.

Frith, Simon. 1987. "Towards an Aesthetic of Popular Music." In *Music and Society: The Politics of Composition, Performance, and Reception,* edited by Richard Leppert and Susan McClary, 133–50. Cambridge, UK: Cambridge University Press.

Gilroy, Paul. 1993. *The Black Atlantic: Modernity and Double Consciousness.* London: Verso.

Kanaana, Sharif. 1994. "Introduction: Palestinian National Identity and the Palestinian Folklore Movement." In *Folk Heritage of Palestine,* edited by Sharif Kanaana, 1–15. Ramallah: Al-Shark.

Kaschl, Elke. 2003. *Dance and Authenticity in Israel and Palestine: Performing the Nation.* Leiden, The Netherlands: Brill.

Massad, Joseph. 2003. "Liberating Songs: Palestine Put to Music." *Journal of Palestine Studies* 32 (3): 21–38.

McDonald, David A. 2009. "Poetics and the Performance of Violence in Israel/Palestine." *Ethnomusicology* 53 (1): 58–85.

Oliver, Anne Marie, and Paul Steinberg. 2002. "Popular Music of the *Intifada.*" In *The Middle East,* edited by Virginia Danielson et al. Vol. 6 of *The Garland Encyclopedia of World Music,* 635–40. New York: Routledge.

Rowe, Nicholas. 2010. *Raising Dust: A Cultural History of Dance in Palestine.* London: I. B. Tauris.

Said, Edward. 1979. *The Question of Palestine.* New York: Vintage Books.
———. 1995. *The Politics of Dispossession: The Struggle for Palestinian Self-Determination.* New York: Vintage Books.
———. 2001. "Orientalism and After." In *Power, Politics, and Culture: Interviews with Edward W. Said,* edited by Gauri Viswanathan, 208–32. New York: Vintage Books.
Scott, James. 1990. *Domination and the Arts of Resistance: Hidden Transcripts.* New Haven, CT: Yale University Press.
Shohat, Ella. (1989) 2010. *Israeli Cinema: East/West and the Politics of Representation.* London: I. B. Tauris.
———. 1995. "The Struggle over Representation: Casting, Coalitions, and the Politics of Identification." In *Late Imperial Culture,* edited by Román de la Campa, E. Ann Kaplan, and Michael Sprinker, 166–78. London: Verso.
Smith, Anthony. 1999. *Myths and Memories of the Nation.* Oxford: Oxford University Press.
———. 2001. *Nationalism: Theory, Ideology, History.* Cambridge, UK: Polity Press.
Smith, Patrick. 2002. *The Children of Ibdaa: To Create Something out of Nothing.* Film produced and directed by Patrick Smith. Arab Film Distribution. DVD.
Swedenburg, Ted. 1990. "The Palestinian Peasant as National Signifier." *Anthropological Quarterly* 63 (1): 18–30.
Tamari, Salim. 1995. "Fading Flags: The Crises of Palestinian Legitimacy." *Middle East Report* 194, 10–12.

7

Realities for a Singer in Palestine

Reem Talhami interviewed by Heather Bursheh

Originally from Shafaʿamr in the north of 1948 Palestine, but for many years living in Jerusalem, Reem Talhami has a successful career as a singer and actor in Palestine. She is currently in the process of producing an album, and in this interview Reem details her background and current life as a singer, as well as the process of producing an album from scratch in Palestine, from the initial thought process and decisions about the theme of the work to the thorny issue of funding.

Heather Bursheh: Can you give me some background about the practicalities of being a singer in Palestine?

Reem Talhami: For as long as I remember, singing has been a challenge for me. From the beginning, I faced social pressures and prohibitions regarding standing on stage and performing other singers' pieces. I found myself fighting against people over my own dream, including my family, extended family, neighbors and acquaintances. Their main claims were basically either social—musicians are seen as socially flawed—or economic, as in "art does not provide bread."

HB: Was there anyone that supported you in your dream?

RT: Of course, there were some friends and teachers who believed in me and in my dream, and those had a great effect on my personality and in believing in me and my decisions later on. Also, friends that I have met outside my hometown Shafaʿamr, filled me with confidence and made me stronger. Through the years, I was invited to sing in so many different places, and I remember feeling so proud and happy to read my name in the newspapers, even though in small letters. But I surrendered for a time, for some years after high school, and tried to do things in the way of people that were pressuring me, but that showed later on its futility. It was a waste of time and years of effort. My decision to go back to school, and this time by my own rules, came in 1991 when I decided to start my singing and music studies at the Academy for Music and Dance in West Jerusalem.

HB: Had you given up singing before that point, or were you singing on an amateur level?

RT: I was singing on an amateur level. I never gave up singing, in fact. When I say "I surrendered for a time," it means that I accepted to leave art aside for a while and head to another direction in life, and keep music as a hobby. You see, I had to leave my town and start my academic studies. Of course, my choice was music and singing, but my family did not think the same. I surrendered by choosing to study social work instead of music. So I tried. Through my two and a half years of studying social work, I realized that I was wasting time and efforts. My decision to quit social work and go back to Shafaᶜamr almost killed my mother. These days were so hard, and I had to prove, first to myself and then to others, that this is not the end of the road, and that I will be going back to study music some day. Someday came very fast, in fact after only one year, and now I know better.

Being in Jerusalem at the beginning of the first *Intifada* [uprising], in 1987, gave other meanings to my music and the issues I wanted to address. The great emotional and national feelings that I was going through, especially coming from the north of 1948 Palestine, carrying the Israeli ID and being called an Israeli passport holder, filled my songs with a weird taste of sadness, sorrow, melancholy, grief, and slowness. Facing all that in the new, strange big city shifted my goal. In fact, my goal became obvious to me. I could feel the tension around and feel the effect of songs over the crowds, both in concert halls and demonstrations. The picture became clearer and my dream started taking shape. Ghurbaih [expatriation/foreignness], was the first group that I was part of. The group was established in 1988 and didn't last long. However, we managed to work on some pieces and perform them in public. Lyrics were taken from famous poets such as Mahmoud Darwish, Samih al-Qassem, Rashid Hussain, and Tawfiq Zayyad. Music was written by Ibrahim al-Khatib and Wissam Joubran. Amer Nakhleh was part of the group, too. The second group I was part of was Washem (Tattoo). It was established in 1992, during my studies. Our efforts in Washem yielded the first album, *ᶜAshiqah* (Woman in love), with lyrics by Wasim Kurdi and music by Suhail Khoury. My music and my voice grew with different kinds of experiences through the years to come. I took parts in children's theater with different companies and productions, sometimes purely acting and sometimes acting and singing. My voice was used in documentaries on the one hand, and I was acting in theater plays on the other hand, which gave my voice new shapes and wider experiences.

I was still facing some difficulties through my work as a female Palestinian artist who was completely involved in the Palestinian community in East Jerusalem, the West Bank, and Gaza. I was trying to achieve more and more through the act of art and in the context of a challenging society that has its own rules and constrictions: to build an audience and to make more songs that will reveal the emotions of the people, their dreams and their hopes, and to be able to talk to the people through the songs. These could be taken as goals that I set for my music and songs. I never saw my songs far from the people. I never saw them far from the political scene. I am a Palestinian singer, and Palestine should be present in my voice. Singing became a sort of a mission to me. As a wife and mother of three daughters, I had to—and still have to—play different roles and characters within my daily life. For some years I was running between nursing my baby and performing on the stage, cleaning, cooking, and rehearsing. I was preoccupied [with] building my name and establishing my music and theater, raising my three daughters, and simply earning my living.

Somebody thought suddenly that I could do some serious stage acting roles, and I was asked to take part in the production *Jidārīyyah* by Mahmoud Darwish, as both singer and actress. That was a marvelous opportunity for my work. The play toured the world for some years, and my theater career took off afterward.

HB: Tell me about your new album.

RT: Carried by the Night—or *Yiḥmilnī al-Layl*—is the title of my new album. It consists of ten new songs written in Gaza by the outstanding poet Khaled Juma. The words are exploring and revealing the dream of the city we dream of and wish to see. The music is written by the great composer Said Murad. *Carried by the Night* is presenting love songs to Gaza and about Gaza, the city that refuses to die. It's not politics, but yet it is. We refuse to remove Gaza from the Palestinian scenery, political-, social-, and cultural-wise. We, by these lyrics, protest the closure imposed over Gaza. We condemn the siege, occupation, division, lack of space and reveal the city and home that we are looking for. The CD has not been released yet. It will be, hopefully, by the end of October 2012, and that is due to production issues and restrictions that I have been dealing with through the whole year.

HB: Can you describe the process of making the CD here in Palestine, right from the original idea of it until its final release?

RT: I must say that this project is considered to be my first personal self-effort project. For years I have been implementing other people's projects, either in music or in theater. That does not mean that I was forced to do so. On the contrary, I did those projects with love, commitment, and passion. Nevertheless, avoiding my own personal voice and the argument I wanted to share with my lyrics and music, I avoided facing myself. Providing myself with the so-called easy road, I kept myself far away from the headaches of paperwork, production management, costs and budgets, up until the point where I had to make my move and decide. No one will ever know exactly what I want to say. Then the problems started! In Palestine, no production companies would sign a contract with me. One reason is because of the lack of these companies.

HB: Are there none, or few?

RT: There are very few.

HB: Could you have gone to an Israeli company, but you chose not to?

RT: Indeed. If I had chosen to go to an Israeli recording company, it would have been easier. I did not, of course. My choice was never there and that is obvious. One can ask: but you chose to go and study in an Israeli music academy! Well, at that point I had not much choice and of course that was the only place that I could choose to study singing if I was not to leave the country. I always thought that Israel, as an occupation state, has the obligation to open doors for education and universities as it does with medical treatments and hospitals, for the occupied Palestinians. It was one of the issues that it seems I will be dealing with my whole life. To be considered both Israeli and Palestinian was a great dilemma that I had to answer always. I was very young, too, and politically complicated questions had to wait for some time. This picture is much clearer now, and Palestinians who have Israeli citizenship by force are more confident and more aware of their steps and thoughts. In fact, I feel much stronger now and no one can disconnect me from my real identity, not even the papers. The music group Ghurbaih was in fact a relevant experience to what we felt at that time. So to choose an Israeli recording company was never an option for me. How could I present my songs through an Israeli channel? I think this would contradict the whole essence of my work.

The second reason I did not produce the CD through a production company is because they would be busy investing in the financial, commercial side of any project and would not care about its essence. This was just a feeling in the beginning, when I always heard specific kinds of music, and the main stream of music that was and still is running was either wedding songs—not Palestinian and not original—or Israeli Radio broadcasting in Arabic. Later on when I lived the experience, it became proven to me. In the past few years I had two offers from two different production companies. Both of them, of course, were interested in the financial side of the project, and I was only thinking music, publicity, and sound. The first company was thinking of using my voice for cellular ringtones, and the project fell through because of the lack of interest from my side. The second company was full of talk about some great ideas for me and my work but suddenly announced bankruptcy. Immediately after announcing that, they bought a restaurant in Ramallah! Experiencing these two companies, I don't think I would count on commercial companies, because in my opinion they would not care about art and music as a mission in life. My work is my way of life. Their work is a way of life too. So I had to step forward and hold the rudder and direct my own business from A to Z. Fear and hesitation were not an option. I called Khaled Juma and started the journey.

I had several ideas in my head from the beginning. Gaza was all over my thoughts. Calling Khaled in the beginning was only the first step. I was not sure of anything. Khaled sent me some of his old songs which were not yet set to melodies. I knew Khaled through his children's songs. Some of them had melodies composed in Gaza by Mahmoud al-Abbadi, and some were composed by Suhail Khoury and Odeh Turjman. I used to sing and teach them for my pupils in schools where I taught music.

My second step was to pick up the poems I loved and lived with most and push them into the hands of composers. No one replied except for one. During this time Khaled went on and began writing new lyrics. The Internet was the only way for our work to be done. Tens of meetings between Jerusalem and besieged Gaza made this work out. Through Skype, email, and Facebook—God bless them all—ten songs emerged.

Said Murad from the Sabreen Association came into the picture later on, agreeing to take part in this work. He began writing the music for the songs I picked, and I was writing down every single detail concerning the songs and the ideas I had in mind.

HB: Can you talk in detail about the issues you faced in funding the CD production, and any internal conflicts you or other people involved in the project felt?

RT: Said was the first to draw my attention to the more practical side of the project. If I wanted to bring my thoughts into action and make them come alive, I had to apply for financial help, especially if I would be working with companies such as Sabreen Association, using their studios, resources, and teams. The cost of my project was quite high, and I was worried it would not be accepted and would not work out. But considering that I had come this far, I was determined that nothing would stop me. I applied for two funds—the Norwegian scholarship administered by the Palestinian Ministry of Culture, and the Qattan Foundation—and waited for their answers. My project was approved in both places and I was thrilled, but even so, the money was not enough. We proceeded with the project anyway, with the knowledge that I would have to search for another resource. Meanwhile, musicians were using the studio for recordings, Said was proceeding with the music, I was running from place to place. Contracts had to be signed between Sabreen, as an umbrella for my album, and myself. Meetings with the donors had to happen, and it looked like everything was moving forward after so many months. However, I had to revise the budget. The budget was high and the money that I was awarded was not enough. The ministry wanted to know exactly where their money will be put, and the Qattan Foundation wanted a detailed budget that included production, marketing, and documentation. The budget was high according to that, and in the end the production was the only line that was funded. At some point the Qattan Foundation wanted a revised budget, according to the money that they approved, and a new detailed implementation plan. Sabreen, as the artistic managers of this project, were also busy with other projects that needed to be completed. So you see, I fall in between, and wait for things to be done on time. With Sabreen we tried to move items and remove some so we could stick within the budget and make things work out.

HB: Did you eventually find more funding, or are you managing to complete it using the money from the two original donors?

RT: I applied for more money from another direction, Afaq Express, and I was denied. I only have the money from the first donors. It seems that when I get to the printing stage of the work, I will have to count on my own personal budget to finish the work. I don't know if this is the case all over the world, but I know for sure that this process in my country, where musicians have to be so involved in funding and running all these projects, is killing the act of making music, the way I know music should be done. This is taking me far away from the essence of the songs. I'm tired and I want to finish.

A committed artist in my country, who has no money and only his art, finds himself or herself in the hands of different players, controlled by composers, musicians, donors, companies, budgets, and papers, waiting for mercy. The big losses here are music waiting to be accomplished on time—and time itself.

HB: Have you performed this program live yet?

RT: Yes, I have performed it. I wanted to try the songs in public and see the direct impact on people. I committed to do that through the annual Jerusalem Festival, run by Yabous in Jerusalem. The lyrics were the first to be noticed. The music, too, had a good impact. I don't think I would say it had the impact I intended yet, because it was not musically ready. I hope that by the time the album is finished, things will change. I believe in this work. I believe in the beauty of Khaled's words, and this is very important to me as the foundation of every project. The music of Said Murad is different from anything that I have ever done. And, yes, I think these songs will attract people. They are closer to the heart and clearer than other songs I presented in the past, and they are modern and lighter. The essence of this project is Gaza, and so I can't wait to see reactions to this work.

Part 3

Resistance

8

Performative Politics: Folklore and Popular Resistance during the First Palestinian Intifada

David A. McDonald

In the many Israeli and Palestinian historical accounts of the first Palestinian *Intifada* (uprising), the role of expressive culture has largely been characterized as epiphenomenal, a mere artistic reflection of larger determinate economic, political, and social forces.[1] In this respect many have argued, perhaps unintentionally, that although the expressive media that emerged during this time was a powerful means of giving voice to experiences of dispossession, it did little more than capture in artistic expression an especially powerful historical moment of resistance to a brutal occupation (Abed-Rabbo and Safie 1990; Bennis 1990; Hass 1996; Hiltermann 1991; Lockman and Beinin 1989; Nassar and Heacock 1990; Oliver and Steinberg 2002; Peteet 1996; Steinberg and Oliver 1994). Yet, in popular memories of revolt, contemporary conversations on the nature of Palestinian resistance, it is striking how many cite music, poetry, song, and dance as a predominant means of mobilizing and sustaining the Intifada. According to people who walked the streets in demonstrations and participated in the boycotts, expressive culture and media did more than simply *reflect* popular sentiment, comment on prevailing power imbalances, or describe national identities and affiliations. Rather, songs, dances, poetry, leaflets, graffiti, and the like *generated* such sentiment, *shaped* national and political identities and affiliations, and provided performative spaces for subverting and re-signifying entrenched power structures. Expressive culture provided an essential integrating tool for the demonstrating masses, allowing for new cultural and political identities to emerge. Collective singing and dancing opened up performative spaces for the integration of new communities, bodies, and ideologies. Such media did more than simply give voice to the subaltern experience of dispossession, but in the act of performance it also offered an essential means of enduring that experience. Through performance new ways of imagining Palestinian bodies and the body politic emerged, opening spaces for contemplating new directions and new possibilities in the nationalist movement.

With this in mind, this chapter seeks to complement the historical literature of the Palestinian national movement by illustrating several ways in which expressive culture both sustained and at times directed the first Palestinian Intifada. In contrast to previous studies, this analysis focuses on the discursive relations between cultural and political spheres, highlighting the essential role of popular folklore in generating national sentiment and integrating a diverse sociopolitical spectrum. In the process this chapter theorizes the essential role of performance in the formation of political movements more generally, outlining why Palestinian leaders of diverse social, political, and religious orientations all sought to use expressive culture in the pursuit of political interests.

Power and the Play of Politics

Central to this argument are two ideas on the nature of power and performance originally asserted by Michel Foucault and widely known throughout the humanities. The first is that power operates not purely as a force of domination, possessed and deployed by agents with a singular location and purpose, but that power must also be understood as a set of diffuse relations that permeate all aspects of society. Foucault explains, "What makes power hold good, what makes it accepted, is simply the fact that it doesn't only weigh on us as a force that says no, but that it traverses and produces things, it induces pleasure, forms of knowledge, produces discourse. It needs to be considered as a productive network which runs through the whole social body, much more than as a negative instance whose function is repression" (1980, 119). The second insight is that power operates in the very constitution of the subject. Individuals do not exist external to power, but rather are produced amid relations of power. Identity, therefore, is the product, the performative effect, of power. That is to say that there is no analytical position from which to theorize subjectivity, or identity, independent of the fields of power from which it emerges. Any analysis of Palestinian identity, therefore, must take into account the interworkings of power, the daily performances through which subjectivity is formed, and the strategic means through which individuals negotiate the contrasting fields of power and agency in their lives.

Antonio Gramsci expands upon these contrasting fields by outlining two distinct yet mutually determined domains of power: *domino* (domination), in which dominant/subordinate structures are maintained through direct violence, repression, fear, and intimidation; and *egemonio* (hegemony), in which power is a joint construction of coercion and collaboration negotiated across various material and cultural sites of engagement (Gramsci 2001; Hall 1986 and 1992). For Gramsci, hegemony locates the social processes through which the people's consent to lead is actively achieved and maintained. It is "the moment when a ruling class is able, not only to coerce a subordinate class to conform to its interests, but to exert a 'hegemony' or 'total social authority' over subordinate classes" (Clarke et al. 1975, 38). While state institutions of power and regulation (police, prisons, military) may compel submission and obedience through the constant threat of violence (domination), it is far more economical and sustainable for a political movement or ruling class to secure obedience through a semiological dialogue of consent *and* coercion (hegemony). In gaining the consent of the people, the threat of regulatory state power (violence) begins to disappear as the population comes to see the movement's goals, values, and tactics as congruent with their own. This feeling of congruence—a performative affirmation of the coherence between a people's fundamental ideas of who they are as individuals *and* as larger social groups (political parties, tribes, nations, etc.)—is absolutely essential for generating consent and securing hegemony. All of this is to say that the struggle for political power and legitimacy, for hegemony, is primarily fought in the reiterative fields of performance and identity; who may lead is determined by popular conceptions of who "*we*" are. By defining the frameworks of acceptable sociality through cultural and educative tactics, state institutions and political movements are able to achieve a consensus whereby the population begins to "internalize the leadership's vision, goals, and actions—its right to lead—as being a part of the natural state of things, beyond question and questioning" (Turino 2008, 194). National leadership formations, national identities, the very notion of "Palestinian-ness," are therefore each actively constructed and reproduced among relations of power and consequence based in a perceived coherence between political, cultural, and ideational fields.

Political movements, therefore, are profoundly cultural and are imbricated within larger processes whereby commonsense understandings of self and other become sedimented into everyday practice. Refracted through the lenses of the first Palestinian Intifada, expressive culture had a constitutive role in shaping political identities, fashioning national intimacies, and integrating a diverse community into a collaborative resistance movement. Through music, dance, poetry, graffiti, and the like, political groups sought to naturalize their political platform as a natural extension of what it means to be Palestinian. Creating a felt and instinctive coherence between signs of identity, the nation, and the political movement enabled political leaders to effectively speak and act on behalf of the nation, determining policy and securing hegemony.

Understanding the processes through which expressive culture is employed to achieve these aims moves beyond essentialist notions of Palestinian identity that seek only to expose the unchanging and primordial essence of the "people" in the project of authenticating nationalist claims. Palestinian identity should not be viewed as an archeological project of uncovering what has been buried by foreign occupation, a search for the pure, primordial, uncontaminated "folk." Instead, national identities—the very notion of the "folk"—need to be deconstructed as the strategic creation of social actors who contour perceptions of the past through the lenses of the present. Therefore, it is worth considering the myriad ways, and for what purposes, national identities may be manipulated and maintained—how belonging is structured and articulated across diverse lines of class, religion, and politics.

Performative Politics in the Nationalist Movement

Throughout the Intifada expressive culture had proven to be a powerful tool in the struggle for hegemony. Competing political and religious factions each dedicated considerable resources to developing sophisticated repertories of expressive culture and ritual in the service of garnering the consent of the people to lead the nationalist movement. Such rituals (demonstrations, protests, meetings) were engineered to experientially link signs of the nation with signs of a particular ideology, political party, or leadership group. Performed repeatedly in everyday practice, signs of the nation (songs, dialect, food, fashion, religious piety, topography, etc.) and signs of political affiliation (flags, images of political leaders, emblems, uniforms, etc.) became linked, creating a perceived "fit" or coherence between what it means to be Palestinian and who best represents Palestinian interests. Through constant reiteration in daily life, signs of the nation and signs of political affiliation became so indexically fused that their relationship, their truth value, was taken for granted, unquestioned, viewed as common sense (Turino 2008, 196–200). Carried over into diverse fields of interaction, the conjoining of various cultural and political sign clusters created a semiotic loop, a *poesis* that, in turn, shaped commonsense understandings of the nation, its people, history, and values (197).[2] For example, Yasser Arafat's skillful juxtaposition of rural dialect, *kūfiyyah* (black-and-white-checkered headscarf, an indexical sign of rural Palestinian lifeways and practices), and green military fatigues (an iconic and indexical sign of militaristic struggle) often blurred the distinctions between the ideational and the political, between *who* a Palestinian is and *how* the nation ought to be established. Over time, this strategically engineered image of the *fidāʾī* (revolutionary) became the normative image of Palestinian-ness throughout the late 1960s and 1970s, and further served to legitimize and validate the actions of the fidāʾīs as an appropriate form of resistance to foreign occupation (Khalili 2007).

There is no doubt that by the early 1980s the established Palestinian political leadership had become masters in the "arts" of propaganda. Music, poetry, dance, imagery, and graphic design were each essential tools in campaigning for political allegiances, defining the nation, and determining appropriate strategies of national resistance. Secular nationalists, socialists, communists, and Islamists alike each made distinct claims to represent the nation. This ideological struggle for position was waged in formal political activities (trade union elections, protests, local leadership councils, and various aid committees) and in the less formal realm of identity politics and performance (music, fashion, graffiti, poster art). Political factions were extremely concerned with manipulating national identity through ritual, imagery, and performance in the project of naturalizing their right to lead. In the process both geographic spaces and the bodies that passed through them became surfaces upon which this ideological warfare was waged. Graffiti, posters, leaflets, music, and fashion served to identify both bodies and spaces within a predetermined political framework, making each legible within competing discourses of national identity.

Among these competing political factions, music was a primary means of fostering identification and belonging. Because of this, the music of the Intifada was profoundly diverse, aesthetically reflecting—and at times shaping—party affiliations, goals, tactics, and ideologies. In general, Palestinian protest song in the years prior to the Intifada could be broken into three interrelated and often overlapping genres, each broadly associated with a specific political and cultural formation. Among secular nationalists, for example, the wellspring of Palestinian protest song was the large repertoire of folk songs and dances (*al-mūsīqá al-shaʿbīyyah*) associated with life-cycle events and practices. *Dabke* (folk dance) tunes, performed at weddings, engagements, and other life-cycle and calendrical festivals were commonly reset with verses of resistance poetry (McDonald 2013).[3] Their melodies, rhythms, and poetic devices were extremely important for signifying a distinct pre-1948 Palestinian "folk" ethos, culture, and history in response to Israeli efforts of cultural erasure and neglect. A long and established tradition of Palestinian culture and practice, rooted in the land and preserved over time, became a powerful means of articulating national sentiment and legitimacy (Barghouti 1998; Sirhan 1988).

With the rise of Marxist/Socialist political parties, the Palestine Liberation Organization (PLO), and the image of the fidāʾī in the late 1960s, Palestinian resistance music fell in line with the militaristic songs of other third-world anticolonial struggles taking place in Latin America, Southeast Asia, and North Africa. Martial hymns (*mūsīqá al-thawrah*) sung in unison male chorus, set to balanced four-bar time structures with running percussion and modest melodic accompaniment, dominated Palestinian radio programming across the Arab world up until the mid-1980s. These martial hymns, stripped of virtually any indigenous Palestinian musical device, were indexical of socialist ideology and its emphasis on class-based anticolonial revolution. In such songs the tight rhythmic accompaniment, narrow melodic range, and constant repetition of short phrases musically reinforced a united political posture. Young, powerful, masculine voices singing in tight unison and low tessitura were iconic of militaristic formations, subsumed individuality, and the strength of the masses in fighting for communal goals. In this way Palestinians presented themselves as engaged in a worldwide storm of resistance (*ʿāṣifah*) communicated through a shared performative of militaristic hymns and rhetorical device. The Popular Front for the Liberation of Palestine (PFLP), Democratic Front for the Liberation of Palestine (DFLP), and Palestine Communist Party (PCP) drew heavily upon this repertoire of song and poetry in their political demonstrations, performances, and literature.

In similar fashion Islamist organizations developed repertoires of expressive culture in the service of the Intifada. While both *shaʿbī* (popular) and *thawrī* (revolutionary) catalogs drew heavily from an established lexicon of Marxist third-world guerilla warfare against imperialism and the preservation of a specific folk ethos, Islamic-inspired resistance song (*al-mūsīqá al-islāmīyyah* or *anāshīd dīnīyyah*) was derived largely from the language of the Qurʾān. References to Qurʾānic scripture and the *sunnah* (the recorded deeds of the Prophet) formed the core vocabulary for imagining Palestinian liberation. To this end, Islamist songs presented a reconceptualized image of the nation framed entirely in religious terms. Land assumed a powerful connection with the greater Islamic world and the history of Islamic expansion. The liberation of Palestinian land was not for the preservation of Palestinian culture and heritage, but for the redemption of the holy sites of Jerusalem. For the sake of the greater Muslim community (*ummah*), Palestine must be redeemed. Essentially the nation was detached from any distinctly Palestinian cultural practices and instead folded into the greater Islamic world. In text these songs often glorified the lives and deeds of famous Muslim heroes (not necessarily Palestinian): the Prophet Mohammad, Salah al-Din, Sheikh Izz Al-Din Al-Qassam, and many others. References to famous battles between Muslim forces and the enemies of Islam were also common.

Musically, the differences between *shaʿbī* (folk/popular) and *islāmī* (Islamic/religious) repertoires were at times strident. Many Islamists believed that the dance-inspired dabke songs of Fatah were at best problematic in terms of religious jurisprudence. By and large, Islamic-inspired protest song rejected many of the core components of the *shaʿbī* nationalists. Indigenous folk instruments such as the *shubbābah* (small end-blown flute) and *yarghūl* (double clarinet), ubiquitous in *shaʿbī* songs, were omitted for their associations with rural folk dancing as well as established schools of religious jurisprudence that dictate melodic instruments should be avoided. Rather, vocalists predominantly sang solo melodic extemporizations on Islamic texts without accompaniment. In song style, accent, vocal timbre, and declamation, these songs emulated the rules of Qurʾānic recitation (*tajwīd*), avoiding local dialect, slang, and idiomatic rhetorical device. The majority of these texts were sung in an unmetered free rhythm and perhaps accompanied by only one or two frame drums (*daf*). Based on an approach that stresses the importance of the message, and not the messenger, music performance highlighted the abstract representation of the land through religious experience rather than focusing attention on the material qualities of the performer.

The Intifada and the Revival of the "Folk"

In the years leading up to the outbreak of the Intifada, the Palestinian national movement had become increasingly fractured along several ideological lines (Hiltermann 1991, 46–49). A series of setbacks, most notably Yasser Arafat's banishment to Tunis following the Israeli siege of Beirut in 1981–1982, left a power vacuum within which several competing political organizations all jockeyed for popular support in representing national interests. During this national corrective, the PFLP, DFLP, PCP, and various Islamist organizations each began to actively campaign for local leadership positions within the West Bank and Gaza Strip. An ongoing struggle quickly emerged pitting populist forces "inside" the territories against "outside" political elites (49). The "inside" masses were becoming increasingly disheartened with the prospects of the "outside" PLO delivering a promised end to the occupation. On the streets and in the refugee camps it became increasingly apparent that an end to the occupation could be achieved only by Palestinians themselves, inside the territories (Hass 1996, 49).

The outbreak of public demonstrations in December 1987 provided just the spark necessary to begin such a campaign. As thousands took to the streets across the West Bank and Gaza Strip, an underground grassroots consortium calling itself the United National Leadership of the Uprising (UNLU) formed, representing each of the four major political factions. Marwan Kafarna (PFLP), Tawfiq al Mabhuh (PCP), Ihab al ʿAshqar (Fatah), and Jamal Zaqut (DFLP) established the UNLU for the purpose of orchestrating the demonstrations, scheduling labor strikes, and defining collective goals and demands. Their leadership, revealed in a series of mass-produced communiqués, proved instrumental in maintaining the collective spirit of the protests, facilitating the means by which the Intifada was to be enacted, and determining the appropriate methods of popular resistance (Hiltermann 1991, 211). The ultimate success of the UNLU in directing the Intifada, however, arose not so much in their tactical efforts to tie down occupation forces in thousands of protests and demonstrations, nor in their expertise at controlling the media, but in their ability to facilitate a widespread cultural transformation of Palestinian society from within. This transformation was based largely on a movement away from the divisive system of political notables and hierarchies (a top-down approach) toward a revival of the shaʿb, the masses suffering under occupation (a bottom-up approach). In its anonymously signed communiqués, grassroots humanitarian efforts, and its persistent calls for national solidarity, the UNLU became a powerful voice for a new direction in Palestinian politics. This new direction promised an end to the occupation—not by protracted military engagement with Israeli forces or guerilla warfare, but through concerted grassroots civil disobedience.

This dramatic political transformation was instigated in part by a profound crisis in Palestinian culture and identity. Beginning in the early 1970s a cultural and political renaissance had begun in the territories, largely founded by a new wave of college professors and young professionals interested in sustainable community efforts aimed at reclaiming and preserving traditional culture and practice. Among these efforts, the Voluntary Work Movement was but one initiative that brought together rural and urban communities, in the process developing a new political consciousness. In an effort to break down the barriers between town and countryside, and to preserve Palestinian culture against erasure, middle-class intellectuals along with professionals and students provided assistance to local farmers during the olive harvest and led education and literacy programs in rural villages (Taraki 1990, 59). These work camps soon became forums for political and cultural expression, reframing rural practices, such as the olive harvest, as acts of political resistance and politicizing a new generation of Palestinian youth.

A central component of this initiative was a rejuvenation of traditional music and dance among cosmopolitan and urban Palestinians. Buttressed by the establishment of many cultural aid organizations, young people who were active in the voluntary work communities began to participate in the widespread effort to document and preserve Palestinian cultural heritage. Foremost among these organizations was the Society of Inash Al Usra (Regeneration of the Family), which spearheaded preservation efforts through the publication of its scholarly journal, *al-Turāth wa al-Mujtama*ᶜ (Heritage and Society), the establishment of a library and archive of Palestinian folklore, and the sponsorship of several folkloric festivals and performance ensembles. The many efforts to preserve and document traditional Palestinian folk song and dance had a profound effect on the larger project of political resistance, shaping perceptions and values of Palestinian identity. As middle-class, educated, urban youth were exposed to, and began to participate in, rural cultural practices, values shifted. Notions of what it meant to be Palestinian were reframed, bringing together diverse urban and rural communities under a shared banner of resistance and enabling a more open and collaborative framework for political action to emerge.

The linchpin of this project was a renewed emphasis on popular heritage (*al-turāth al-sha*ᶜ*bī*), most clearly articulated through formal and informal music and dance performances. In his ethnographic study of Palestinian folklore during the Intifada, Nimr Sirhan identifies two determinate factors in generating the uprising: the subjugation and repression of everyday life (material anxieties), and the attack on indigenous Palestinian culture and practices (cultural anxieties) (1988, 10–14). In addition to deplorable living conditions and social, economic, and political oppression, Palestinians were expressing widespread fears of losing their "indigenous selves," their "Palestinian roots," to foreign occupation and encroachment (Barghouti 1998; Sirhan 1988). Those communities (largely urban, educated, cosmopolitan), feeling dislocated from their roots, sought them out in traditional practices and popular folklore. According to Sirhan's research, the Intifada was as much a cultural uprising as a political one. By taking to the streets Palestinians were making a statement that was both political and cultural: the occupation must end, and "traditional historic Palestine" must live.

The UNLU strategically articulated both of these anxieties in its many directives. The desired political transformation to grassroots activism was indexically linked to a revival of the "authentic," "pure" Palestine of pre-1948. In folding together the political project of ending the occupation with an ongoing cultural renaissance of indigenous Palestinian folklore and practice, the UNLU and other political institutions working at the time fostered the development of a new political consciousness among segments of the population that had often been neglected in nationalist discourse (Taraki 1990, 60–62). As a tool for integrating diverse rural and urban communities under a shared banner of nationalism, the revival of Palestinian folklore through music and dance served to encourage rural and poor communities to join the demonstrations. To do this, explicit political demands and instructions were layered between poetic references to Palestinian history, nationalist leadership, and the importance of solidarity in confronting the enemy. In public communiqués, graffiti, music, and dance, signs of the "folk" were employed as an educative tool, bringing diverse segments of the population together and teaching appropriate means of resistance to Israeli forces.

From Freedom Fighters to Children of the Stones

In order to better articulate both the political and cultural anxieties brought forth by the occupation, political leaders, artists, and intellectuals very strategically sought to reconceptualize the resistance movement away from the once ubiquitous image of the uniformed freedom fighter (fidāʾī) to the more sympathetic image of adolescents demonstrating in the streets. These *aṭfāl al-ḥijārah* (children of the stones) quickly superseded the uniformed fidāʾī as the primary sign of the nation and the resistance movement. In song, imagery, and rhetorical device the *klashin* (Kalashnikov) and RPG were replaced by the *ḥajar* (stone), the *maqlāʿ* (sling), and the *muqlayʿah* (slingshot) as tools of national resistance and affirmation. This demonstrative transformation from rifle to stone was a powerful means of resignifying resistance from military engagement to grassroots civil disobedience. The stone and sling were powerful signs of indigenous Palestinian lifeways and practices due to their associations with rural shepherds. Moreover, this resignification successfully indexed the enormous power imbalance between Palestinian demonstrators and the Israeli army.

In taking up the stone and slingshot against heavily armored Israeli tanks, Palestinians were developing a new resistance performative that was intended to articulate with both political and cultural discourses. Essentially such a tactic expressed the political need for an end to the occupation and the cultural need to preserve indigenous Palestinian history, lifeways, and practice. As the technologies of modern warfare (RPGs, Kalashnikov rifles, uniforms, etc.) had proven themselves ineffective at stopping Israeli attacks in the refugee camps of Lebanon, Palestinians interpreted the adoption of nonlethal resistance, epitomized in the stone, slingshot, and Molotov cocktail, as a return to their Palestinian roots. Indeed, among political leaders, artists, and intellectuals the strategy of stone throwing, labor strikes, and demonstrations harkened back to the Palestinian peasant revolts of 1834 and 1936 (Barghouti 1998; Sirhan 1988; Swedenburg 1990 and 1995). To lay down the klashin, take off the green army fatigues, and instead walk the streets wearing the kūfiyyah around one's head and neck, singing folkloric songs, signified a return to the folk, the embodied "pure" Palestine.

Such a dramatic transformation in the tactics of resistance rested upon and was driven by a transformation in the ways Palestinian identity was articulated across various fields. In demanding self-determination it was imperative to confront occupation forces armed with implements of Palestinian history and indigeneity, signs that reinforced and legitimized their struggle for recognition against colonial encroachment. Songs, poetry, posters, graffiti, scarves, and stones were all framed as powerful weapons of resistance, signs of history and presence in the land long before Jewish colonization. Yet in the early phases of the uprising, there was immense pressure to resort back to small-arms warfare. Demonstrators were reluctant, perhaps fearful, of taking on the enormous resources of the Israeli military with such limited weaponry. However, confronted with ubiquitous signs of national sentiment, sacrifice, and the sacredness of the stone, land, and history, across multiple fields of sociality, people became more and more convinced. Verses of folk songs chanted in the streets and painted on the city walls hammered home this ideational shift through their redundancy and affective power (Barghouti 1998, 19–21; Sirhan 1988, 11–15).

There is no fear, There is no fear	*mā fī khawf mā fī khawf*
For the stone has become the Kalashnikov	*al-ḥajar ṣār klashnikūf*
Oh world take a look, and people come see	*yā dunyā tull w yā bashar shūf*
Our stones are stronger than the Kalashnikov	*w ḥajarnā aqwā min klashnikūf*
Now is the time of defiance and not of fear	*waqt al taḥaddī mā ʿennā khawf*
Whoever opposes us will become crazy	*w illī yʿādīnā yaṣbaḥ majnūn*

Palestinian folklorist Nimr Sirhan, in researching the significance of the stone in Intifada folklore, goes so far as to say that among Palestinians under occupation it had become increasingly apparent that "there ultimately was no cure for the contamination of the land, but for the stone" (Sirhan 1988, 12). The binary of pure/

impure, sacred/profane that is alluded to in Sirhan's prose is found throughout the folkloric research, expressive culture, and media of this time and further reinforces the ways in which expressive culture was operationalized as a means to determine and direct mainstream notions of Palestinian identity and resistance. To cleanse the nation of its contamination required the resurgence of the "pure" Palestine, embodied in the sacred relationship between the people and the homeland.

To throw a stone, a piece of the homeland, at a foreign occupying soldier was a powerful resistance performative that was strategically engineered to reinforce the sacred relationship between the nation and the land. This relationship was further solidified in the act of transforming pieces of the land into implements of national resistance. The conflation of people and land is further exemplified in the act of throwing. In throwing a stone, Palestinians were metaphorically throwing pieces of the nation, pieces of their bodies, and pieces of the body politic at their enemies. The following folk song, based on a traditional poetic form, *murabba^c*, further explains the performative relationship between stone and man (Sirhan 1988, 12).[4]

Oh stones, oh stones	*yā ḥijārah yā ḥijārah*
Do not leave our cramped quarters	*uwʿī trūḥī min al-ḥārah*
You and I were raised together	*anā wiyāk trabbaynā*
Like the sea and the sailor	*mithl al-baḥr wa biḥārah*

For many Palestinians, the sling and slingshot were equally powerful signs of folk resistance and indigenous practice. In Palestinian dialect the words *al-maqlāʿ* and *al-muqlayʿah* are each derived from the same root (*qlʿ*), meaning to throw or cast out, to expel, oust, or evict. As young boys took to the streets with their slingshots, they were in essence giving a performative display of expelling and evicting, casting out, occupation forces from Palestinian lands, utilizing the tools or implements of Palestinian history. Similar to the shepherd's flute, the slingshot was a sign of rural folk practice, youth culture, and linkages to an idyllic Palestinian past. Among Palestinians seeking to revive indigenous culture in the service of the nationalist movement, such practices carried with them powerful associations of rural purity, family, protection, and masculinity.[5] Young boys tending their family's flocks would typically utilize a leather sling or slingshot to fend off predators. Boys would later hone their talents with larger stones while tending the fields with their fathers or while hunting sparrows. The more proficient a young boy became with the sling and slingshot, the more he could be trusted to assume the full duties of tending the flocks and hence take on some of the responsibilities of being a man and head of household. From this the sling and slingshot became important tools for protection and for demonstrating one's burgeoning masculinity.

While Sirhan's notion that the Intifada brought people back to their "authentic" selves may have been quite popular—even to the point of cliché—it nevertheless reveals an important strategic essentialism operating at the time. As is certainly true in earlier periods of Palestinian history, popular folklore became a tool for uniting people for political ends by reducing complex subjectivities to a core set of aspects that were projected as fundamental and immutable to Palestinian identity (Turino 2008, 104). From the post-1948 *jīl al-ṣumūd* (generation of steadfastness) to the post-1967 *jīl al-thawrah* (generation of revolution), this new *jīl al-ḥijārah* (generation of stones) was carried forth in popular folklore as a strategically imagined Palestinian identity, one that served to reinforce the leadership of the "grassroots" UNLU and reframe Palestinian resistance away from the image of the fidāʾī. The so-called return to the "authentic Palestine" was yet another example of how politico-nationalist groups strategically used different facets of identity to serve their causes, often shifting dramatically depending on context.

Ṭāq Ṭāq Ṭāqīyya

In a similar fashion, popular folklore, in the form of children's games, dances, and nursery rhymes, was appropriated into the resistance movement. For example, the well-known children's game *Ṭāq Ṭāq Ṭāqīyya* became a powerful resistance performative during the uprising (Sirhan 1988, 17). In this game, played by young boys and girls, participants chase each other in a kind of "hide and seek" around a circle, singing a prescribed folk song. Participants sit in a circle, facing inward, while a chosen player walks around the outside of the circle carrying a knotted handkerchief. The one carrying the handkerchief is marked as "tagged," the leader of the game. The object of the game is to safely pass off the handkerchief to another player so as not to be tagged. In the course of walking around the circle, the tagged player secretly places the handkerchief behind the back of one of the players in the circle, passing off the handkerchief to another player, in essence tagging a new player. The tagged player must then grab the handkerchief and chase his opponent around the circle, trying to catch the one who tagged him. If the evading player circumvents the entire circle and sits in the vacant spot without being tagged with the handkerchief, he is safe and may remain in the circle. However, if the chasing player is able to tag the evading player with the handkerchief before he circumvents the circle, then the evading player remains tagged, and must attempt the entire process again. While walking around the circle, the tagged player leads a call-and-response folk song as the seated players clap their hands and respond after each line (Hijab 1997, 201–203).

Taq Taq Taqiya	*Ṭāq Ṭāq Ṭāqīyyaih*
Response: Two hats on the rooftop . . .	*ṭāqīytayn bʿillīyyaih*
It takes two shots for freedom	*ṭaleqtayn lil-ḥurrīyyaih*
Response: Two hats on the rooftop . . .	*ṭāqīytayn bʿillīyyaih*
Pop! Pop! Oh my goodness!	*ṭuq ṭuq yā salām*
Response: Two hats on the rooftop . . .	*ṭāqīytayn bʿillīyyaih*

Catch me if you can	*ilḥaqnī ilḥaqnī ʾan kannak humām*
Response: Two hats on the rooftop . . .	*ṭāqīytayn bʿillīyyaih*
Taq Taq Taqiya	*Ṭāq Ṭāq Ṭāqīyyaih*
Response: Two hats on the rooftop . . .	*ṭāqīytayn bʿillīyyaih*
Ring! Ring! Oh bell	*rinn rinn yā jaras*
Response: Two hats on the rooftop . . .	*ṭāqīytayn bʿillīyyaih*
Turn and mount the horse	*ḥawwil w irkab ʾal-faras*
Response: Two hats on the rooftop . . .	*ṭāqīytayn bʿillīyyaih*
Taq Taq Taqiya	*Ṭāq Ṭāq Ṭāqīyyaih*
Response: Two hats on the rooftop . . .	*ṭāqīytayn bʿillīyyaih*
Give freedom to the land	*ʿalā blād al-ḥurrīyyaih*
Response: Two hats on the rooftop . . .	*ṭāqīytayn bʿillīyyaih*
Line up! Line up straight	*ṣaf ṣaf bi al-niẓām*
Response: Two hats on the rooftop . . .	*ṭāqīytayn bʿillīyyaih*
Stay awake, and do not fall asleep	*ẓal ṣāḥī wa lā tnām*
Response: Two hats on the rooftop . . .	*ṭāqīytayn bʿillīyyaih*

Based on its associations with rural folk practices, poets and musicians frequently drew upon the many layers of meaning associated withṬāq Ṭāq Ṭāqīyya, the sling, and the slingshot to articulate new imaginings of national resistance. For example, in Abdellatif Barghouti's collection of popular Intifada songs he documents how the well-known nursery rhyme that accompanied Ṭāq Ṭāq Ṭāqīyya was rewritten to reflect nationalist themes and issues (Barghouti 1998, 302).

Taq Taq Taqiya	*Ṭāq Ṭāq Ṭāqīyyaih*
I am without identity	*wʾanā balā hawīyyaih*
Ring! Ring! Oh bell	*rinn rinn yā jaras*
For there is a dagger in my back	*khanjar fī ẓahrī ingharas*
Taq Taq Oh Father of strength	*ṭāq ṭāq yā bū el-ṭūq*
For my country I am filled with longing	*la-bilādī ʾanā kullī shūq*
Arise! Arise! Oh those who hunger	*ʿin ʿin yā juʿān*
You are steadfast while others are disloyal	*inta el-ṣāmid w ghayrak khān*
Taq Taq oh roaming patrols	*ṭāq ṭāq ṭawwaqnā*
Our situation changed but we did not wake up	*ṣār al-ḥal w mā fiqnā*
We need more effort from the revolutionary	*shiddū el-himmaih yā thuwwār*
We have been patient for too long, we want revenge	*ṣabarnā kthīr bidnā thār*
In the West Bank and Gaza Strip	*bi al-ḍaffaih w kull al-qitāʿ*
Taq Taq Taqiya	*ṭāq ṭāq ṭāqīyyaih*
With the sling and the slingshot	*bi al-moqlayṭah w al-maqlāʿ*
Revolution, Popular Revolution	*thawrah thawrah shaʿbīyyaih*

Chanted in call and response, this well-known children's song became a powerful means of communicating national sentiment, history, and resistance utilizing a familiar set of musical signs. What is more, through constant reiteration in protests and other public performances, the game of Ṭāq Ṭāq Ṭāqīyya became a metaphor for the uprising itself, a musical image of Palestinian identity based on the confluence of youth culture, popular folklore, and resistance. Young adolescent boys (*shabāb*) taking games of Ṭāq Ṭāq Ṭāqīyya into the streets against the Israeli army were in essence affirming the ideational construct of the "children of the stones," legitimizing local grassroots leadership, and making a powerful political statement. Associations of burgeoning masculinity and family protection, indigenous rural lifeways and practices, and political protest all coalesced into a powerful resistance performative against the occupation.

Folklore and Performative Solidarity

In her analysis of the Palestinian national folklore revival, Lisa Taraki (1990) concludes that the incorporation of popular folklore into the national movement served several strategic purposes. First, among cosmopolitan nationalists espousing a leftist political ideology, folklore affirmed and valorized indigenous Palestinian lifeways and practices. Artists, politicians, and intellectuals worked diligently to revive and preserve Palestinian folklore and introduce and disseminate it among the urban middle class as a means to pacify cultural anxieties. Folklore festivals spread throughout the Occupied Territories along with the publication of journals, magazines, and books dedicated to folklore preservation. Music ensembles and theatrical groups traveled throughout the Occupied Territories in an attempt to bring distanced communities into the national movement, solidifying a new political consciousness based in popular heritage (65). Second, as folklore became a highly valued cultural artifact among urban middle-class intellectuals, rural Palestinians suddenly found themselves thrust into the national spotlight. Their indigenous life ways and practices were now highly valued weapons against colonial encroachment and occupation. This ideational shift had the effect of mobilizing new segments of the population into nationalist discourse, decentering "outside" political elites and intellectuals, and further reinforcing local grassroots leadership. The cultural and political divide between the largely urban cosmopolitan base of the national movement and the rural indigenous masses was bridged in folklore and the articulation of new national identities. Facilitated by a complex network of institutions, labor organizations, universities, and other social groups, women, youth, rural poor, and urban refugees were recruited into the nationalist discourse in ways that had never been done before (Hiltermann 1991; Taraki 1990, 61–66). The overall effect of this mobilization was the development of a new national consciousness at the heart of the resistance movement.

Throughout the Intifada, performance was an essential force in propelling and sustaining the uprising, generating national sentiment, and forging the indexical linkages between the political goal of ending the occupation and the cultural goal of preserving a sense of the historic Palestinian nation against colonial erasure. In the streets mass singing was a primary process for helping unite people to action across the political spectrum. The act of unison singing and dancing, central to indigenous life-cycle events and later appropriated into political activities, facilitated powerful communal experiences. Political rallies, demonstrations, and meetings were each forums for performance and communal integration. For demonstrators, the overall effect of such performances was extremely powerful. Voices coming together in song, feet coming together in rhythm, would often produce strong feelings of solidarity in purpose, history, and identity among those participating. Such feelings of group solidarity were then indexically linked with the musical and linguistic signs carried forth in the performance. Texts advocating a particular political ideology were easily associated with latent feelings of community and history, creating a powerful political tool. Merging their collective voices together in song, participants iconically resembled the political movement as a whole. In this way music became a particularly significant resource for generating group identities and bonding individuals together into larger social groups.

From the beginning of the uprising, political leaders were quite aware of the power of music to shape popular conceptions of self and society. The UNLU in particular called on musicians and other artists to assume leadership roles in the Intifada, composing songs, slogans, and poems to help shape both the form and content of the uprising.[6] Local political organizations, cultural societies, and grassroots aid organizations were equally supportive of indigenous Palestinian folklore, poetry, language, dress, food, music, and dance (Taraki 1990, 62–64). Cheaply produced music cassettes found their way past Israeli censors into the Palestinian marketplace throughout the West Bank and Gaza Strip. These newly released protest songs were then blasted on street corners, in coffee shops, and from passing taxicabs. Local music production became a powerful instrument of political resistance, with musicians risking severe consequences.

From the beginning of the Intifada, public music performances were strictly banned by Israeli authorities, who feared incitement in the streets. Musicians produced and recorded cassettes in makeshift underground studios and then distributed their work under pseudonyms at rallies and demonstrations. Suhail Khoury's influential Intifada recording, *Sharar* (Spark), for example, was originally produced in his home and featured many significant Palestinian musicians such as Issa Boulos and Reem Talhami. It became incredibly popular and was distributed through informal networks of bootlegged recordings. The circulation of protest songs and poetry via underground networks of cassettes served important cultural as well as strategic purposes, informing the people of current events, encouraging them to take to the streets against armed soldiers, and articulating and enacting collective identity structures essential for political action (Boulos, pers. comm. 2010). Among local political leaders, music and poetry offered a powerful means of communicating political ideology, broadening constituencies, and advocating for cultural legitimacy necessary to lead the movement.

The songs on these cassettes were largely pre-composed indigenous folk songs with altered or newly composed poetic texts, similar to the various examples quoted above. Couched in Palestinian folklore and thick dialect, such politicized texts were easily remembered by participants and, through constant reiteration, had the effect of lingering in the mind long after the performance was finished. This process involved a type of creative indexing where familiar rhythms and melodies were layered with contemporary political messages and imagery, fusing together powerful associations of indigenous Palestinian lifeways (the past) and the new popular resistance (the present) (Turino 2008, 208). Over time, these protest songs so effectively signified a revival of indigenous Palestinian identity within the politics of the contemporary moment, that the revival of indigenous practices and the resistance movement became mutually constitutive, two sides of the same coin: in order to preserve one's Palestinian identity, one must take to the streets in protest; and in order to end the occupation, one must return to one's Palestinian roots. Through constant repetition across various sites of performance, such media created new relations between history and nation, satisfying political and cultural anxieties.

Most importantly, in developing a new resistance performative founded on the revival of indigenous folklore, musicians, artists, and other intellectuals were in essence establishing new discursive frameworks for imagining the nation. Music, poetry, graffiti, leaflets, and so forth provoked people to reassess long-sedimented understandings of Palestinian history and identity. In performance Palestinians were offered spaces for collectively thinking about new ideas. Signs of national intimacy and political affiliation were drastically reconfigured so as to create new solidarities, new strategies, moving beyond the established politics of exclusion toward a new national movement based on shared history and collective experiences of dispossession. Performative media offered a means of imagining an end to the occupation and a revival of the "pure," pre-1948 Palestine through nonlethal civil disobedience. It provided an image of what the Palestinian people could accomplish and prescribed essential strategies for actualizing these goals.

Notes

1. This chapter expands upon material concurrently published in my book *My Voice Is My Weapon* (2013).

2. My usage of the term "sign clusters" is indebted to Turino's discussion of semiotics and political movements (2008, 197). He distinguishes "indexical clusters" as groupings

of unrelated signs that begin to be organically connected through repeated experiencing of them together. Turino explains that such indexical clusters are a primary tool for political movements to shape commonsense perceptions of the self and the world.

3. The Palestinian dabke is an indigenous participatory line dance comprised of various song types native throughout the region. Among Palestinian communities the dabke is a treasured cultural artifact, preserved as an embodied sign of the nation and its long history in the land.

4. The murabba[c] is a popular form of Palestinian folk song structured around the improvisatory rendering of four-line stanzas within a predetermined poetic structure. The murabba[c] is typically associated with the performance of wedding singers, *zajjālīn,* throughout historic Palestine.

5. Gustaf Dahlman's 1901 study of Palestinian folklore, *Palastinischer Diwan: Als Beitrag zur Volkskunde Palastinas,* prominently features a picture of a young boy using a sling to tend his flocks of sheep. Several Palestinian folklorists point to this photo as further evidence of the importance of the sling and slingshot in Palestinian folklore and of its use as a weapon in the resistance movement.

6. The UNLU's fifth communiqué called upon intellectuals to "participate actively in the uprising whether by extending aid or through writings, songs, and slogans. Also [to] participate in the information campaigns against the occupation policy."

References

Abed-Rabbo, Samer, and Doris Safie, eds. 1990. *The Palestinian Uprising: Facts Information Committee, Jerusalem.* Belmont, MA: Association of Arab-American University Graduates.

Barghouti, Abdellatif. 1998. *Diwān al-Intifāḍa al-Sha[c]bīyyah* [Encyclopedia of Intifada Folklore]. Birzeit, Palestine: Birzeit University.

Bennis, Phyllis. 1990. *From Stones to Statehood: The Palestinian Uprising.* Brooklyn, NY: Olive Branch Press.

Clarke, John, Stuart Hall, Tony Jefferson, and Brian Roberts. 1975. "Subcultures, Cultures, and Class: A Theoretical Overview." In *Resistance through Rituals: Youth Subcultures in Post-War Britain,* edited by Stuart Hall and Tony Jefferson, 9–74. London: Hutchinson and Co.

Dalman, Gustaf H. 1901. *Palästinischer Diwan: Als Beitrag Zur Volkskunde Palästinas.* Leipzig, Germany: J. C. Hinrichs'sche Buchhandlung.

Foucault, Michel. 1980. *Power/Knowledge: Selected Interviews and Other Writings, 1972–1977.* New York: Pantheon Books.

Gramsci, Antonio. 2001. "Selections from the Prison Notebooks of Antonio Gramsci." In *Selections from the Prison Notebooks of Antonio Gramsci,* edited by Quintin Hoare and Geoffrey Nowell-Smith, 131–47. London: Electric Book Co.

Hall, Stuart. 1986. "Gramsci's Relevance for the Study of Race and Ethnicity." *Journal of Communication Inquiry* 10 (2): 5–27.

———. 1992. "The West and the Rest: Discourse and Power." In *Modernity: An Introduction to Modern Sciences,* edited by Stuart Hall, David Held, Don Hubert, and Kenneth Thompson,184–228. Oxford: Blackwell Press.

Hass, Amira. 1996. *Drinking the Sea at Gaza: Days and Nights in a Land under Siege.* New York: Henry Holt.

Hijab, Nimr Hassan. 1997. *Aghānī alʿāb al-Aṭfāl fī Falasṭīn* [Children's Songs and Games in Palestine]. Amman, Jordan: Wizārat al-Thaqāfah.
Hiltermann, Joost R. 1991. *Behind the Intifada: Labor and Women's Movements in the Occupied Territories.* Princeton, NJ: Princeton University Press.
Khalili, Laleh. 2007. *Heroes and Martyrs of Palestine: The Politics of National Commemoration.* Cambridge, UK: Cambridge University Press.
Lockman, Zachary, and Joel Beinin, eds. 1989. *Intifada: The Palestinian Uprising against Israeli Occupation.* Boston: South End Press.
McDonald, David A. 2009. "Poetics and the Performance of Violence in Israel/Palestine." *Ethnomusicology* 53 (1): 58–85.
———. 2013. My Voice Is My Weapon: Music, Nationalism, and the Poetics of Palestinian Resistance. Durham, NC: Duke University Press.
Nassar, Jamal R., and Roger Heacock eds. 1990. *Intifada: Palestine at the Crossroads.* New York: Praeger.
Oliver, Anne Marie, and Paul Steinberg. 2002. "Popular Music of the Intifada." In *Garland Encyclopedia of World Music: The Middle East,* edited by Virginia Danielson, Scott Lloyd Marcus, and Dwight Reynolds, 635–40. New York: Garland Press.
Peteet, Julie. 1996. "The Writing on the Walls: The Graffiti of the Intifada." *Cultural Anthropology* 11 (2): 139–59.
Sirhan, Nimr. 1988. *Arshīf al-Fulklūr Al-Falasṭīnī: al-Intifāḍah fī al-Fulklūr al-Falasṭīnī* [Archive of Palestinian Folklore: The Intifada in Palestinian Folklore]. Ramallah, Palestine: Dāʾirat al-Maktabāt wa al-Wathāʾiq al-Waṭanīyyah.
Steinberg, Paul, and Anne Marie Oliver. 1994. *The Graffiti of the Intifada: A Brief Survey.* Jerusalem, Palestine: PASSIA: Palestinian Academic Society for the Study of International Affairs.
Swedenburg, Ted. 1990. "The Palestinian Peasant as National Signifier." *Anthropological Quarterly* 63 (1): 18–30.
———. 1995. *Memories of Revolt: The 1936–1939 Rebellion and the Palestinian National Past.* Minneapolis: University of Minnesota Press.
Taraki, Lisa. 1990. "The Development of Political Consciousness among Palestinians in the Occupied Territories." In *Intifada: Palestine at the Crossroads,* edited by Jamal R. Nassar and Roger Heacock, 53–71. New York: Praeger.
Turino, Thomas. 2008. *Music as Social Life: The Politics of Participation.* Chicago: University of Chicago Press.

9

Hamas's Musical Resistance Practices: Perceptions, Production, and Usage

Carin Berg and Michael Schulz

The Palestinian Islamic resistance organization Hamas (*Ḥarakat al-Muqāwamah al-Islāmīyyah*) frequently uses and even produces music in order to unite, inspire, and strengthen Palestinian resistance against the Israeli occupation of Palestinian lands. Music is seen by Hamas not only as a form of entertainment and religious practice but also as a form of discursive resistance and a kind of weapon for struggling against unjust regimes, rules, and systems. Not solely for Hamas's followers, but among many Palestinians as well, music is used to create a political space for expression beyond the reach of Israeli authorities. As much as Hamas was established in response to the Israeli occupation, so too is their music. Despite widespread interest in Hamas and in Palestinian expressive culture, there are few studies of the organization's use of music. This chapter seeks to fill this research gap by exploring how Hamas's music can be understood in relation to the organization's actions and stated goals.

Previous Research on Hamas and Palestinian Music

There is a need to place the cultural study of music in relation to power, resistance, and identity. Usually studies of Hamas rely solely on a political analysis of power and national struggle for Palestinian self-determination, in which popular culture and the arts are underrepresented. Here expressive culture is seen as less relevant for understanding or explaining Hamas's political behavior. We argue in line with Rebecca Stein and Ted Swedenburg that one needs to take "popular culture seriously as a space, practice, and/or discourse . . . popular culture in Palestine and Israel is fundamentally one of politics and power" (Stein and Swedenburg 2004, 5–6). We argue that through an analysis of music we can better our understanding of the role it plays in the formulation and organization of resistance strategy. It then becomes important to analyze what kind of places, meanings, and roles Hamas gives to music. Through a performative analysis it is possible to identify how Hamas perceives, produces, and uses music in the context of occupation, resistance, and the articulation of Palestinian national identity. A performative analysis places a particular *activity* in focus—in this case, resistance—and musical performance is seen as "constitutive modalities for the negotiations of power and resistance, social interaction, and identity" (McDonald 2006, 5). Further, resistance activities are seen as a practice applied by a subaltern and could be defined as "a subordinated agency's response to power, a practice that can challenge and undermine power" (Lilja and Vinthagen 2009, 51).[1] Hence, resistance can be seen as an act by the subordinated and can include cultural acts such as using, playing, making, or becoming inspired by music. Music becomes a resistance tool for the subaltern as a means to undermine oppressive power structures.

Much has been written about Palestinian music in general, and what has been described is closely linked to the analysis of Palestinian national identity formation, sometimes referred to as "the sounds of struggle" (Morgan and Adileh 1999, 385). Analyzing the history of Palestinian liberation songs "parallels in many ways the history of the Palestinian struggle itself" (Massad 2003, 21). It has been a way of being heard to the outside world and has been a "translation process, through which the deeply felt and often incomprehensive emotions of distrust and hopelessness can be heard" (Wong 2009, 282). However, music is not solely a tool for fostering national coherence and identification; it is also a tool to be used to ensure that the outside world recognizes Palestinian existence and suffering under Israeli occupation. It is a way to mobilize resistance against oppressive power and to gain external support. Suffering is a leitmotif in many musical performances in Palestine. Unsurprisingly, and due to the harsh everyday experiences of Palestinian life under occupation, music focused on resistance and identity plays an important role in Palestinian life.

Previous research has shown that music may be used as a tool of inspiration among soldiers preparing for combat (Pieslak 2009). Understanding and explaining the violence of everyday life under occupation has also been the subject of various analyses of musical performance. Music can be seen through the lenses of performative acts given that "performances, aesthetics, and other artistic practices structure in many ways how violence becomes meaningful, beautiful, and appropriate" (McDonald 2009, 60).

However, very little previous research exists on the Islamist movement, specifically Hamas. In addition, the forms of music that Hamas uses and produces, such as Islamic *anāshīd* (anthems), are often connected to religious followers but not solely to Hamas. Levitt mentions briefly that "reports on the Islamic Charity Association described an assembly line of Palestinian men and teenage boys packing food items to the tune of inspirational music praising Hamas" (Levitt 2004, 7). However, this is an indirect link, not to how Hamas uses music internally, but rather to how it can influence Hamas-affiliated supporters. In-depth studies on Hamas rarely discuss musical practices (see, for instance, Roy 2011; Milton-Edwards and Farell 2010; and Gunning 2009). Due to lack of previous research on musical practices specifically, there is a need to work with these empirical questions.

Background

In what way does Hamas complement and add its music to the rich fauna of different Palestinian and Arab music traditions? Before answering this we need to place Hamas within the historical development of Palestinian resistance music and the overarching struggle for Palestinian statehood. Much of Palestinian resistance music, such as protest and liberation songs, has been linked to the Palestine Liberation Organization (PLO). Since the 1970s a number of bands, such as the Central Band (*al-Firqah al-Markazīyyah*), were associated with the Fatah organization within the PLO. The PLO also established its own radio that was broadcast in Egypt and Jordan (*Sawt al ʿĀsifah* [Voice of the Storm]), and one in Lebanon, Radio of the Revolution (*Sawt Falasṭīn Sawt al-Thawrah al-Falasṭīnīyyah* [Voice of Palestine and Voice of the Palestinian Revolution]). These broadcasts became well known to most Palestinians and to people in the Arab world. Many Palestinian singers broadcast via these stations were associated with the PLO guerrilla movement. For instance, Abu Arab, a prominent Palestinian artist based in Beirut, became an inspirational source in the resistance efforts of the PLO (Massad 2003, 31ff.).

However, there is little written about Hamas's approach to and utilization of music since its establishment in December 1987. With Hamas's establishment by previous members of the Muslim Brotherhood, the organization became another political force, influencing Palestinian cultural and societal norms. At the time of its establishment at the beginning of the first Palestinian *Intifada* (uprising), Hamas was considered to be an alternative and challenger to the secular PLO, and in particular Fatah. Hamas became the main critical voice against the PLO after the signing of the Declaration of Principles in 1993. Hamas was not ready to let down the armed resistance against Israel in the same way as the PLO had agreed to, and the organization gained increasing political support as it became more apparent that the Oslo peace process was failing. In 2006 Hamas participated in the national elections and won a majority in the Palestinian Legislative Council (PLC), able to form a new Palestinian Authority (PA) cabinet. Despite running on a unity government platform, Hamas soon ended up in political rivalry with

Fatah. When Hamas assumed political control over the Gaza Strip in June 2007, after violent clashes with Fatah rivals, it implemented official rules and regulations on public policy. Fatah responded by taking sole control over the West Bank, creating two different Palestinian governments. With full administrative control over the Gaza Strip, Hamas began a program for safeguarding public life, including cultural life, in accordance with the organization's political and religious norms and values. In addition, Hamas began enforcing its policies in the formation of cultural spheres, including music. Hence, Hamas had a major political role in how to define and frame how music should be linked to the struggle against Israeli occupation.

Hamas Defines Its Perception of Music and Resistance Music

There exists a debate over the content of Palestinian national identity and what role religion should play not only in relation to this identity (see Robinson 1997) but also in the spheres of culture and music (Otterbeck 2008). Although no official policy exists to ban music, discussions on the permissibility of some genres of music such as pop, hip-hop, and rock are taking place. There are different opinions about music and musical taste among Hamas members, and occasionally music has been questioned by members or those associated with the organization. There is a wide spectrum of views on what music they prefer and accept and on what role music should play in internal inspiration and external representation of Palestinian society. Not solely within the Hamas movement, but occasionally during the last two decades, quite intense fears and confrontations concerning musical issues have occurred in both the West Bank and Gaza Strip.[2] Thus, it becomes of interest to understand how Hamas positions itself within the larger historical developments of the Palestinian resistance music.

Mark Levine underlines that "it's impossible to understand Israeli and Palestinian music today apart from the abysmal failure of Oslo to deliver on its promises of peace, independence, and development for either Palestinians or Israelis" (2008, 113). Levine goes even further by saying that it is because of the harsh past that today one can find the best hip-hop and heavy metal bands in the world in the Palestinian territories. Chuen-Fung Wong also underlines the importance of music in the light of the failed Oslo peace process, or, more specifically, related to the two Intifadas. Wong explains that "protest songs have been composed to mobilize the Palestinian people for uprisings against the Israeli state, disseminated quickly through audio cassettes and other mass media" (2009, 270). Palestinian songs have had a major impact on the struggle during the Intifadas, alongside the contributions of musicians from neighboring countries such as Fairuz and Mansour al-Rahbani. Artists from nearby countries have sung about the Palestinian struggle in a nationalistic manner, which Palestinians have used as a tool for mobilization and inspiration against Israeli forces.

Music Censorship

Music is often the object of censorship and control as ruling parties struggle to maintain their rule. Authoritarian governments typically censor music as a means of preventing criticism, and in places where Sharia (Islamic law) influences the legal code this is certainly no exception. Jonas Otterbeck writes: "As a reaction to changes, some states and local authorities have taken actions against heavy metal musicians, female singers, music videos, and public concerts" (2008). But music censorship is also frequently related to politics with the aim of controlling the spread of political messages and exhortations. The main reason for censorship within the Islamic world is often related to Western-style music, which is feared to "threaten the established order, and through it their political power" (Levine 2008, 5). However, local musicians performing songs in their native language and singers trying to mediate nationalistic or political messages are exposed to similar restrictions. This shows that it is not simply the Western message of art in itself that is a threat, but rather the fast spread of musical messages that imply a loss of control. The question that is raised is, how has Hamas coped with critical music?

In the Palestinian territories, one can see tendencies of Hamas to ban certain musical performances. The Gaza Strip, where Hamas has exercised sole governance since 2007, is historically the most conservative and strictly controlled Palestinian area in terms of lifestyle, dress codes, and other aspects of culture. Musicians from Gaza have often reported that Hamas bans all kinds of music not performed in accordance with Islamic norms. From the data we have received, two explanations stand out as to why certain performances have been banned. One is linked to how proper—in relation to Islamic correctness—the performance is seen to be, and the other has a political motive—that is, preventing what is seen as Fatah-affiliated music and musicians.

For instance, in events where mixed dancing occurs, authorities argue that this behavior should be prevented due to arguments that it is non-Islamic behavior.[3] Hence, what has led to reactions from Hamas authorities is not that music is performed per se, but how and during what circumstance the music is performed. A question that needs to be addressed is whether there is a consensus within Hamas regarding these actions or if these are single reactions from particular Hamas-affiliated persons. From our interviews we find that it is typically allowable for any non-Hamas member to attend music performances with mixed sexes in closed areas (for instance, in a restaurant or hotel) (Yasir Ali, interview 2011).

However, reports claiming that Hamas has closed down musical performances in Gaza when groups were using instruments other than percussion (drums and tambourine) are common, given that these instruments are mentioned in the *Qur'ān,* or concerts with mixed sexes in the audience or in the group itself, even if it concerns traditional Palestinian music. Hamas officials have always denied that such things have happened under the name of government (Mousa Abu Marzouk and

Yasir Ali, interviews). There have also been reports of Hamas members beating up musicians performing in bands affiliated with Fatah. This is obviously a manifestation of the power struggle between the two rival groups rather than a stand against music itself.[4]

In the West Bank town of Qalqiliya, in 2005, for example, the Hamas-led local government decided to ban the Palestine International Music Festival for being inappropriately organized.[5] The same municipality "also ordered that music no longer be played in the city's zoo," backed by a religious edict issued by Mufti Mustafa Sabri.[6] In this particular case it was the opposition to mixed male-female social contexts rather than the music itself that led to the decision. Also, this event created an internal rift within the movement over the extent to which the government should impose restrictions in the cultural sphere. After much internal debate, the majority within Hamas opposed placing restrictions on public behavior, fearing that doing so would harm their position in the broader public who were critical of these actions (Yasir Ali, interview 2011).

In the late 1980s and early 1990s tensions arose between different social groups when Hamas tried to create a code of moral conduct by burning certain video shops and books argued to be dissenting toward Islam.[7] This has led to accusations that Hamas wants to prevent the performance of certain music. However, according to interviews with Hamas leaders, there is no Hamas policy or strategy to ban any certain kinds of music. Nevertheless, there are some within the movement who believe in more strict codes of conduct in relation to music festivals, weddings, and so forth. They also underline that individuals who have left Hamas, or Salafi groups in Gaza, are those who harass people in public places. This is not something Hamas is supporting, but the organization is often falsely blamed for these single actions. In any case, even if there is a will of a particular regime to apply censorship, the whole Arab world has reached a point where governments have increasing difficulties controlling the flow of musical media.

But in the case of Hamas it is quite different, given that the organization was initially democratically elected and at the same time plays an important censoring role on different levels of the public sphere. Hamas has a unique ability to exert control over the public sphere, in contrast to other Islamic organizations that are not in a state governing position. One example of Hamas taking control over the musical public sphere is the closing down of the rap performance by Mothafar Assar in Gaza in March 2009. Hamas's motivation for shutting down the concert was not the performance of music in itself, but that they believe the mixing of sexes in public places is forbidden (*ḥarām*). Moreover, in relation to the same incident, it was reported that Hamas discouraged studios in Gaza from permitting Assar and other bands to record their music (Sherwood 2010). And the Danish organization Freemuse, for freedom of musical expression, also reported several incidents where masked gunmen (sometimes specifically identified as Hamas) have obstructed musical performances and kidnapped or used violence against singers. However, it is unclear whether this was due to the power struggle with Fatah (if, for example, Fatah members were members of the performing group), or whether it was a reaction to how the performance was being conducted (female singer, mixed sexes, etc.). Further, it is also unclear whether it was Hamas or whether some members, parts of the movement, believe they have the right to intervene because of their position of power and moral beliefs. It is quite obvious, however, that within Hamas various opinions on the forms and usage of music (or any other moral/cultural issues) exist and are discussed in much the same way as they are in other Palestinian political movements and Palestinian society in general. It is not the most politically important issue, and hence a difference of opinion on the topic is allowed within the movement. On the other hand, the use of new media is as important in Gaza as in other places, and it is widely used in the hip-hop scene, at least, to subvert attempts at control. After the Arab Spring it remains to be seen how these new social media will be used in the sphere of music. There are no record shops in Gaza, so the musicians send out their songs by Internet or cell phone (Freemuse).

Interviews with Hamas members reveal that there is no singular Islamic principle for music, and they argue that no single Hamas member, or no religious leader, organization, and so on, can solely (a priori) prohibit or decide on matters of religion, but has to refer to judicial texts and teachings (the Qurʾān, Ḥadīth, and Fatāwī). Among many Hamas members, it is the democratic (preferably consensus) vote from all Palestinians that offers the correct interpretation in relation to music, or any other matter. The Qurʾān is available for legal support on questions regarding music. Even if the Qurʾān itself does not bring up the legal standards of music specifically, it is used by all sides in the debate on the permissibility of music (see also Shiloah 1995; Al-Faruqi 1985, 1980).

Hamas-Produced and -Used Music

Since its establishment in 1987, Hamas has produced its own recorded music in the form of cassettes (1990s), CDs, and via the Internet. This repertory of song has historically contributed to and challenged music and musicians supported directly by the PLO and its dominant Fatah party. Since Hamas serves as both a social and political movement, it is particularly interesting to investigate the roles and functions of music produced and promoted by the organization. Is the music simply an outlet for frustration and inspiration to rise up against Israeli occupation? Or, rather, does the music foster social affiliation, spreading the message of Hamas in order to gain popularity? In many ways it serves both purposes, as songs are often seen to express collective feelings of belonging. As a social movement Hamas is sensitive to public opinion. And acting within a particular Palestinian cultural context, it strives to avoid imposing a particular Islamist model for how the public should act in the public sphere, including music.[8] As Hamas representative Osama Hamdan expressed it, "We seek consensus before we implement, not imposition, because this is how we believe democracy works" (Hamdan, interview 2009).

Hamas anashīd (Anthem) for the Leader

Sleep in peace, the sleep of the heroes, and let Hamas attack like an earthquake; as a hero you lived in the colors of the prayer call, so you die today like the heroes!
When you left
You left behind you a nation who like an infant, nursed from you the milk of revenge so long before! (x2)
You were the leader, even although you died your revenge will be by our hand, leader! (x2)

Sleep in peace, the sleep of the heroes, and let Hamas attack like an earthquake; as a hero you lived in the colors of the prayer call, so you die today like the heroes!
You stood in front of the strongest country and you were victorious against it despite your being crippled, God has chosen you because you are immaculate and the others flirted in the dirtiness!

Sleep in peace, the sleep of the heroes, and let Hamas attack like an earthquake; as a hero you lived in the colors of the prayer call, so you die today like the heroes![9]

Although much of the music affiliated with Hamas fits within the general rubric of Islamic devotional song (*anāshīd*) in terms of lyrics, message, melody, instrumentation, and performance practice, this is not always the case. While most anāshīd pay tribute to the Prophet Mohammed, those associated with Hamas typically pay tribute to many different leaders. However, the Islamic message of encouraging *jihād* (holy struggle) is repetitively used, not only for the sake of God but also to create an Islamic Palestinian nation-state. Links between the land of Palestine and Islam are asserted, as the music is intended for inspirational and religious purposes. This music seeks to place the listener in relation to God and the land of Palestine. It establishes meaning, place, purpose, and expectations for the Palestinian listener. It positions the individual within the collective struggle, functioning as both a source of inspiration for individual members and external followers and a tool of social and political mobilization.

Much of the music produced and promoted by Hamas members is transmitted and disseminated through online music videos and other social networking sites. They are generally belligerent in their appearance, specifically toward Israel, depicting it as an evil to be destroyed. These videos follow the general trend of presenting liberation music among other Palestinian political factions, with specific markers of character and style. Similar to other Islamic groups in the Middle East (Hezbollah in Lebanon, or Shia Islamic groups in Iraq, and others), Hamas relies on online music videos to present and circulate their political messages. Overall these videos show snapshots of masked fighters carrying rockets and other weapons, Palestinian children dressed in the traditional scarf (*kūfiyyah*) throwing stones and using slingshots, pictures of various political leaders, and cartoon images of Israelis oppressing Palestinians.[10]

The Return of the Qassam Falcons

Hit Hit (x4)
Hit the Qassam rocket, shoot it into the liver of the oppressor, hit your terror as a coming storm, roaring in bombs. (x2)
Hit, so the glory is calling us, shaking the nests of our enemies. (x2)
Don't worry, it is time to answer, so fix the rocket, fix it. (x2)

Hit hit hit
Hit the Qassam rocket
Hit the Qassam rocket, shoot it into the liver of the oppressor, hit your terror as a coming storm, roaring in bombs. (x2)
This is by our hand, and God is protecting us (x3)
Hey you extorter, my people will not kneel, my rocket has surpassed the cannon (x2)

Hit hit hit
Hit the Qassam rocket
Hit the Qassam rocket, shoot it into the liver of the oppressor, hit your terror as a coming storm, roaring in bombs. (x2)
Ask Gaza about us, ask about us, the occupier became weak and we didn't. (x3)
Prepare your winding-sheets (of surrender) extorter, you will be shocked by our coming reaction. (x2)

Hit hit hit
Hit the Qassam rocket
Hit the Qassam rocket, shoot it into the liver of the oppressor, hit your terror as a coming storm, roaring in bombs. (x2)
Zionist if you come back we will return, you didn't provide but we did. (x2)
So prostrate oneself and go on, the glorious rocket has warmed up. (x2)

Hit hit hit
Hit the Qassam rocket

> Hit the Qassam rocket, shoot it into the liver of the oppressor, hit your terror as a coming storm, roaring in bombs (x2).[11]

Even if Hamas's political, military, and social wings include women, all songs are sung by men or boys and often in chorus. Frequently, martyrs are depicted as heroes in the struggle against Israeli occupation. Images of Palestinian national personalities and symbolic or otherwise important places, such as Al-Quds (Jerusalem), are shown. Also, images of collaborative negotiations between rival Fatah and Israel are presented, often as a sign of failed attempts for justice and independence.[12] In this sense, Hamas aims to show that they are the only serious resistance movement capable of liberating Palestine. This also implies that political negotiations are failing and that armed resistance is a necessary means of ending Israeli occupation. It also gives the implicit message to the listener that Fatah is not capable of achieving liberation through negotiations.

While many of the videos vary in their instrumentation, particularly percussion, Hamas-affiliated music draws from the tradition of religious devotional songs (anāshīd). It remains largely monophonic, rhythmically simple and stable, with very little instrumental accompaniment. This structure of performance has an inspirational affect on many Hamas followers. As one Hamas-affiliated young man claimed: "Personally when I hear Hamas music, I get very active and I am ready to fight! I think I share that feeling with all people who hear it. But Hamas music is not in itself created for the sake of creating violence" (interview in Nablus, March 23, 2011).[13] Likewise, another young man expressed a very common sentiment with regard to Hamas-affiliated music:

> It is a moral war to get our rights back, and in this aspect music is important. The Hamas music supports my friends to blow themselves up. I had an eighteen-year-old friend who was a Hamas member, and he tried to conduct a suicide bombing in Israel, but he failed. Afterward I asked him what made him do this thing, and he said that he listened to Hamas music and was triggered to do it. (interview)

This is not to say that the music triggered the eighteen-year-old friend to conduct the act. The decision was probably made long before, but at the time, when it was the right moment to launch the mission, the music inspired, triggered, and strengthened him to proceed with the violent mission.

The aim of Hamas's music is first and foremost to strengthen the courage of fighters, but it is also to spread political messages to the people and encourage them to fight against Israeli occupation of Palestinian land. Political exhortations are either general, with phrases like "Hit the Qassam rocket," "Shoot in the liver of the oppressor," as seen above, or expressly directed at Israel, "If the whole world will give in, we will not admit the presence of Israel," or "Ask about us, the occupier became weak and we did not" (see song lyrics below).

We will not admit the presence of Israel

The leader Ismail said: we will not admit! We will not admit! We will not admit the presence of Israel!
The leader Ismail said, this is the procedure and there is no change, if the whole world will give in, we will not admit the presence of Israel. (x2) . . .

We will not admit the presence of Israel. (x2)
Jaffa and the free Nazareth and the Galilee of glory and revenge, Gaza and West Bank and Jerusalem, Haifa and the ancient homes. (x2)
All my country exclaimed loud. (x2)

We will not admit the presence of Israel. (x2)
No peace for a piece of sand which is an Islamic entity, and these are our guns on the way to uproot the oppressive people. (x2)
We have announced it in a war. (x2). . . .

We will not admit the presence of Israel. (x2)
The leader Ismail said, this is the procedure and there is no change, if the whole world will give in, we will not admit the presence of Israel. (x2)[14]

Political slogans or powerful phrases are often repeated several times in the songs of Hamas, stressing particular messages like a mantra. The songs often contain fatal incidents, often historical, as triggers of resistance, such as different Israeli attacks. Some songs are specifically made for what seems to be battle songs for Hamas's military wing, the al-Qassam Brigades. The song mentioned above, "The Return of the Qassamist Falcons," is one particular example. The repetitive refrain in this song goes, "Hit, hit, hit. Hit the Qassam rocket. This is made by our hands and the only God is protecting us."[15] Such phrases encourage and foster bravery for the forthcoming struggle and tell the listener that one should not be afraid, because it is their duty in the name of God.

Moreover, many of these songs pay tribute to particularly brave persons indirectly or directly, showing respect to fallen martyrs and honoring martyrdom. One example of such is the song specifically produced to honor the late Hamas political leader and spokesman in Gaza Abdel Aziz al-Rantisi, who was assassinated by the Israeli air force in 2004. Phrases from that particular song, mentioned above, are an example: "Sleep in peace, the sleep of heroes, and let Hamas attack like an earthquake." "You were the leader. Even though you died, your revenge will be by our hand, leader!" It is important to note that these songs are never solely of grief, but rather combine political messages of struggle or resistance with regard to the position and performance of the honored person. Although having many similarities with music videos made by other Palestinian political organizations, but with its own specific characteristics, Hamas-associated music has developed into a modern form of Islamic devotional song. As much as members of Hamas produce the songs for internal usage, the music can easily be recognized and adopted into mainstream Palestinian society. Any Palestinian can identify with the music's depiction of historical and present disasters affecting the population as a result of the Israeli occupation. The message is a political slogan: fight for, and in the name of God, obliterate the state of Israel and retake Palestine, obey the leaders, and honor the martyrs.

Hamas and Musical Resistance

Within the context of the occupation and the harsh everyday life of Palestinians in Gaza and the West Bank, Hamas has devoted significant resources to cultural performance. Hamas-affiliated music has become a performative means of instigating and strengthening the armed political resistance against the Israeli occupation. Using music for political purposes, in motivating resistance fighters, triggering political mobilization, and fostering political recruitment, Hamas has adopted music as a primary means of resistance practice. Such music provides explanation and meaning to resistance activities. Hamas uses music to inspire but also to comfort and mourn when fighters have been killed. Our findings follow similar research that reveals how music is part of Palestinian identity formation and also becomes a cultural performative practice in the resistance against oppressive powers. Hamas-affiliated music is a practice taking place in several spheres: internally (to strengthen, motivate, and comfort), domestically (to motivate, mobilize, and challenge), and regionally (to mobilize and generate support).

Our findings fall in line with those of Sara Roy (2011) and Beverly Milton-Edwards and Stephen Farell (2010), who show the many ways in which the approach to and permissibility of music is a contested issue within Hamas. What is music? How should it be used? And what are appropriate Islamic values? These are all questions subjected to rigorous debate among Hamas members and affiliates. Further, as Jeroen Gunning (2009) and Roy (2011) have shown, Hamas, as an Islamic organization that seeks to place Islam at the center of society, uses many different tools and remains dependent on the larger Palestinian social and political setting in which it operates and is influenced. As a social and political organization it does not seek to impose an Islamic model of societal practice over the public, especially in places like the Gaza Strip, where Islamic values have always been more conservative than in the West Bank (Roy 2011). Despite this, a wide spectrum of different positions exist, including a high level of individual freedom of choice on what to listen to. It is not music itself that makes Hamas, or its affiliated members, occasionally judge it as forbidden (ḥarām). Rather, it is context, surroundings, and details in the content and language of the lyrics, dance, or other elements like dress codes that become the subject of dispute. Roy underlines that Islamic social institutions in civil society are not formally or institutionally linked to Hamas, and they speak with diverse voices. Hence, Hamas has a "certain, albeit limited, acceptance of social and political pluralism" (2011, 187), and issues such as deciding on what is proper music, and in accordance with Islamic values, is for most leaders not an important political issue.[16]

How the debate on what music is preferred and for what purposes will proceed, and in what direction it will go within the movement itself as well as in the broader Palestinian society, is something that needs further systematic research. Meanwhile, music produced by Hamas will continuously be used by its members as a tool to resist Israeli occupation as its popularity increases among the general Palestinian public.

Notes

1. Authors' translation from the original Swedish text.

2. See, for instance, "Angry Islamists Break up Hip-Hop Concert with Kalashnikovs," Freemuse, October 6, 2005, http://www.freemuse.org/sw10796.asp.

3. See, for instance, "Ramallah Refuses to Dance to Hamas Cue," Haaretz, April 28, 2008, http://www.haaretz.com/print-edition/news/ramallah-refuses-to-dance-to-hamas-cue-1.244740.

4. "Angry Islamists."

5. Mustafa Sabri, Hamas spokesperson, quoted in "Hamas Council Bans Music Festival," Jihad Watch, July 2, 2005, http://www.jihadwatch.org/2005/07/hamas-council-bans-music-festival.html; see also "Hamas Council Bans Music Festival," BBC News, July 1, 2005, http://news.bbc.co.uk/2/hi/4641765.stm.

6. "Palestine: Taliban-like Attempts to Censor Music," Freemuse, August 17, 2005, http://www.freemuse.org/sw10095.asp.

7. See ibid.

8. Interviews with Abu Khaled, Hassan Mohammed, Mohammed Abu-Chakra, Mousa Abu Marzouk, Osama Hamdan, Raafat Morra (Abu Yasir), Salaheddin, and Yasir Ali.

9. See Hamas Nasheed, http://www.youtube.com/watch?v=M3FMLDQ93EY&feature=related. All song lyrics in this chapter are translated from Arabic to English by Rafic Sayyed.

10. See ibid.

11. http://www.youtube.com/watch?v=_5Jnj-EQ3Zo&feature=share (accessed 03/10/2013).

12. See Gaza Nasheed 2, http://www.youtube.com/watch?v=qsDEq0D371M&feature=related (accessed 3/19/13).

13. Fieldwork with observations, conversations, and interviews with Hamas members and sympathizers has been conducted by the authors since 2006.

14. http://www.youtube.com/watch?v=v9qUIU9THvE&feature=youtube (accessed 03/10/2013).

15. http://www.youtube.com/watch?v=_5Jnj-EQ3Zo&feature=share (accessed 03/10/2013).

16. Underlined by, for instance, Ayaman Daragmeh (PLC member on Change and Reform List), Ramallah, Palestine, March 21, 2007, and Ramallah, Palestine, March 23, 2011; Khaled Meshal (head of Hamas), Damascus, Syria, May 24, 2009; Osama Hamdan (head of Lebanon office), Beirut, Lebanon, November 28, 2008; and Yasir Ali (Hamas member), Beirut, Lebanon, October 28, 2011.

References

Al-Faruqi, Lois Ibsen. 1980. "The Status of Music in Muslim Nations: Evidence from the Arab World." *Asian Music* 12 (1): 56–85.

———. 1985. "Musicians and Muslim Law." *Asian Music* 17 (1): 3–36.

Al-Taee, Nasser. 2002. "Voices of Peace and the Legacy of Reconciliation: Poplar Music, Nationalism, and the Quest for Peace in the Middle East." *Popular Music* 21 (1): 41–61.

Bayat, Asef. 2007. "Islamism and the Politics of Fun." *Public Culture* 19 (3): 433–59.

Butcher, Tim. 2007. "Hamas Boy Band to Bring Harmony to Gaza." http://www.telegraph.co.uk/news/worldnews/1567852/Hamas-boy-band-to-bring-harmony-to-Gaza.html.

Freemuse. 2005. "Palestine: Taliban-Like Attempts to Censor Music." http://www.freemuse.org/sw10095.asp.

Funch, Johnny. 2000. "Vi saluterar Ahmed Yassin—En diskussion kring Hamasmusik" [We Salute Ahmed Yassin—A Discussion about Hamas Music]. Bachelor's thesis. Lund, Sweden: Theological Institution (in Swedish).

Gunning, Jeroen. 2009. *Hamas in Politics: Democracy, Religion, and Violence.* London: Hurst and Company.

Hjärpe, Jan. 2004. *99 Frågor om Islam* [99 Questions about Islam.] Stockholm: Leopard Förlag (in Swedish).

Levine, Mark. 2008. *Heavy Metal Islam.* New York: Three Rivers Press.

Levitt, Matthew. 2004. "Hamas from Cradle to Grave." *Middle East Quarterly* 11 (1): 3–15. http://www.meforum.org/582/hamas-from-cradle-to-grave.

Lilja, Mona, and Stellan Vinthagen. 2009. *Motstånd* [Resistance.] Lund, Sweden: Studentlitteratur (in Swedish).

Massad, Joseph. 2003. "Liberating Songs: Palestine Put to Music." *Journal of Palestine Studies* 32 (3): 21–38.

McDonald, David A. 2006. "Performing Palestine." *Jerusalem Quarterly* no. 25, 5–18.

———. 2009. "Poetics and the Performance of Violence in Israel/Palestine." *Ethnomusicology* 53 (1): 58–85.

———. 2010. "Geographies of the Body: Music, Violence, and Manhood in Palestine." *Ethnomusicology Forum* 19 (2): 191–214. http://www.tandfonline.com/doi/abs/10.1080/17411912.2010.507463.

Milton-Edwards, Beverly, and Stephen Farell. 2010. *Hamas.* Cambridge, UK: Polity Press.

Morgan, A., and M. Adileh. 1999. "Palestinian Music: The Sounds of Struggle." In *World Music: The Rough Guide,* edited by S. Broughton, M. Ellingham, and R. Trillo. London: Rough Guides. 1: 385–90.

Otterbeck, Jonas. 2008. "Battling over the Public Sphere: Islamic Reactions to the Music of Today." *Contemporary Islam* 2 (3): 211–28.

Pieslak, Jonathan. 2009. *Sound Targets: American Soldiers and Music in the Iraqi War.* Bloomington: Indiana University Press.
Richert, Annika, Suzanne Unge, and Ulla Wagner. 1985. *Islam: Religion, Kultur, Samhälle* [Islam: Religion, Culture and Society]. Malmö, Sweden: Gidlunds Bokförlag (in Swedish).
Robinson, Glenn E. 1997. *Building a Palestinian State: The Incomplete Revolution.* Bloomington: Indiana University Press.
Roy, Sara. 2011. *Hamas and Civil Society in Gaza: Engaging the Islamist Social Sector.* Princeton, NJ: Princeton University Press.
Sherwood, Harriet. 2010. "Last Rapper in Gaza Struggle to Make Voice Heard." *Guardian* online. October 20, 2010. http://www.guardian.co.uk/world/2010/oct/20/gaza-street-band-rappers.
Shiloah, Amnon. 1995. *Music in the World of Islam: A Socio-Cultural Study.* Detroit: Wayne State University Press.
Stein, Rebecca L., and Ted Swedenburg. 2004. "Popular Culture, Relational History, and the Question of Power in Palestine and Israel." *Journal of Palestine Studies* 33 (4): 5–20.
Wong, Chuen-Fung. 2009. "Conflicts, Occupation, and Music-Making in Palestine." *Macalester International* 23, article 19, 267–84. http://digitalcommons.macalester.edu/macintl/v0123/iss1/19.

Interviews with Hamas Members

Abu Khaled, Bas Camp in Tyreh, Lebanon, June 25, 2009
Abu Rami, Camp Badaawi in Tripoli, Lebanon, June 26, 2009
Ayaman Daragmeh, Ramallah, Palestine, March 21, 2007, and Ramallah, Palestine, March 23, 2011
Hassan Mohammed (pseudonym), Palestine, Nablus, March 23, 2011
Karem Taha, Wavell Refugee Camp, Lebanon, May 29, 2009
Khaled Meshal (head of Hamas), Damascus, Syria, May 24, 2009
Khaled Thwaib, Bethlehem, Palestine, March 24, 2007
Mahmoud Abu Mustafa, Burj al Shamaleh Refugee Camp, Lebanon, June 25, 2009
Maryam Saleh, Ramallah, Palestine, March 27, 2007
Mohammed Abu-Chakra, Beirut, Lebanon, October 28 and 29, 2011
Mousa Abu Marzouk (deputy head of Hamas), Damascus, Syria, May 24, 2009
Osama Hamdan, Beirut, Lebanon, November 28, 2008, and May 22, 2009
Raafat Morra (Abu Yasir), Beirut, Lebanon, June 17, 2009
Salaheddin, Nablus, Palestine, March 23, 2011
Sheikh Hijam il Hajj Musa, Bas Refugee Camp in Tyreh, Lebanon, June 25, 2009
Yasir Ali, Beirut, Lebanon, October 28, 2011
Zaidan Abdel Rahman, Ramallah, Palestine, March 22, 2007

10

Palestinian Music: Between Artistry and Political Resistance

Stig-Magnus Thorsén

In this essay Palestinian music is used as a case study in an attempt to understand the use of music as resistance. The discussion and the cultural production that I met during recent travels in the country revealed to me richness not only in the music but also in the discussion about the music. I realized that the study of this specific case could be beneficial to a more general discussion. I think that everyone can learn from the informed statements and cultural praxis manifested by Palestinians. The country is subjected to specific cultural and political circumstances that make issues concerning cultural resistance more explicit—more on the edge. As human rights activist Omar Barghouti told me:

> Artists cannot be neutral or apathetic. Under conditions of colonial oppression particularly, neutrality is not an option, basically. Even artists who pretend to work under the concept of *l'art pour l'art* cannot do it. Because as Palestinians they are subject to the same conditions as the rest of the population. (Barghouti, interview)

I interpret this statement as a reminder of the conditions all music is subject to. And in order to understand the meaning of music as such, I raise the questions underlying this essay: How does politically committed music sound? What is the relation between aesthetics and politics? How does music function in an aesthetic field charged by resistance?

The Investigation

During the years 2006–2011, I gathered interviews, observations, and texts relating to Palestinian music and its context. At an early date (2007), an interview with Omar Barghouti inspired me to let my investigation take a certain direction. The activist, author, and former choreographer of the distinguished El-Funoun dance group described various ways of thinking that opened my eyes to the Palestinian scene of cultural resistance. He emphasized the difference between the evolutionary art of the oppressed and the defensive art of the oppressed.[1] This categorization explained the various functions art could have when reacting to political oppression. Evolutionary art sought development away from a vulnerable situation, whereas defensive art accepted the status quo and expressed only the complaints of the victims.

Barghouti's statements (see also Barghouti 2004) deepen our understanding of music used among Palestinians and indicate the risk of music being used only as an instrument for political purposes. He claims that the inner laws of music must be considered as meaningful; otherwise the humanness of the Palestinians will be corrupted. The victims are the losers, but Palestinians must manifest their general value as human beings.

This essay reflects on how various artists and producers look upon the role of music seen against the backdrop of the other essays in this volume. Especially relevant is David A. McDonald's text describing the political and artistic mechanisms involved in cultural production during the first *Intifada* (uprising). Elsewhere he also points out the role played by music in shaping national unity. "In developing a new resistance performative founded on the revival of indigenous folklore, musicians, artists, and other intellectuals were in essence establishing new discursive frameworks for imagining the nation" (McDonald 2006a, see also 2006b).

What Is Music of Resistance?

It is intriguing to explore the music of resistance. How does it sound? What constitutes its power and agency? I have not found easy answers to such questions, as resistance is not in the music per se. It is therefore necessary to understand the relationship between music and several extra-musical factors. In the first place comes context: the human, social, and political environment surrounding musical actions. The context is a structure containing people who are agents in the musical event, such as composers, lyric writers, performers, media, and listeners. The physical environment and adjacent objects taken together make up the context that determines how the sounds will be perceived. I see aesthetic activities as human and therefore always emerging from social situations. A tone can exist in isolation, but as soon as it is produced by a specific person, in a specific space, on a specific occasion, and listened to by a specific audience, we cannot escape the fact that each single tone exists in a human context.

Following the contextual relation are the connotations that connect to the context but at the same time are tied to a musical strophe by other means. Thus music signifies a special text, a special occasion, a special performance, or a special perception. Such connotations often follow the music into new contexts. Harmonies, melodies, rhythms, and even single intervals actually become a symbolic language charged with extra-musical meanings. The opposite effect is possible as well: when performed in a new context, the meaning of tones can alter and the music gains new layers of significance.

This aesthetic reasoning is grounded in the fact that a musical sound does not in itself contain features symbolizing a particular political standpoint. However, music signifies political standpoints by virtue of its connotations. Resistance can be acted by whistling the "wrong" melody in the "wrong" situation. Music as political resistance thereby relies on the connection between the sounds, contexts, and connotations. It is also obvious that we must deal with the function of music—that is, how music in its context acts as an agent for human beings and society.

Almost all research on the music of resistance deals with the texts. Words connected to the nonfigurative sounds not only guide the total experience but also control the way a song is interpreted. The vast majority of what is generally regarded as music of resistance is song. Censorship of music is mostly aimed at the messages in the texts performed (Kirkegaard 2011). However, accompanying music often makes a difference regarding efficiency in communication and the way a text is perceived and memorized. Here I have chosen to reflect first and foremost on the music of commitment that can serve resistance without using text. I encountered a broad discussion on that theme in my interviews among Palestinian musicians.

First I need to provide some notes about what is obvious in the text-based music of resistance in Palestine. The composer and singer Mustafa al-Kurd mentions how deeply rooted text is in Arab society. Poetry and elaborated verbal utterances permeate the aesthetics of Arab culture. This is, according to al-Kurd, even more pronounced in times of conflict: "If I lived in different surroundings, I wouldn't have to make songs, I would simply make music, because in my music there is this entire message. However, in this context I can't do without the words, because that's what people focus on" (al-Kurd, interview). When the Lebanese *ʿūd* (lute) player Marcel Khalife composed and performed songs with texts of Mahmoud Darwish, he was under fire not for the music but for the texts, which were, however, not written by him. Music as the conveyor of text was regarded as more subversive and obviously more penetrative than just the poems as printed or as read. Part of the calamity was the fact that the original words were a text from the *Qurʾān*. In any case the act of singing harshly exposed sensitive words.[2]

Even the title of a piece steers the experience. Ahmad Al Khatib, an internationally touring Palestinian ʿūd player, has experienced discussions about the song titles on his latest CD, *Sabīl*: "Exode" (Exodus), "Moses," "Canaan," and "Two Rivers." People in the audience have claimed that these titles imply dubious messages and that the word "Exode" carries connotations mostly directed toward the Jewish diaspora (Al Khatib, interview).

The modus operandi in the music of resistance is not only built on context and connotation; at the same time, the perceived expression inherent in the music also plays an important role. In discussions I often have met the opinion that music in itself has a power. Beauty, a strongly expressive melody, a coherent form, a provocative and interesting setting, outstanding instrumentation, voice, and timbre are ingredients that have inherent musical qualities, but they are also part of the combined aesthetic/political utterance. The content denoted becomes changed through the music because of new signs coded into the music.[3]

An aesthetic expression relates to context and connotations in various ways. From the aim, text, function, and context of the music, different aspects emerge that give an indication of the music's general human or specifically situated values. We might construct a scale on which different performances can be looked at according to their degree of aesthetic or societal dominance. However, I have rejected such a simplified theory in favor of a perspective where I look at music as a result of the combined effect of aesthetic and societal aspects. Nevertheless, it is important to regard aesthetics and politics as two paradigms having discrete qualities and logics that must be respected. An aesthetic expression has a language and rules, and artistic value is an essential feature. In the same way, politics must be regarded within its own paradigm. An efficient political action is not always beautiful, but it is judged by its consequences. The complexity we need to understand is that music and politics are dialectically intertwined.

Expectations and Intentions

The absurd question of whether a Palestinian person is normal or abnormal is discussed by many intellectuals—for example, Maya Abu Al Hayyat (2010). Can Palestinians, who have been subjected to much suffering and harassment, still be considered human, or have they been transformed into either victims or heroes? Are they equal to Israeli, Arab, or American people (111)? Consequently, the music of Palestine is often regarded with differing attitudes. Uninformed external listeners, who often have a picture of the country as being violated and terrorized, expect cultural products to be permeated by frustration and devastation. The music is interpreted in terms of one-sided political information. Palestinians I have met talk about this as a trap that they encounter that forces them to fulfill external expectations (Al Khatib, interview).

Another theme running through my interviews counters this stereotyped attitude. Being a Palestinian is not the main focus of a cultural utterance. Accordingly, artistry as a general human activity is what is being sought. Nevertheless, the two attitudes are unavoidably present in the musical discourse. The music of Palestine contains influences from specifically situated geopolitical facts as well as those based on general human values. This situation can superficially be regarded as a conflicting ambiguity, but in order to understand the conditions for artists, it must be looked upon as an aesthetically compelling complex. Musician and writer Khaled Jubran explained it in these terms: "Artistic awareness is, to me, by definition political awareness . . . My music is an attempt at making something different that is still Arab, but not simply derivative. What are the sounds you want to hear? Those that reflect your sense of self and your awareness" (Khaled Jubran, interview). The music ensemble Sharq—comprised of Palestinians based in Amman, Jordan—illustrates how such double attitudes can be combined. Lara Elayyan (singer) and Tareq Al-Jundi (ʿūd player) described their internal discussion in the group, a dichotomy between their political and aesthetic views on music and how these talks have led to certain musical choices (interview). Primarily, in spite of their awareness of the extremely bad conditions for their professional lives as artists, they have rejected any kind of commercial music for giving concerts or for releasing CDs. However, within their group a dialogue developed.

Elayyan is clear about her position regarding her engagement as a performer. Its explicit purpose has been built on political statements: she wants to preserve and sing out the traditional heritage of the Palestinians in order to conserve ethnic knowledge and skills. She searches for texts and folklore connected to the people. And her songs are coupled with the struggle for liberation. She has a pedagogical urgency: "Talking about our problems is good art."

She chose to leave her studies at the Amman Conservatory in favor of her work to find materials and to "develop" folklore into modern art. For her, melodies and customs are urgent themes. The choice of a political theme—for example, the *Nakba* (catastrophe)—might set limits on what is possible to sing, but at the same time the limits stimulate concentration and intensity in the manifestation. She claims that the vocal training she needed was provided through practice and performance with the Sharq ensemble. She has been able to develop her political and artistic expressivity at the same time. Altogether she means that the work with the group has been an intrinsically political act that mirrors a multifaceted vision of art.

In the first place, she wants her music to be situated in a context where she can understand the audience and what she wants to tell them via her music. "The only thing I can do," she says, "is to remind our generation." Thus she has focused on a presentation of the historical heritage being threatened with falling into oblivion by choosing music related to the Palestinian people. She sings about Palestinian places, and she uses the traditional Palestinian names instead of the contemporary Hebrew ones. There is a rich treasure of traditional songs and dances related to work, weddings, and funerals, for example, that she identifies as her pedagogical task to transfer. Elayyan sings the song "Ka Makaber Al Shuhadʾa" with a text by Mahmoud Darwish on the CD *Bayna Bayn*. The text is about a folk hero, and the song is performed a cappella, showing talent for both the folk elements and the artistic expression. It is obvious that she is renewing the heritage in a modern aesthetic manner with a luminosity that is effective in up-to-date media and on contemporary stages.

Elayyan is aware of the limitations of her choice of material and singing style. If she sings for an audience that is uninformed about the conditions of Palestinian life today, explanations are needed. This is actually not a problem as long as she is aware of the audience's reactions. The more concretely political part of the content is accompanied by a general aesthetic presentation that can be accepted by any kind of person.

Al-Jundi gives more attention to the general Oriental musical material. To him, political action also means an unfolding work with new artistic utterances. "Arab music stresses the emotions. And to develop a method for expressing emotions one needs to use the instruments in new ways." He has a vision of improving the instrumental form *taḥmīlah*. Current ways of composing music and playing ensemble are "not mature" at the present stage, he says. A new society craves new ways of making music, and he talks about changing the idiomatic praxis to give each instrument an individual voice. A dialogue between voices might thereby enhance both the ensemble feeling and the individual instrument's technique and sound. According to al-Jundi, this is a way of building on the tradition of *maqām* that has prioritized monophonic music. He said in a modest manner that in a hundred years' time there might be new musical forms developed by his generation.

Thus the members of the Sharq ensemble are aware of both the difference between political and aesthetic values and the possibility of integrating the two. Their creative workshops focus on several qualitative goals that can be seen as divergent but in a deeper perspective actually benefit from each other. Mustafa al-Kurd, who claims that he has never faced a situation where he had to compromise his artistic values for the sake of politics, likewise underlines this concept (interview).

Identity

The need to reinforce the identity of the Palestinians is a recurring theme in these interviews. It is about both boosting an inner strength and making a manifestation toward other people. This is a general human need, but in the issue of identity it has become specifically urgent for Palestinians. The country has been occupied since the Persian rule (538 BC), through Hellenistic, Roman, Arab, Ottoman, British, and other rule, up to the present Israeli occupation. Many of these autocratic forces, of course, have left their mark on the people ethnically and culturally. However, Palestinians still talk about one nation with one people living on a certain area of land, well aware of the relative possibility of this claim. The interviewees often refer to Greater Syria as a common cultural home. Yet it was only after 1948 when the Nakba struck the people that a decisive fight for a Palestinian National identity started. This came as a response to the awareness of the ethnic cleansing that was part of the Nakba (Pappé 2007, 13). And music became a vital ingredient in this struggle. Mustafa al-Kurd underlines the strong relationship between the human being, the dream, the past, and the place in his songs (al-Kurd, interview).

The concrete events entailed in the establishment of Israel influenced the life of individuals, organizations, and the country. Forced transfer and exodus affected a majority of the population. Many left the country and live today in diaspora mainly in Jordan, Syria, and Lebanon but also in the United States, the United Kingdom, Canada, and many Arab countries. "There are today on the United Nations rolls close to four million Palestinian refugees (the Palestinian Authority says five million)" (Morris 2004, 1). Around 1.5 million live within the borders of the Israeli state. These are often defined as Palestinians even if the term is disputed (Waxman 2012). The rest of the population (3.8 million) lives on the fragments of land remaining on the West Bank and Gaza Strip. Israeli settlement on the West Bank has further diminished the land and the life conditions of the Palestinian people. It is obvious that geopolitical circumstances have cut off and still threaten the country and its people's existence. Apart from these changes of life conditions for the residents, Israel is also in combat against Palestinian culture and thereby the cultural identity of Palestine (Jubran, Hammad, Hashhash, Khoury, interviews). In this war Palestinian culture, buildings, historical sites, and cultural infrastructure have been destroyed. Cultural events like concerts or theater performances are often hindered.

Palestinians feel that their history, culture, and ethnic identity are at stake, and many of my interviewees mentioned that a strong culture could raise resistance toward the occupiers. However, the struggle for a characteristic culture is under pressure also because Israeli/Jewish culture is not homogenous; rather, it is a mixture of cultures from all countries where Jews in diaspora have settled (Khoury, interview). People from many places around the world that now constitute bases for Israeli/Jewish culture bring back—while moving to Israel—cultures fertilized in such various contexts as Arab countries, Asia, Europe, Africa, and both South and North America. Thus the shared Arab background complicates the maintenance of a distinct difference between Israeli and Palestinian heritage. Both peoples are in need of asserting and manifesting their historical roots. A conflict around the present ownership of lands is thus connected to claiming a historically cultural legacy. Many cultural workers point out what they feel to be deliberate Israeli destruction of cultural sites: "By demolishing the cultural heritage, by coming every night of the year in order to arrest, execute, tear down houses, et cetera—in that way the identity of the Palestinians was destroyed. We are supposed to become culture-less" (Hammad, interview). Palestinian artists express a natural reaction toward the Israeli attempts to wreck their identity via the culture of resistance.

However, a contradiction emerges between using art for this specific purpose and the essence of art. "The political issues are consuming the artistry to a degree that is becoming really annoying" (Al Khatib, interview). The result is a lack of freedom.

Freedom

"I just live the situation I find myself in and try to reflect it." Ahmad Al Khatib rejects deliberate politicizing and the concept of a special genre called the music of resistance. "I am expressing myself then as a human being, as a world citizen." He is a Palestinian living in exile since 2002 due to a conflict with the Israeli state. He has not been able to work in Palestine since, and he continuously experiences the predicament of being a Palestinian. This gives him a role as a musician in which he cannot avoid the audiences seeing him as political. He finds himself in ambivalence between taking responsibility and being annoyed. "For me resistance is being able to continue your creativity, not to surrender and be a victim of circumstances . . . to always be able to go on playing music, producing, and performing" (Al Khatib, interview).

> Music to the CD *Sada* was written during a curfew in Ramallah in 2002. There was not much sound in Ramallah, which usually is a very active city. And suddenly you saw the city like in a picture. So I got inspiration from the silence of the city. I did not think of the bigger political issue, but more like the psychological effect of seeing Ramallah in this echo of sounds of very soft breeze and such sounds. I was trying to translate what I saw and heard. That was the main aim and the main attention. Of course it all was happening due to the political situation. (Al Khatib, interview)

Al Khatib points out that just the fact of having a concert, whatever the music is, has a certain value for the Palestinian people in the occupied territories. For him, the music of resistance has come to denote musical performances as such and not just a specific kind of music. This manifestation of being able to live and to indulge in cultural and social values is important, and it broadens our discussion on the features of music of resistance. The Palestine Youth Orchestra is sometimes criticized for playing works by Beethoven and other Western composers. But in the light of this expanded concept of resistance it becomes logical. Connotations are not neglected, but they do not follow a politically correct stereotype.

Striving for freedom is thus tied to striving for artistry and humanness. Omar Barghouti writes about shattered dreams and shaken identities that need reconstruction just as material things do (2004). On the question "Isn't dance a very low priority in time of war?" Barghouti claims:

> Restoring our humanity, our dreams, our hopes and our will to resist and to be free, therefore, becomes even more important than mending our in-

> frastructure. Thus, we dance . . . Cultural expression to us, then, serves dual purposes: self-therapy and expansion of the "free zone" in our collective mind, where progressive transformation can thrive. In response to all the attempts to circumscribe our aspirations, we must push on, dreaming and being creative, boundlessly. Thus we dance. (2004)

Zakaria Zubeidi—involved in the Freedom Theater in Jenin—points out the fact that promoting a Palestinian identity is dependent on freedom (Zubeidi, interview). He argues that social and collective freedom must be combined with the freedom of individuals. An individual identity has to be freed from other people's opinions and influences—freed from local, Israeli, and Western pressure.

Folklore and Identity

The Popular Arts Center (PAC) has been instrumental in identifying and gathering folkloric material. The center was established in 1987 and has since documented about 220 hours of songs, dances, and interviews with artists. For many artists, the archive has become a haven for the preservation and development of their heritage. However, it is not just a museum for preserving tradition; it is also playing a role in the front line of the development and education of new generations. With a vast outreach program and onsite projects, the PAC plays an important role for many independent groups and individuals. Iman Hamouri, the leader of the organization, situates the PAC's aim and activities in a general developmental plan both for Palestinian artists and for Palestinians taking part in projects as audience or as participants: "We have four principles. I have pre-thinking, I can communicate, I can create, and I have the sense of belonging" (Hamouri, interview). The PAC was connected to the dance group El-Funoun, which took a leading role in creating the historical memory of the people. The group (established in 1979) performed with traditional costumes, dances, and songs with both historical and modern forms. The aesthetics of the group influenced the work of a whole generation in terms of creating an identity. The conflict between being an ethnic museum and their shaping of a modern, urban, and international expression was part of El-Funoun's everyday life. According to Mohammad Yacoub, a member of El-Funoun, for the first time in Palestine they performed dances with both male and female participants (Yacoub, interview). This was a breach of tradition that was influenced partly by the transformation of folk art to stage performances and partly by internal trends in modern Palestinian culture, a kind of internal revolution (Khoury, Yacoub, interviews). There were naturally differences between urban and rural culture and music, but songs from the countryside that were still alive in the villages and among farmers were the most obvious base for emphasizing the uniqueness of Palestinian identity.

Early on, El-Funoun encountered problems with Israeli attempts to prevent the activities of the group. During certain periods they had to work underground

(Yacoub, interview). The members of El-Funoun were even challenged by curfews from time to time. Defying the ban put every individual at risk when meeting for rehearsals. Omar Barghouti described how the members had to fight their own fears. There was a choice between staying at home or carrying on with their work; every member had to make a private decision. Nevertheless, people came in full force to every meeting but were exhausted by their powerlessness. Thus the work at the rehearsals became an internal process that strengthened political decisiveness for the individuals and the group. Here we can note how artistry played a central role in political resistance. Actions of cultural resistance were aimed not only at the occupying power but also at the Palestinian society: "We should face up to our internal problems as Palestinians. Addressing sound and healthy survival under bad conditions—and the conditions themselves . . . otherwise you can never fight against the other side. There is no neutrality under occupation" (Yacoub, interview).

An Artistic Heritage

El-Funoun reshaped their work during the 1980s. The earlier phase was connected to the group's political role and its relation to the Palestine Liberation Organization (PLO) (Yacoub, interview). After 1986 they wished to reach a wider audience with artistically more advanced programs. "We were no longer a documentary group that staged folklore. We started to study artistically what the body language meant, the ideas and themes of the songs, and the story that was performed from the deep Palestinian heritage" (Yacoub, interview). This change was an answer to the need to communicate with the national and international stage.

Reem Talhami (actor and singer) points out the necessity of conveying the sense of belonging to a people: "Mainly my song has to do with where I come from . . . I see a love song as connected to me, connected to me as a Palestinian living in Palestine."[4] Talhami is aware of the dilemma between superficial political messages or ethnic markers and a more-worked-through artistic expression. She emphasizes the urgency of passing on an artistic heritage: "It's the Palestinian and the Syrian kind of art music."

Talhami regards her music as a weapon directed toward two enemies. On the one hand it is aimed at all those who deny Palestinians the right to develop their own culture, and on the other hand it is aimed at the inner enemy, the devastating despondency mirroring the failure to achieve success in the fight for freedom. The first struggle is underpinned by a wish to tell the world about the conditions under which the Palestinian people live. The other struggle is personal and against Talhami's feeling that her persistent work to improve the situation for her people is in vain (Talhami, interview).

Other cultural workers have likewise pointed out the need to show that Palestinian identity contains a substantial history of artistry. Sami Hammad, who runs the project Nablus the Culture, talks about the importance of the new possibilities of staging music performances and investing in music education: "We were abandoned by the rest of the world. We wanted to revive human values" (Hammad, interview). He is of the opinion that this activity functions as an act of resistance toward the occupation of Nablus and the limitation of freedom for the citizens. As long as the Israeli presence in terms of cultural destruction in Nablus exists, Nablus the Culture and other cultural activities must react by proclaiming Palestinian dignity.

"*L'art pour l'art*" is a concept that brings to our mind lack of sensitivity for social and societal contexts. Nevertheless, music and dance, typical nonverbal expressions, carry structures corresponding to our minds and ways of thinking and feeling (Langer 1957). Thus cultural expressions can mean a dialogue between the creator, performer, and audience. An evolutionary art can enforce changes in our mind-sets through new artistic structures and forms. New music, developed according to inherent musical factors, can induce alternative and utopian ways of thinking, which is a decisive fact in times of conflict and hardship. The development that Sharq's Al-Jundi aspired to is part of logical steps toward freedom not only of expression but also of thinking.

Khaled Elayyan, choreographer and technical director of Sareyyet Ramallah Troupe for Music and Dance (the First Ramallah Group) as well as executive director of Al-Kasaba Theater and Cinematheque in Ramallah, underlines that identity matters: "We used the arts before to keep our identity—using music and dance is an indirect form of struggle against Israel. Most of our songs, most of our dance, most of our plays, are about the Palestinian people, to tell the people that we have an identity and that we are here" (Elayyan, interview). Elayyan was one of the pioneers among cultural workers and started his dance group at Sareyyet Ramallah in 1985.

Elayyan emphasizes the fact that after the Oslo Accords, communication with the world expanded as part of the efforts to show that Palestinians exist and that they have an artistic potential. This became even more urgent after the 9/11 attacks on America in 2001 as the reputation of all Arabs (including Palestinians) was called into question by the Western world.

The Oslo Accords

The Oslo Accords provided a means for strengthening the identity of the Palestinians. Areas ruled by the Palestinian Authority (PA) in the West Bank and the Gaza Strip were able to establish administrative infrastructures including Departments of Culture and Education. Before 1993 a strong dream about a future Palestine was nurtured by song, music, and dance performed according to the tradition of the Palestinians (Hashhash, interview). After the accords were made, emerging administrative structures stabilized these aesthetic utterances by way of education, production companies, and performance venues. At the same time, a more individualistic aspect appeared in the artistry. This trend lifted much of the music to an international scene, where the ethnic Palestinian markers no longer seemed to be that important. We can thus see how the Oslo Accords influenced two aspects of the music of resistance. On the one hand, improved aesthetic quality demonstrated the strong competitive potential of the music; on the other hand, music characterized by an ethnic quality did not mean very much to an international audience. The contradiction between these two aspects permeated much of the aesthetic discussion that followed. (A broader view is unfolded in Yara El-Ghadban and Kiven Strohm's essay in this volume. They describe the phenomenon as a dilemma between subversion and seduction.)

Mahmoud Abu Hashhash is involved with funding several Palestinian artists and groups through his work at the A. M. Qattan Foundation's program "Art and Culture." He mentions the importance of the growth of local groups. This was especially obvious during the first Intifada when new settled groups supported the struggle. They had a greater role compared to more established performers. One consequence of this phenomenon was the emergence of new musical styles, maybe not with the same artistic aspirations, but rather an outburst of spontaneous expression. "The first Intifada has witnessed a lot of national stories, especially local dance and local initiatives that came out of nothing. Because this was the spirit of the Intifada, its very creative spirit, collectively wise and individual. But after the Oslo agreement things changed on all levels: music, literature, and theater, whatever—the whole discourse changed" (Hashhash, interview). To Hashhash, art before the Oslo Accords was a tool of resistance, but after Oslo art became more personal. Even the concept of resistance changed after Oslo, because people thought at first that to resist was to sing a national song, but later they realized that resistance can be shown by performing a very good artistic piece of music. To resist, according to Hashhash, is, among many things, to represent your country in international arenas:

> Artistic standards took the priority over political standards, because it's easy to make something political that people will like. But it's not easy to make something apolitical that people like, because the taste of the people was rooted in politics . . . In a sense I don't want to say that everything good in culture and music is because of Oslo, but Oslo was a heroic moment where history changed; the change in history was reflected in cultural practice more than anything else . . . Israelis never wanted Palestinians to express themselves in creative way. The Israelis resisted this from the beginning. We did not have any fine art department before the Oslo agreement, because this was not allowed, and Israel will never welcome that. Because to Israel, I think, the most dangerous thing is to start seeing the Palestinians with artists and singers and musicians who can express and convey the spirit of the times. (Hashhash, interview)

The consequences of this new international relationship are also complicated by relations with international donors. From both Palestinian organizations and artists, and from the funding organizations we can find demands and expectations that do not always go hand in hand.

> Artists and musicians end up in a dilemma. On one hand, adaptation to foreign donors means that one may change one's aesthetics in order to please foreign organizations. Western aesthetics often emphasize the uniquely individual, which means that the political function of Palestinian art has to be sacrificed. On the other hand, Palestinian artists are striving for more individual forms of expression. It is essential to seek a balance between the demands of the donors and one's own ambitions. (Hashhash, interview)

Mohammed Maragha, activities coordinator at the Edward Said National Conservatory of Music, notes another change after the Oslo Accords: "The Palestinians were tired because they discovered during the second Intifada that the Israelis did not care. And international opinion accepted everything, the massacres and all the weapons, and it was a shock. The Palestinian Authority had to compromise even more than before. And they started to establish some kind of individualism. Forget Palestine, focus on your daily life now." As a consequence, popular music gained the attention of audiences, music that did not aim to awaken and motivate resistance. Popular singers comforted and entertained the young generation instead (Maragha, interview).[5]

Musical Genres

Two aspects of identity reinforcement were prominent in the interviews. On the one hand we find music and song that were rooted in a local tradition, stamped with ethnic collective characteristics. On the other hand we find music expressing the distinctive nature of Palestinians as individuals as well as their belonging to humankind.

The first genre came from cultural activities connected to major life events—for example, weddings, celebrations, and other functions. In these contexts the dance *dabke* dominated (McDonald 2006b), but many other dances and songs were performed at home feasts and sung for and among children. Songs sung at funerals reflecting feelings and relationships have had a significant role. One can say that this art has a more static connotation, but at the same time it is obvious that this genre is developing in modern society, not least by way of adaptation to modern media and sometimes furnished with new texts. Typically during the first Intifada (1987–1991), many songs were of popular origin, but after being charged with new texts they reflected the suffering that imprisoned Palestinians faced. At the same time, songs for mobilization and motivation (*tāᶜbiʾah*) were also being written (Maragha, interview).

The second genre grew out of traditional Oriental poetry and music and has a wider Oriental and Greater Syrian connection. According to Said Murad, founder and leader of the Sabreen Association, this genre stems from another historical source but is also subject to a development influenced by international contacts and artistic development (Murad, interview).

A third genre is based on contemporary international movements, such as pop and hip-hop. A regional trend has developed music that has spread from Egypt to Lebanon and throughout the Arab Middle East. This modern genre connects to both local groups and international stars. Hip-hop has lately exploded as a genre and has a special feature in that it combines musical creativity from the local to the global environments. The genre has also become important for bonding within the fragmented Palestine and with a vast diaspora (see the essays by Randa Safieh and Janne Louise Andersen in this book). Hip-hop is at the same time regarded as alien to the Palestinian tradition. A difference exists between countryside villages and the urban settings: "Hip-hop is more for the privileged groups, whereas if you go to the young people in the villages, they are more involved in traditional art. There is a drastic gap between the villages and the urban settings. I believe personally that each village has its own traditions. Even between Nablus and the villages around Nablus there are differences" (Hamouri, interview). We can perceive here how the meaning of music shifts. In the villages the dabke dance is part and parcel of folklore. If used in a rebellious situation, new connotations will appear. That has happened with this dance. It is no longer only folklore, but now it is also charged with political meanings. It has been converted to a show dance where men and women take part. The art of resistance creates new functions where both the artistic form and the content become transformed (see the essay by Sylvia Alajaji in this book).

Said Murad explains how various genres are differently anchored in various community groups. The social characteristics of music gained different meanings in the resistance struggle. Before the first Intifada this division was evident, but during the new era several political bodies founded their own music groups (PLO, Fatah, etc.).

Later, after the Oslo Accords took place (1993), there was the possibility of receiving foreign funding for infrastructure and events. The ensemble Sabreen was first established in 1980, but new opportunities came its way after Oslo. In 1987 they became the Sabreen Association. One of their new missions was to merge groups of listeners by combining different styles representing various genres. Their new way of composing and performing made an impact on artistic development as well. The Sabreen group experimented with a "high artistic standard that took the priority before political standard." This, coupled "with a human and a national content," enabled them to "survive . . . as a fashionable group" (Hashhash, interview).

Sabreen and other similar groups facilitated the development of a musical Palestinian identity that made an impact at concerts abroad. This time the identity was not founded on rural music, but sought to embrace various social groups, specifically including younger urban generations (Khoury, interview). Thus differences between traditionalists and innovators were coloring the aesthetic and political discussion on music after 1993. The effect of using traditional rural music and song was strong, but it held back a development showing human and artistic progress.

Said Murad noted that a consequence of this change was that this music lost its sense of political direction after the first Intifada. He pointed out Sabreen's chain of CD releases as mirroring the development of the music of commitment. The first record, *Smoke of the Volcanos* (1984), was a display of folklore. The second, *Death of the Prophet* (1987), was an act of resistance with a clear-cut message. The third CD, *Here Come the Doves* (1994), was an illustration of post-Oslo hopes, whereas the fourth, *Where To?* (2000), reflected the Palestinian people's despair and frustration caused by the failure to free themselves from the occupation.

Education as Resistance

A constructive infrastructure is a consequence of the striving for improved artistry. Since the Oslo Accords took place, education and financial support have been part of the establishment of structures that have strengthened music production. There are many organizations and institutions flourishing on foreign and domestic money (Hashhash, Maragha, Murad, Khoury, interviews). They have constituted a deliberate act of resistance in terms of improving artistic skills and performances. The aims of these endeavors indicate an underlying idea about the need for good art aimed at a domestic Palestinian public, Palestinians in diaspora, and also as a means of demonstrating the features of Palestinian art to a broad international audience. Thus educational institutes and production companies have been part of establishing a Palestinian nation. Suhail Khoury was one of the founders of the Edward Said National Conservatory of Music, and he drew attention to the role of the conservatory as part of the Palestinian identity. This comprehends working with both classical and modern Arabic music taught side by side with Western music.

Educational institutions have been closely linked to prominent performers. At the same time, several projects, many of them run on foreign funding, are part and parcel of schools' or production companies' programs. (An educational project developed by Sabreen is described in Andersen's essay in this book.) It is obvious that the funding of musical education is entangled between Palestinian cultural integrity and surrender to foreign cultural forces. The West-Eastern Divan Orchestra project run by the Barenboim-Said Foundation has been criticized for actually promoting Western values (Beckles Willson 2009). The foundation runs several educational projects in Palestine. (See the essay by El-Ghadban and Strohm in this book.)

Music of Resistance Balances Aesthetics and Functions

The initial question "How does politically committed music sound?" has not been answered via clear statements emerging in a review of my collected material. However, it has raised a discussion about the use and function of the music of resistance and thus underlined the discursive aspects of their activities. Since the sociological and anthropological perspective has been my starting point, such aspects were awaited. So the question now is, how can we understand the results that have been displayed in this essay?

In his discussion of the phenomenon "cultural resistance," Stephen Duncombe (2002) points at differing positions according to expectations and effects. He describes five kinds of action: from the proactive ideological and material creation of a free space to the absorbing of cultural resistance by the dominant power. His description gives us some guidance as to how to analyze the issue.

In the interviews among Palestinian artists, I have met many of Duncombe's levels of activity, but most of what I have encountered belongs to the proactive side. "Space to create new language, meanings, and visions of the future" and "place to build community, networks, and organizational models." Another of his positions that is applicable here describes how cultural resistance is political activity: "writing or rewriting political discourses and thus political practice" (2002, 8). However, in my material I have found more developed discourses than those suggested by his scheme.

The discourse that runs through the material is related to the dialogue or conflict between artistry and political resistance. These discourses are well anchored in both the political and aesthetic practice. Typically they relate how to keep several aspects alive and in focus at the same time. The music/politics dichotomy is replaced by a discussion on humanness, freedom, identity, and recognition. The connections between and the mutual dependence of politics and aesthetics are nurtured.

Identity is one of the concepts most commonly brought up in interviews that I have carried out concerning the music of resistance. It is also a feature that many scholars have described as being double-edged, as it limits the audience's expectations (Hall 1981, 187f). This concept of identity connects in this essay to several aspects of the individuals and the society. For instance there were changes toward a more individualistic Palestinian art after 1993. Questions raised by this shift pointed at changes that were included in the general cultural policy. Had cultural activities reached new audiences with new demands? Were there new expectations from internal and external agents? Did the desire to draw from foreign funding change the outcome of art production? Were the attitudes from different donors built on an empathetic wish to support the resistance? Or were they based on a common colonial wish to control the troublesome Middle East and to reinforce the wealthy countries' relationships to Palestine? We can see how this reflects the inner game of art as crucial for the being and development of any given individual. As Barghouti formulated it:

> From my experience, nothing can imitate the profound, transformative effect of an art that impacts the hearts and the minds of the oppressed . . . In the process, we realise that dancing our tragedies can help us rehabilitate our injured souls, to heal our buried collective trauma, and to make peace with our past, with all its pain, remorse, and haunting guilt. And in dancing our dreams, we can take the process a step further, to fulfil our aspirations for justice, peace and dignified living. (Barghouti 2004)

Talhami discusses the role of the individual artist when she points out her dual address: the inner and the outer enemy. This ambivalence underlines a profound function of art situated in a space embracing both person and society.

Collective aspects of identity were not lost along the road. Much of what happened after 1993 was done in the name of worldwide Palestinian nation building. The discourses—as I perceived them—were permeated by a conscious seeking for contact with authentic roots and a communicative internationalism. And we have seen various usages of music as resistance covering many aspects of collective life: commonly shared artistic styles, folkloric traditions, political events and phases, social strata, and general education. We have seen how different outcomes of these societal relationships are formulated: Al Khatib exemplifies one aspect when he describes how he interacts musically with political oppression: "I just live the situation . . . and try to reflect it." He explains this with reference to his commitment as a musician. True and reliable reflection is only possible for him through artistry with integrity.

A statement by Iman Hamouri shows another perspective: "I don't think we use art for art's sake here at the PAC. It's a tool for social change. Also when we talk about art's role in the society—improving appreciation—we see art as something that can create change in society. We are also talking about the social aspect. Art is a vital component in the social need and development" (Hamouri, interview). The way she formulates the relationship between art and social change indicates not only an awareness of the necessity of art as such but also, simultaneously, an awareness of its role in society. We can also recall the way dabke dancing has become symbolic and changed function and thus become loaded with new connotations and meanings.

The conclusion of the investigation points to a wholeness that can be described as consisting of layers of relationships between music, individuals, and society. All of these relationships strive toward scrutinizing and developing our understanding of the world. Thus the sound of the music of resistance emerges from the music actually used in the community and from the needs of the situation in question. It does not sound unique, but it functions in a unique way. Barghouti expresses a broader vision of a crucial relationship to the entire world: "In the evolutionary art you do have a certain balance between authenticity—your roots—and modernism and universality. Authenticity does not negate universalism. You can be authentic and universal as well. You can be original and in touch with the world" (Barghouti, interview).

Notes

1. Barghouti's term *evolutionary* seems to refer to a balance between authenticity (your roots) and modernism and universality. It is thus different from a *revolutionary* change that does not always recognize tradition.

2. "On December 14, 1999, a Lebanese court found Marcel Khalife innocent of blasphemy" (Freemuse). "The charges stem from a complaint about the lyrics to the song 'Oh My Father, I am Yusif,' lyrics written as a poem by Palestinian Mahmoud Darwish and published in 1992 . . . Khalife set it to music and recorded it on a 1995 album titled 'Arabic Coffeepot' ('Rakwat Arab'). The lyrics include a quote inspired by the Koranic version of Joseph, a figure mentioned in both the Koran and the Bible; the lyrics compare Joseph's suffering to that of the Palestinians" (Chalala 1999).

3. This double aspect of the meaning of music is explored by Nicholas Cook (2001). He describes two examples of onesidedness, which ascribe causality to either internal or external musical factors. As a better alternative, Cook explains meaning in music as a constantly ongoing negotiation between immanent and arbitrary musical features. "Music never *is* 'alone,' . . . it is always received in a discursive context, and . . . it is through the interaction of music and interpreter, text and context, that meaning is constructed" (180).

4. See the interview with Reem Talhimi in this book.

5. In some quotations above "Israelis" are mentioned as if they all participated in a cultural war against Palestinians. I interpret "Israelis" as meaning representatives of the Israeli state. In fact many Israelis also struggled for a respect of Palestinian values. But the harsh political conditions do not give space for more nuanced relations. Thus I have often found standpoints from Palestinians that at first sight are not negotiable, but when closer to the situation I have come to admit that the war-like occupation does not allow respectful relations.

Sources

Interviews

Mahmoud Abu Hashhash, September 18, 2007
Omar Barghouti, September 22, 2007
Khaled Elayyan, September 20, 2007
Sami Hammad, September 16, 2007
Iman Hamouri, September 20, 2007
Khaled Jubran, September 17, 2007
Suhail Khoury, September 21, 2007
Ahmad Al Khatib, September 14, 2011
Mustafa al-Kurd, September 24, 2007
Mohammad Maragha, September 3, 2009
Said Murad, September 7, 2009

Reem Talhami, September 7, 2009
Mohammed Yacoub, September 7, 2009
Zakaria Zubeidi, September 19, 2007
Sharq (Tareq Al-Jundi, Lara Elayyan), February 17, 2010

Primary References

Al Hayyat, Maya Abu. 2010. "Den palestinska författaren" [The Palestinian Author]. *Glänta* 3–4, 109–13.

Barghouti, Omar. 2004. "The Crucial Fire." *Peace News.* March-May, Issue 2454. http://peacenews.info/node/3869/crucial-fire.

Beckles Willson, Rachel. 2009. "Whose Utopia? Perspectives on the West-East Divan Orchestra." *Music and Politics* 3 (2): 2–21.

Chalala, Elie. 1999. "Marcel Khalife Faces Charge over Darwish Poem' Arab Intellectuals Rally to Defend Creative Freedom." *Al Jadid* 5 (28). http://www.aljadid.com/content/marcel-khalife-faces-charge-over-darwish-poem-arab-intellectuals-rally-defend-creative-freed.

Cook, Nicholas. 2001. "Theorizing Musical Meaning." *Music Theory Spectrum* 23 (2): 170–95.

Duncombe, Stephen. 2002. *Cultural Resistance Reader.* London: Verso.

Freemuse. 2011. "Marcel Khalife—The Blasphemy Trials." January 1, 2001. Freemuse. http://freemuse.org/sw6542.asp.

Hall, Stuart. 2002. "Notes on Deconstruction of 'The Popular.'" In Duncombe, *Cultural Resistance Reader.* (Originally published in Raphael Samuel, *People's History and Socialist Theory,* London: Kegan Paul–Routledge, 1981.)

Kirkegaard, Annemette. October 2011. Email correspondence.

Langer, Susanne. 1957. *Philosophy in a New Key: A Study in the Symbolism of Reason, Rite, and Art.* Cambridge, MA: Harvard University Press.

McDonald, David A. 2006a. "Performing Palestine: Resisting the Occupation and Reviving Jerusalem's Social and Cultural Identity through the Arts." *Jerusalem Quarterly* 25 (1): 5–19.

———. 2006b. "My Voice Is My Weapon: Music and Nationalism in the Palestinian Resistance Movement." PhD diss. University of Illinois at Urbana Champaign.

Morris, Benny. 2004. *The Birth of the Palestinian Refugee Problem Revisited.* Cambridge, UK: Cambridge University Press.

Pappé, Ilan. 2007. *Den etniska rensningen av Palestina.* Stockholm: Karneval. (Published in English as *The Ethnic Cleansing of Palestine.* Oxford: OneWorld Publishing, 2006.)

Rakha, Youssef. 2002–2003. "Khaled Jubran: To be a Palestinian musician you play at the edge of the abyss. A selfless sensibility." *Al-Ahram Weekly* online. Issue 618. http://weekly.ahram.org.eg/2002/618/profile.htm.

Waxman, Dov. 2012. "A Dangerous Divide: The Deterioration of Jewish-Palestinian Relations in Israel." *Middle East Journal* 66 (1): 11–29.

Music

Al Khatib, Ahmad, and Youssef Hbeisch. 2012. *Sabîl.* Paris: Institute Du Monde Arabe. Harmonia Mundi.

Sharq. 2009. *Bayna Bayn.* CD. Amman: eka3.

11

The Ghosts of Resistance: Dispatches from Palestinian Art and Music

Yara El-Ghadban and Kiven Strohm

In the summer of 2010 Palestinian artists Emily Jacir and Yazid Anani installed two billboards in downtown Ramallah as part of a public intervention called *al-Riyāḍ*. Visually mimicking the urban-development genre, the two billboards ironically questioned the erosion of a collective Palestinian political project through the building of gated communities (that look conspicuously similar to illegal Israeli settlements in the West Bank) and the creation of a Dubai-style business tower that was to be constructed atop Ramallah's fruit and vegetable market. Their work was part of a larger exhibition titled *Ramallah: The Fairest of Them All?* produced by the Birzeit Ethnographic and Art Museum and the Ramallah municipality. Yet within twenty-four hours the municipality, calling the billboards "problematic," removed them. Despite demands from the artists and the organizers of the exhibition to discontinue such acts of censorship, both the mayor of Ramallah and the director of the municipality remained steadfast in their decision and offered no further clarification of their problematic nature.[1]

While the Ramallah municipality had initially approved Jacir and Anani's public intervention, the problem with the works arguably centered on their exposure of the destruction of a collective political project through the neoliberal and neocapitalist agenda being pushed through by the Palestinian National Authority (PNA). In other words, it exposed the divide between the political program of the PNA and the collective political project of the Palestinian people, whereby causing embarrassment for the PNA. More importantly, however, the works exposed the complicated role of culture and cultural practices in a paradoxical context in which occupation, continued colonization, and state-building initiatives coexist.

For years Palestinian artists and musicians have struggled against their work being interpreted exclusively within the paradigm of liberation politics,[2] which sees the task of art and music, their raison d'être, as the emancipation of Palestinians and Palestine from the stranglehold of colonialism and occupation—in short, art and music at the service of politics.[3] Yet, while constantly trying to escape the reductive discourses surrounding culture and politics, including those defended by Palestinian political representatives like the PNA, many refuse to give up engaging with it in their work. This tension between nationalist liberation discourse and the creative strategies of Palestinian artists and musicians has been exacerbated by the interest taken by international cultural actors, organizations, and institutions with Palestinian artists, and by the gradual move by international nongovernmental organizations (NGOs) and humanitarian aid agencies toward funding cultural projects in the Occupied Palestinian Territories. Together these have resulted in an unprecedented dissemination of Palestinian cultural production, both locally and globally. Palestinian artists and musicians are confronted today with an increasing range of brokers and mediators that include, among others, the PNA, Western and Palestinian humanitarian aid agencies and NGOs, art museum and gallery curators, and connoisseurs and music industry representatives from all over the world. Why are these international actors taking an interest in Palestinian culture now? How is the link between culture and politics being articulated in this context? What are the political and aesthetic repercussions of the internationalization and humanitarization of Palestinian art and music? And, finally, how does the current situation affect the discourse on "culture as liberation" and "culture as resistance" that dominated studies of Palestinian art and music during the twentieth century and continues to inform most sociocultural analysis of Palestinian culture today?

We argue that Palestinian music and art have been represented through three ideological frameworks that have informed the roles and meanings attributed to cultural practices in Palestinian society: culture as survival, culture as resistance, and culture as a site for humanitarian intervention and development. Although emerging at different moments over the last one hundred years, these frames of reference tend to overlap and interact, creating tensions with which musicians and artists continue to struggle. In making this argument, we are admittedly taking a step back from music making and art making as practice and focusing on the discourses that have surrounded them. These discourses have been mobilized to varying degrees by scholars, by Palestinians in their daily representations and interactions with music and art, as well as by mediators and cultural brokers like NGOs. In other words, this is not about Palestinian music and art per se, but about the discourse on Palestinian music and art. As such, our argument is not ethnographic, but epistemological and historiographical. We revisit the theoretical and discursive framework that has surrounded Palestinian cultural production, mainly music and art, and build on ethnographic studies, some of which are represented in this book, as well as on our own field research, to propose a moment of reflection on the profound changes that have occurred with relation to the meanings and roles attributed to Palestinian cultural practices like music since the end of the nineteenth century and on their implications for the future.

When Things Fall Apart, All That Remains Is Culture: Cultural Survivalism in and after Palestine

The tension between culture and politics is not unique to Palestine.[4] In societies that have been through traumatizing historical experiences, such as colonization, the forced uprooting of a people, or a civil war, cultural practices take on meanings and roles that go well beyond questions of creativity and aesthetic appreciation. Whether it is in Palestine, or in South Africa during or after apartheid, or in Lebanon during and after the civil war, cultural practices are intimately implicated in projects of nation building and have been used for political propaganda, resistance against colonialism, and to criticize corrupt postcolonial governments, among other things. Anthropologists and ethnomusicologists today tend to focus on the many ways cultural production is entangled in the formation of national and transnational imaginaries in the face of globalization, economic, political, cultural, and social fluidity, instability, inequality, and heterogeneity (White 2012; Marcus and Myers 1995). They investigate how cultural practices such as music making participate in the generating and reinforcing of hegemonic representations and ideologies just as they can be mobilized for resistance, critique, and the subversion of power (Nooshin 2009; Clayton, Herbert, and Middleton 2012).

These sometimes contradictory roles attributed to the arts and cultural production are not mutually exclusive. That is especially the case with Palestinian cultural production since the last quarter of the nineteenth century, when it emerged as an object of study (and fantasy) in Orientalist literature only to become the gravitational core around which Palestinians' attempts at reconstituting a shattered homeland would develop after the *Nakba* (catastrophe) of 1948. While these two perspectives differed on many levels in terms of the representations associated with Palestinian culture, they both tended to frame it within a survivalist ethos, albeit for very different reasons. Indeed, in the decades preceding the Nakba, the "manners and customs of the indigenous Arabs of Palestine" (to use the language of that era) were central to European archaeological and theological studies of the "Near East." This interest was not motivated by a sudden appreciation for the history and culture of Palestinians, but by the belief that the customs and traditions of Jews during biblical times had survived among Palestinian peasants. According to Khaled Furani and Dan Rabinowitz, the interest was so great that "the biblical rediscovery of Palestine triggered more European writing on Palestine in the nineteenth century than on any other Arab territory save Egypt" (2011, 477). Citing the enormous amount of literature produced during that period, they add, "This conjuring of biblical time objectified contemporary Palestinians as living fossils, mumming a historiography that serves Europeans" (478).[5]

Over the next two decades, scholarship on the subject of Palestinian customs would continue to grow, prompting the foundation of the *Journal of the Palestine Oriental Society.* And as it did, Palestinian researchers increasingly got involved. Tawfiq Canaan (1882–1964), a leading Palestinian scholar of that period, wrote several articles on traditional medicine, as well as on the myths and beliefs of villagers, including the "folklore" of the Palestinian family home (1934, 1932). Canaan was partly driven by the need to correct the shortcomings of Orientalist literature and partly by a sense of imminent danger as the first waves of Jewish immigrants arrived at the ports of Palestine and Zionism began changing the political, economic and cultural landscape (Al-Qush 1994). As Furani and Rabinowitz have noted:

> Canaan, with a circle of mostly Christian contemporary Palestinian intellectuals, (e.g., Totah, Stefan, Haddad, al-Bargouthi), portrayed Palestinians as a vibrant, cumulative assemblage of modern and ancient civilizations that included Israelites, Egyptians, Syrio-Aramaics and, not least, Arabs (Canaan 1931:34). This depiction was strategic. It challenged a colonial British version of Palestinian history that saw Arabs in Palestine as transient and ephemeral, offering a narrative that contested the endorsement by the Balfour Declaration of a national Jewish homeland in Palestine. Within the biblical and Oriental modalities of ethnographic work on Palestine we have reviewed, Palestine as the cradle of Christianity and the contemporary Orient as the key to understanding the Bible's inception was the theory. (2011, 479)

Even though much could be said about the legacy of Orientalism in his own work, Canaan is recognized as the pioneer of Palestinian heritage studies and among the first researchers to adopt the methodological and theoretical principles of anthropology—that is to say, conducting fieldwork and approaching Palestinians as individual subjects.

This approach would be taken up by Hilma Granqvist (1890–1972), who arrived from Finland with a delegation of German theologians and archaeologists during the same period. She dropped her original project to investigate the status of women in biblical times and decided to focus on the present lives of Palestinians, signaling perhaps the growing influence of anthropology and ethnography as tools for the production of knowledge during the colonial era. One might also say that constructing Palestinians as the survivors of a biblical past was becoming increasingly problematic, as it belied growing Zionist claims that the land was uninhabited and that those who did live there were mostly nomads without deep roots in the area. Nevertheless, Granqvist invested several years studying life in the Palestinian village of Arṭās between 1920 and 1930. Although her doctoral dissertation was rejected in 1932, and her ethnographic approach embodied much of what classical anthropology would later be criticized for (Fabian 1983, Clifford and Marcus 1986), including a static conceptualization of culture, Granqvist's portrayal of Arṭās offers a rare glimpse of life in Palestine during the British mandate (1947, 1931). It would also be an important reference in what would later become the Palestinian folklorist movement and one of the markers of the "salvage and preserve" turn in studies of Palestinian culture.

In the first two decades that followed the 1948 Nakba, survivalism in the Palestinian context took on new connotations as Palestinians went from being the custodians of practices that were thought to have survived through two thousand years of history to being the victims of ethnic and cultural cleansing. Consequently, the 1950s and early 1960s tend to be portrayed as years of loss and passivity, during which Palestinians were reduced to life-sustaining strategies (Peteet 2005). It was thought that staying alive in the terrible conditions of the refugee camps or as virtual hostages in the newly constituted Israeli state did not allow time, space, or energy for any creativity in terms of music and cultural production.

In fact, far from being a period of cultural inertia, these twenty years (1948–1967) set the foundations for the gradual development of a distinctively Palestinian musical and artistic expression. Indeed, a new generation of Palestinian scholars emerged, the majority of whom graduated from European universities and institutions in various fields of cultural and social studies. Their aim was to research, collect, and preserve all aspects of Palestinian culture as it became increasingly threatened by the dispersal of the majority of the people; the destruction of the villages; the uprooting of farmland; and the cultural, social, and political confusion that sprouted within the refugee camps. It was without doubt a question of survival, albeit not of a millennial past but of a present that was systematically being erased. Their work was published in the 1960s, initiating one of the richest and most productive periods of the Palestinian folklorist movement (Alqam 1994, 1977). Among these pioneers we may count Abdellatif Barghouti, who earned a PhD from the School of Oriental and African Studies (SOAS) in London and produced an invaluable collection of studies on traditional Palestinian song (1963, 1986, 1990). He was followed by Abdulla H. Lutfiyya, who worked in the village of Baytīn (1966), and Khalil Nakhleh, whose research focused on Palestinian citizens of Israel (1975).

Nakhleh's work was particularly interesting as a counter-narrative to Israeli representations of Palestinians. While Palestinian scholars were keen on salvaging the memory and culture of destroyed villages in diaspora and in the refugee camps of the West Bank and Gaza, Israeli scholars constructed their own narrative on Palestinians by taking advantage of the access they had to the Palestinians who had remained within the newly established Israeli state:

> Propelled by an Israeli culturalist desire to fabricate a secular and modernized Israeli identity, many of these writers worked within the dual dismissal

> of the Jewish diaspora and Arab culture. They largely generated functionalist accounts that portrayed Palestinians as "traditional," resistant to modernization and politically detached—a trope diametrically opposed to the self-image of a rational, forward-looking, modernizing Israeli. (Furani and Rabinowitz 2011, 480)

Paradoxically, many of the first publications on Palestinian culture, including music, and those that followed, emphasized the village and rural traditions and practices as well. Even though emphasis by Palestinian scholars was driven by very different reasons, which we will discuss later, it has tended to overshadow an equally vibrant urban music heritage that was going through its own brand of survivalism in the 1950s and 1960s.

Surviving in the City

At the time, a wave of nationalization and modernization (greatly influenced by Western models) was transforming the politics and aesthetics of music in the metropolises of the Arab world (Castelo-Branco 2002), as pan-Arab nationalism was brought to the forefront by Gamal Abdel Nasser and the brief unification of Egypt and Syria. Citing the founding of *firqat al-mūsīqá al-ʿarabīyyah* (the Arab Music Symphony Orchestra) in Cairo in 1967, Salwa E. Castelo-Branco summarizes some of these changes as follows: "A large chorus of twelve men and twelve women replaced the solo vocalist . . . The concert hall was established as the performance setting for Arab music, and the norms of performance by Western symphony orchestras were imposed" (2002, 561). However, these events did not have the same impact on Palestinian urban music; after all, Palestine had not experienced decolonization or independence. Furthermore, anxiety over Zionist attempts at assimilating Palestinians into an all-encompassing Arab identity compelled Palestinians to resist some of the homogenizing and Western-oriented aspects of pan-Arab nationalism. As a result, they maintained a tense but productive relationship with both trends: Arabism and Westernization.

In the West Bank, performers of art music, or *ṭarab,* embraced modernization strategies that reflected a stronger commitment to the *maqām* tradition. While the *firqah* (symphonic orchestra) and the *ughnīyyah* (popular song) were taking over the Arab musical sphere through cultural centers like Egypt (Racy 2003), the smaller *takht* ensemble and the *waṣlah* (suite of vocal and instrumental performances) continued to be prominent in Palestinian cities, including cities like Nazareth that were now part of Israel. In fact, a localized genre of waṣlah called *nasrawīyyah* (of Nazareth) continues to be part of contemporary Palestinian musical practice (Libbis 1994, 1989). The survival of this repertoire and its ensemble is evident today with the central role that instrumental groups such as the Oriental Music Ensemble, Sabreen, and Karloma, who draw on the takht formation, continue to play in the contemporary Palestinian music scene.

Besides maqām-centered urban music practices, the religious status of Palestine and Jerusalem endowed it with a strong Christian liturgical music tradition rooted in Western music idioms and practices. As ethnomusicologist Christian Poché notes, many musicians who had developed their skills through that repertoire went on to perform and compose Western music during the first half of the twentieth century:

> The various Christian communities and their liturgies were important in the musical life of Jerusalem. These included the Armenian, Coptic, Ethiopian and Roman Catholic ("Latin") liturgies performed in their various languages. Franciscan and Dominican monks trained local musicians to provide music for the religious services, and the musical techniques of the West were most readily adopted by the Arab Christians practising the Latin rite. (Poché 2001, 935)

Counting among those composers are Salvador Arnita; Yousef Khasho, whose musical legacy includes a repertoire inspired by Italian-style nineteenth-century romanticism; organist Augustin Lama; and ethnomusicologist Habib Hassan Touma, who composed Western contemporary music before dedicating himself to the study of Arabic music (Poché 2001). These two repertoires, Arab maqām music and European tonal music, existed in parallel without necessarily converging, as was the case in Egypt. Therefore, according to Poché, art music in Palestine maintained what he described as a "traditionalist spirit," which we believe served to revive the takht and its instruments in Palestine today.

Resistance and Catharsis

As the implications of the 1967 defeat of Arab forces by Israel started to sink in, the question of survival among Palestinians was in many ways indigenized. No longer associated with the survival of an imagined Israelite peasant life during biblical times, or the survival of urban musical practices that had been profoundly transformed in the rest of the Arab world, investigating Palestinian culture and music took on new meanings as part of a concerted effort by Palestinians to take their fate into their own hands.

Anthological projects that went beyond specific aspects of expressive culture to cover all aspects of Palestinian village life emerged in different parts of the Palestinian diaspora. Years of research and collaborative work would lead to important publications in Arabic and other languages during the 1980s and early 1990s, including the multivolume *Encyclopaedia Palaestina* (1984–1990) and Nimr Sirhan's *Encyclopaedia of Palestinian Folklore* (1989). These projects were not motivated by grief and nostalgia alone, nor by an irrational urge to recreate an idealized homeland through the model of the Palestinian village, but by a determination to counter attempts at erasing Palestinian rootedness to the land that had become Israel, to fill in the flagrant gaps in Western literature on Palestinians, and to cauterize the wounds of displacement. The desire to "re-member" the dismembered parts of Palestine through the nucleus of the village was understandable, as the majority of Palestinian refugees were of peasant origins (see Bisharat 1997). They would also become the main constituency of the Palestine Liberation Organization (PLO)—the principal source of funding for most of these studies—and act as primary sources of information for scholars. The production of knowledge on Palestinian culture was also propelled by the conviction among Palestinian refugees that return to the homeland was only a matter of time. These uprooted practices must be kept intact until they are reinscribed in their original context when the refugees finally return. When approached from this angle, the Palestinian folklorist movement can no longer be interpreted through the sole lens of a posttraumatic reaction to the Catastrophe of 1948. It also indicated the beginning of the resistance movement as a political and cultural force that was geared toward a future in which return was not only possible but also an inevitable event that must be prepared for.

This new emphasis on action, emancipation, and self-preservation through the appropriation of their own cause translated into two tendencies in terms of music making: the explosion of political songs and of musical theater onto the Palestinian cultural scene. Political songs evoking Palestinians' plight and their fight spread in the Arab world. Combined with the repertoire that the Palestinian folklorist movement was making accessible to the general population, both tendencies resulted in the emergence of several popular arts and music groups. El-Funoun's elaborate theatrical productions in the Occupied Territories, on the one hand, and Al-ᶜAshiqeen's patriotic performances in diaspora, on the other, are some of the best-known representatives of these trends. The term "popular arts" replaced other terms such as "traditional" or "folk," as it allowed these groups more flexibility in the kind of repertoire they drew from for their productions and in the way they reimagined and transformed it through performance. Musicians invested heavily in field research, collecting songs from elders or from folklore books. In the case of Al-ᶜAshiqeen, these songs were then politicized through changing the lyrics, citing the names of destroyed or occupied towns and villages, famous martyrs and revolutionary figures from the British mandate era, or by recalling important dates in the history of Palestinian resistance.[6] Aesthetically they included elements of Western harmony and modern instruments, such as drums and synthesizers. Performances often began with passionate speeches on the Palestinian cause. Sometimes one or two stanzas of engaged poetry would precede the songs. Other times they would begin with a *shubbābah* (traditional flute) or the *mijwiz* (double clarinet) solo followed by a *dabke* (circle dance), thus referring to the false tranquility before the storm of revolution. Musicians and dancers would be dressed in *fidāʾī* (guerilla/revolutionary) military uniforms or traditional costumes, with emphasis on the peasant roots of the resistance movement.

In the case of El-Funoun, the group developed an aesthetic inspired by Palestine's cultural heritage but aiming at modernization in the hopes that it would remain relevant to Palestinians' contemporary lives and concerns (Al-Kurdi 1994). The repertoire of musicals were partly inspired by the Rahbani brothers' popular operas in Lebanon but also based on stories from Palestinian rural life. Here, too, traditional music and dance were set in counterpoint with complex choreography that was reminiscent of Arabic modern dance and ballet, and original musical compositions were created and performed by Palestinian musicians who were equally immersed in Arabic art music and Western art music, such as Said Murad and Suhail Khoury.

In both of these styles of performance, past and present were nested within each other, giving the music a sense of authenticity while captivating the audience, either with an overtly political message or one that was translated through a strong aesthetic project. These performances spread through solidarity events or festivals held throughout the Arab world and, subsequently, recordings of these performances that were then copied, shared, and distributed through largely informal channels.

While many of these modernizing initiatives were a product of the urbanization and transnationalization of Palestinians, they did not displace the village as the nucleus of Palestinian identity in diaspora. If anything, the lifestyle of villagers became mythicized. As anthropologist Randa Farah notes, talking about a specific culture to refugees implied recognition of a new existence, that of the refugee, an existence considered abnormal, artificial, inauthentic by Palestinians in exile: "Remembering the 'way it was there and then' became a cultural form through which refugees re-claimed their history in a particular territory . . . Put in other words, remembering the past became a way to re-historicize a territory and re-territorialize a history" (1999, 222). As a result, diaspora discourse during the 1970s and 1980s tended to place cultural practices and the realities of life in exile in different temporalities, countering the daily trials of a present in exile with cultural practices that were firmly anchored in the past. Indeed, cultural practices did not function as mere reflections of refugee life, but offered a counter-narrative, or, rather, an antidote to it.

While it is tempting to interpret these positions as stemming from a state of denial, it would be more appropriate to approach them as part of a process of catharsis (Delvicchio-Good and Good 2008). Beyond its use to inspire or legitimate political and armed resistance, culture also became a site where suffering could be differed. No one perhaps said it better than Antonin Artaud (1964), who describes theater as the scene on which there is a collective emptying out of an abscess that can either end in healing or in death. Keeping this in mind, it is no coincidence that after poetry, theater is the form of art that blossomed the most in the Arab world following the disaster that was the 1967 war (Stone 2008).

In diaspora, amateur musical theater—in particular, combining music, dance, theatrical sketches, and poetry readings, inspired by groups like El-Funoun—has become a common occurrence among Palestinians (El-Ghadban, 2004). In most Palestinian communities today, regardless of country, there are equivalents of what

Yara El-Ghadban (2004) observed during field research among Palestinian youth in Montreal, Canada: the organization of culture nights, in which younger generations of Palestinians who had not experienced the uprooting directly, recreate the before and after of the Nakba, wear Palestinian traditional clothes, play recordings of Palestinian songs like *dalʿūnā,* and choreograph dabke dances alternating with poetry and theatrical sketches of significant moments of loss and triumph in the Palestinian experience. The youth participating in such events were not naïve about what they were doing. As one of El-Ghadban's interviewees eloquently explained, they weren't dancing to bring awareness to the Palestinian cause within the international community. They weren't educating ignorant but well-meaning outsiders. The point was to give Palestinians in diaspora a sense of community and to transmit the memory of the Nakba to the next generation (2004). In many ways they were dancing for themselves, talking to themselves, dreaming collectively. In such events, memories, true and invented, mythical and real, would circulate among an audience almost exclusively composed of Palestinians, feeding and bouncing off each other, answering each other, creating and recreating Palestine in an immense transparent bubble that excluded everyone but those who knew the secret of being Palestinian in diaspora. Far from being introverted and self-isolating, however, art making and music making in this context acted as a form of catharsis—in other words, as a process of emotional cleansing. As these theatrical performances played out, the audience was confronted with what Julia Kristeva (1982) calls the abject—in this case, the Nakba and its aftermath. By expressing and reflecting horror and violence, these performances simultaneously served to release it, thus contributing to a healing process.

In the Occupied Territories catharsis was not an option, as the realities of life under occupation and daily confrontation with Israeli soldiers left no space for any kind of distancing. The explosion of political music as a form of resistance and counterattack would reach its peak with the first *Intifada* (uprising) in 1987. The symbol of the revolutionary peasant was gradually overshadowed by that of the children of the stones and of the martyr.[7] Hundreds of secret recordings circulated among the Palestinian people that glorified children of the revolt and encouraged their audience to action. According to ethnomusicologists Anne Marie Oliver and Paul Steinberg (2002), the aesthetics of the music of the Intifada reflected the different political ideologies that competed for Palestinian public opinion—that of nationalists, who defended the notion of a Palestinian secular state, as opposed to that of Islamists, who advocated a transnational vision of Palestine within the vast Muslim *ummah* (nation).

It is primarily in reference to the period of the 1970s and 1980s that most studies on Palestine and Palestinians tend to emphasize resistance as a dominant political and cultural paradigm. In many ways it has become an unquestioned premise on which most subsequent literature on Palestinian music is built. As a result, it has also become a discourse toward which Palestinian musicians and artists today are compelled to position themselves. By focusing on meanings, representations, aesthetic idioms, and connotations, other dimensions of that period—particularly those related to the role that mediators such as political factions, grassroots organizations, and international NGOs played in the way Palestinians constructed their own subjectivities and cultural identity—have tended to be overlooked. If we are to understand what has become of the "culture as resistance" discourse since the 1990s, a period marked by the rise and fall of the Oslo peace process as well as by the increasing impact of globalization, we must pay attention to these mediators and track their genealogy in the Palestinian context.

Committing to Culture: The Story of Palestinian Grassroots Organizations

In the Occupied Territories, culture, its valorization, and its preservation were indeed enlisted, so to speak, as important components of Palestinian resistance to the occupation and one of the central concerns of the nationalist movement up to the end of the first Intifada. As we have indicated, the recognition and promotion of culture contradicted Israeli claims that Palestinians had no real or rooted relationship with the land. However, a new social and economical dimension, which had already emerged in the camps in earlier decades, became increasingly influential as the potency of culture when a means for economic support and development began to be fully recognized. A network of cultural committees established as part of socially and politically engaged Palestinian organizations or affiliated with Palestinian universities had already emerged in the 1970s and 1980s, which, in turn, led to the founding of departments dedicated to the study of culture (Craissati 1998).Each village, town, or refugee camp had one or more such groups that were centered on culture and acted independently or as part of regional or national political organizations. One of the first was the Committee for Social Research and Palestinian Folklore, which counted among its members prominent artists such as Sliman Mansour and researchers, historians, and folklorists including Sharif Kanaana, Ibrahim Muhawi, Nabil Alqam, andAbdellatif Barghouti, among others. Published individually and in partnership, members of the committee produced several books on various aspects of Palestinian culture.[8]

As Dina Craissati explains, the tendency to create committees, with the encouragement of the PLO, was "aimed at the mobilization of the population in the Occupied Territories in building an infrastructure of national institutions to sustain a process of self-reliance and of disengagement from the occupation. In a way, one could venture to concede that the politics of *ṣumūd* (steadfastness) represented aspects of a traditional welfare system carried by a 'quasi-state,' that is the PLO (which had by that time a well-developed bureaucracy outside the Occupied Territories)" (1998, 121). Palestinian organizations in the Occupied Territories and in diaspora launched embroidery projects that served to preserve this tradition and to employ women in the camps. These initiatives went beyond culture, focusing on education, health services, and employment. Undertaken individually and collectively, with the financial and logistical support of the PLO, they contributed to the birth of a new educated generation and the development of a Palestinian civil society outside the parameters of an independent state or geopolitical boundaries.

With the PLO weakened after the 1982 invasion of Lebanon by Israel, the West Bank became the center of a new form of social activism, propelled by such committees that would later develop into local grassroot NGOs. Social and cultural organizations comprising, among others, Inash al-Usra, the Popular Arts Center, and the Khalil Sakakini Cultural Center took an active leadership role during the first Intifada by mobilizing popular classes and organizing collective resistance efforts through the recording and dissemination of a Palestinian cultural narrative. Other aspects of this movement would eventually challenge some of the presumptions associated with PLO-initiated committee programs by opting for "alternative, decentralized, more open democratic structures, through grass roots voluntary work and within a spirit of egalitarian social transformation" (Craissati 2005, 186). As Craissati notes, "When the Intifada began in 1987, they could provide the organizational basis and the agenda to sustain the movement" (186).

A further challenge to the PLO's monopoly on the production of Palestinian culture began to appear through the increased presence of international aid through international NGOs and development agencies that, during the Intifada, had been funding professional centers, providing "support, technical assistance and training to other organizations, to charitable societies, to grass roots committees and to various unions and cooperatives" (Craissiti 2005, 186). All of these players would later be at the heart of what Sari Hanafi and Linda Tabar have described as a fundamental shift in the political economy of aid to Palestinian NGOs in the early 1990s:

> Solidarity-based support . . . withered and was replaced by bilateral and multilateral relations between Southern NGOs, [including Palestinian NGOs] and European as well as North American governments and development agencies. Regionally and locally, this period coincided with the 1991 Gulf war and the onset of the Madrid peace talks, through which Palestine's geopolitical status was reconfigured and the West Bank and Gaza Strip recast as a site of "peace-making." (2005, 25)

This shift to "peace-making," as opposed to the marginalization of occupation through grassroots activism, brought a new organizational order within the NGO network in the Occupied Territories. Voluntary work was gradually replaced with professionalized paid work as Western NGOs funded by international development agencies offered well-paying positions to local personnel and trained them to implement projects following international management standards and funding criteria. In order to compete for funds, Palestinian NGOs, which tended to be affiliated with various political factions and ideologies and counted activism among their central activities, were under increasing pressure to disengage from direct action and focus instead on witnessing, democracy and rights advocacy, relief, and development, all of which are framed within an apolitical rights-based and civil-society-building framework, as opposed to fighting the occupation (Nakhleh 2012). As Hanafi and Tabar have argued, this led to a process of "disembedding and disassociation" wherein Palestinian NGOs were separated from their role as "the nexus of the popular movement of the first intifada" and pushed toward workshops and training programs (2005, 26). Mufid Qassoum goes further by arguing that this shift to advocacy has "put an end to mass social movements," dismantled "the triad affinity between the intellectual, the masses, and the progressive and revolutionary ideas," in effect, leading to demobilization, de-radicalization and depoliticization (Qassoum cited in Hanafi and Tabar 2005). While many of these scholars have pointed to health, human rights, and women's rights as the main areas in which this shift was enacted, culture also became an important arena for this new form of intervention.[9] As we will see below, this trend can be traced back to the foundation of the *United Nations Educational, Scientific, and Cultural Organization* (UNESCO) in 1945. However, engagement with culture on humanitarian and developmental grounds has intensified over the last two decades, propelled by globalization and the expansion of humanitarianism's boundaries as an ideology and set of practices in realms beyond relief (Gabiam 2012).

Since the early 1990s, and particularly in the wake of the optimism that followed from the Oslo Accords, Palestinian society underwent a veritable explosion in terms of culture and arts, partly due to the interest taken by the international community in Palestinian culture and to the presence of international NGOs and agencies on the ground as mediators. From the Edward Said National Conservatory of Music to the Institute for Palestinian Art, the last two decades have been a watershed in terms of cultural production and funding. Importantly, this resurgence of Palestinian culture has not been confined to the local scene. It has been wholly embraced through international music festivals, museums, and galleries. This is not the same cultural scene that existed in the 1970s and 1980s, as there has been a shift not only in the type of works being produced but also, and more importantly, in the attitudes of artists and musicians themselves.

By 1993, with the recognition of the PNA and a formal government in place, the conditions of the survival of music and art became increasingly dependent on international support, both politically and economically. Two agendas were at work: economic development and state building by enforcing the role of NGOs as active partners in reinscribing the already existent Palestinian civil society networks within the parameters of a state-in-the-making. For foreign donors, that involved the establishment of a cultural policy that would allow freedom of expression and the right to culture for Palestinians. Culture became the new buzzword, the new commodity for foreign investment with the belief that culture would provide the basis for a modern liberal and democratic Palestinian society, a society, in the words of UNESCO, built on "co-existence, evolution, dynamism" and that questions patterns of thinking and acting (Eriksen 2001). Central to this project was the establishment and flourishing of cultural institutions, which provided space and support for writers, musicians, painters, performers, media artists, and so forth. For Palestinians, this attention to their work provided an opportunity to continue to relate to their cultural traditions in light of their political plight while also transmitting and communicating the language of Palestinian culture to the world. However, it also meant yielding part of their ownership and control of their creative process and musical practices to mediators like NGOs. Individual Palestinian artists and musicians, and the various Palestinian liberation movements, are no longer the only, nor even the principal, agents handling the production of Palestinian art and music and its meanings.

In Palestine, in the aftermath of the 2006 election that brought Hamas to power, NGOs were handed an enormous amount of power and resources as a way for Western countries to absolve themselves of the guilt of cutting aid to the Palestinians. Besides Christian missionary organizations that have been present for multiple decades, musicians and other artists rely heavily on funding from Scandinavian development agencies, such as the Swedish International Development and Cooperation Agency (Sida), which supports institutions like the Edward Said National Conservatory of Music in the West Bank. Other organizations and foundations worth mentioning are the A. M. Qattan Foundation; the Ford Foundation; UNESCO; the Prince Claus Fund; Regional Social and Cultural Fund for Palestinian Refugees and the People of Gaza (Germany); EuropeAid (ENPImed); the Danish Center for Culture and Development; the Qatar Foundation; the Khalil Sakakini Cultural Center; and the Aventis Foundation, based in Germany, which funds the West-Eastern Divan Orchestra, whose mission is to bring Israeli and Palestinian children together through music.

What lies behind such interest in the funding of Palestinian culture is a discourse that has moved away from art and music as a form of resistance and nation building to its becoming an instrument of redemption and a new avenue for humanitarian intervention. This is in line with what George Yudice has identified as the redefining of "culture" in the era of globalization, first and foremost, as a resource:

> *Culture-as-resource* is much more than a commodity; it is the lynchpin of a new epistemic framework in which ideology and much of what Foucault called disciplinary society (i.e., the inculcation of norms in such institutions as education, medicine, and psychiatry) are absorbed into an economic or

> ecological rationality, such that management, conservation, access, distribution, and investment—in "culture" and the outcomes thereof—take priority. (2003, 1; emphasis in original)

Further on, he adds: "High culture becomes resource for urban development in the contemporary museum. Rituals, everyday aesthetic practices such as songs, folktales, cuisine, customs, and other symbolic practices, are also mobilized as recourses in tourism and in the promotion of the heritage industries" (4). All of these are endeavors that the above-mentioned funding agencies are happy to participate in, especially because they do not involve critiquing the occupation, but contribute to state building.

To be sure, in places where the state is powerless, and where power is still in the hands of colonial actors, as in the Palestinian Territories, NGOs become the channels and networks through which culture as a resource is put to work. Drawing on the uses of culture to improve social conditions in Brazil's favelas, Yudice observes: "The most innovative actors in setting agendas for political and social policies are grassroots movements and the national and international NGOs that support them. These actors have put a premium on culture, as a resource already targeted for exploitation by capital and as a foundation for resistance" (2003, 6). While we fully agree with Yudice's argument, we do not follow him in his optimistic assessment of culture's use by NGOs as a resource for resistance under conditions such as those facing Palestinians, especially when we consider the work of scholars such as Hanafi and Tabar (2005), Nakhleh (2012), Craissati (1998, 2005), Fassin (2009, 2010), and Feldman (2010), to name but a few, on the negative effect that the internationalization of NGOs and the humanitarization of the conflict in Palestine has had on mobilization and popular movements in the last two decades. If culture is a resource in the Palestinian Territories, it has been mainly constructed within a paradigm of development and humanitarian intervention. As such, it provides an effective alibi for the international community to keep deferring a lasting and just resolution to the political situation of the Palestinians.

An important contributor to culture as a form of humanitarian intervention is the Prince Claus Fund (PCF) in the Netherlands, whose funding is based on the principle that "culture is a basic need." It has recently pushed this ideology even further by creating the Cultural Emergency Response (CER) program, which acts as a type of International Red Cross for culture in situations marked by violence and unrest. Created in response to the looting of Baghdad's museums following the U.S. invasion of Iraq and the destruction of the Bamiyan Buddhas in Afghanistan, the PCF has also been active in the Palestinian Territories. Through its emergency program, it contributed to the reconstruction of the Center for Archaeological Heritage at the Islamic University of Gaza, which was completely destroyed by Israeli bombing in 2008. It has also funded the Three-Dimensional Virtual

Museum (3DVM) at Birzeit University. Both projects are worthy of praise in their own right. However, the justification the Prince Claus Fund uses to underline the importance of funding such projects raises questions as to their ultimate legacy in the context of conflict. Citing the virtual museum, the PCF website promoting the project notes:

> The 3DVM is expected to be of great importance in Palestine, where restriction of movement, checkpoints and siege . . . are the reality of everyday life. In this environment, and with the paucity in the number of professionally run galleries or museums, a 3D Virtual Art Space will stand as a *substitute* [our emphasis], offering visitors wherever they are, in cities, villages or refugee camps, the opportunity to experience going online to a gallery or museum.[10]

While the fund's engagement is commendable on many levels, its statement is indicative of the new role culture is playing when it comes to international support for the Palestinian struggle for their rights. Creating a virtual museum to overcome checkpoints is much less risky than actually calling for the removal of the wall and the checkpoints. Similarly, building a music school is much easier to achieve than demolishing Israeli colonies.

Perhaps the most dramatic demonstration of this movement toward culture as a substitute for political resolution is the recent attempt by the PNA to obtain recognition for Palestine as a full-member state of the United Nations. The move was immediately rejected by its main opponents—namely, the United States and Israel—and even among sympathetic states it was portrayed as unjustified "unilateralism." A few weeks later however, UNESCO, which is the UN's main cultural organization, admitted Palestine with great fanfare and loud but empty protests by the United States, who threatened to cut its contribution to UNESCO. UNESCO's decision was represented in the international media as a big step toward the recognition of Palestine and as a big sacrifice (or loss) for Israel and the United States. The refusal to recognize Palestine as a member of the United Nations was swept under the rug as Western countries congratulated themselves for the UNESCO decision.

The implication of such a move in terms of the politics of culture become clearer when one considers UNESCO's history and its way of functioning. In his ethnographic study of UNESCO, anthropologist Philip Rousseau (2011) recalls the origins of the institution, which was founded in 1945 as a response to the devastatingly effective Nazi propaganda machine. The first director of the institution, Julian Huxley, laid down the orientation of the institution in 1947 as the principal protagonist for a good and "true propaganda" using education, science, and culture as tools "and deliberately bending them to the international tasks of peace, if necessary utilizing them . . . to overcome the resistance of millions to desirable change" (Huxley cited in Rousseau 2011, 113). Although UNESCO would provide the ideological framework in the name of which culture would be promoted, as an institution composed of independent member states it would still be up to those states to ensure the implementation of cultural policies in line with UNESCO's ideals. By including Palestine into UNESCO but refusing it full state membership in the UN, Palestinians are being asked to adhere to UNESCO's ideology through peace-making cultural projects, even as they still suffer from occupation and denial of their right of return, while simultaneously depriving them of the very legitimacy and autonomy to implement cultural policy as they see fit, since Palestine is not an internationally recognized state.

The long-term impact of international aid on Palestinian cultural practices needs to be examined. While the culturally informed pedagogical/relief projects of Western national development agencies in the Palestinian Territories has provided Palestinian artists and musicians much-needed financial support, the political and aesthetic implications of such support cannot be ignored. What does it take for Palestinian cultural practices to be recognized by institutions like UNESCO? What are the criteria they have to correspond to? What interpretative frame are music and art being confined to in order to receive funds? Regardless of the individual agency of the artists and musicians, their works increasingly depend on being able to sell an artistic project to a given funding organism. The aesthetic norms and tools of art and music production are influenced by implicit and explicit criteria that artists and musicians have to grapple with in order to get funding regardless of their discourse. These criteria act as terms of recognition through which the work of Palestinian artists and musicians is legitimized or not.

Two funding and promotion ideologies seem to have emerged. On the one hand, Palestinian musicians are encouraged to embark on creative projects that emphasize collaboration and dialogue with Israelis and Jewish counterparts in general. These are the buzzwords that are constantly used in what appears to be a cultural reincarnation of the peace process. Imposing such criteria on artists and musicians today takes on highly political significations when we consider the growing call for the political, economic, and cultural boycott of Israel. On the other hand, a trend supported by international activist groups frames Palestinian art and music as part of a globalized resistance movement, whereby the struggle of Palestinian musicians and artists is inserted within the larger postcolonial struggles of indigenous peoples for their autonomy. The risk here is that the long and rich histories of different peoples and nations are reduced to one traumatic experience—the colonial experience—and that everything else these peoples and nations produce in terms of culture, knowledge, politics, and economics is a product of, or a reaction to, the West, and not first and foremost for themselves. Furthermore, artists are all seen as a collective that is acting in a sort of choir of postcolonial critique, but not as individuals. In this case the discourse on art as resistance is paradoxically turned into a commodity, where artists who do not fit neatly into that frame, either aesthetically or politically, tend to be ignored.

How do musicians and artists deal with all of these challenges and the cultural brokers that are behind them? How do they negotiate the tension these brokers have created between culture as resistance and the framing of culture as a "basic need" or a peacemaking tool, in their creative processes?

I Make Music, Therefore I Am Human: The Globalization of Palestinian Culture

The question we ask is complicated by the fact that this shift in the politics of culture came hand in hand with the globalization of Palestinian cultural production. In many ways the humanitarization and the globalization of Palestinian music are two faces of the same coin. The promotion of Palestinian music and art as site for peace-making and for developing cross-cultural and cross-musical dialogue cannot be separated from the emergence of a global market for "third world" artists. Events such as the World of Music, Art, and Dance (WOMAD) festival have become launching pads for Palestinian musicians onto the international scene. Despite severe restrictions on their mobility, they rode the wave, performing for Palestinian and international audiences in the diaspora. Palestinian art experienced a similar resurgence as the art market was globalized and opened its doors to Palestinian artists. Consider that in 2008 artist Emily Jacir was the winner of the prestigious Hugo Boss Prize, which was followed by a major show at the Guggenheim Museum in New York City in 2009, while Sharif Waked, an artist based in Haifa, recently sold pieces of his work to the Guggenheim and other museums.

On the international scene the ideological underpinnings of this recent interest in Palestinian art and music has been the idea that Palestinian art and music can foster cross-cultural understanding, in this case providing the West with an image of Palestine and Palestinians that challenge specious media stereotypes. It follows from this that art and music are evidence of a Palestinian humanity. In her discussion of this phenomenon with respect to Palestine, Jessica Winegar refers to the press release accompanying an exhibition of contemporary Palestinian art that traveled (with great opposition) through the United States starting in 2003 titled *Made in Palestine,* in which the director of the Station Museum in Houston is quoted as saying, "It is our conviction that the American public deserves to be made aware of Palestinian art as a profound manifestation of the humanity of the Palestinian people" (Winegar 2008, 672).

On the local scene this overture took place at a time when the hope for peace following the Oslo Accords was still strong. The PNA had yet to establish itself as the new authority in cultural policy, and NGOs were not viewed with the same skepticism and suspicion as they are today. As a result, artists and musicians felt free to engage actively in bringing culture back into Palestinians' lives as an expression of life beyond mere survival and struggle. Most importantly, after decades of enlisting musicians and artists in the struggle to liberate Palestine through cultural revival, folklore, and resistance songs, there was an effort to get out from under the political rug. Encouraged by international funding, musicians in the West Bank were deeply involved in music education and transmission through institutions such as the Edward Said National Conservatory of Music or by organizing creative workshops.

Undoubtedly, all of these developments on the local and global front, compounded by the discourses brought in by NGOs and other cultural brokers, not to mention the fluid political situation since the 1990s, have had an important impact on the kind of music and art Palestinians are making today.

Instrumentalizing Palestinian Music

In terms of music, one important trend has been the move from the politicized lyrics of the 1970s and 1980s toward a greater emphasis on instrumental music. The Edward Said National Conservatory of Music (ESNCM) counts within its network today no less than five orchestras: the ESNCM Orchestra, the ESNCM Wind Band, the Palestine Youth Orchestra, the Jerusalem Children's Orchestra, and the Palestine National Orchestra, not to mention the chamber ensembles composed of the conservatory's professors, like the Oriental Music Ensemble (OME). Other ensembles worth mentioning are Le Trio Joubran, Sabreen, Karloma, and the Gaza Orchestra. What are we to make of this move toward instrumental music? And how is it linked to larger phenomena such as the globalization of music and the increasing intervention of governmental and nongovernmental organizations in the Palestinian cultural realm?

In a wide-ranging article documenting the aesthetic and political effects of globalization on musics from the Middle East and Central Asia as they have traveled beyond local performance contexts, ethnomusicologist Jean During (2011) highlights a series of aesthetic transformations that many of these musics share. First, they undergo a process of "metropolization" as practices that were once mostly embedded in rural or regional contexts are lured into "world cities" like London, Paris, and New York, where demand for world music is great. According to During, metropolization tends to discourage music centered on solo performers based on improvisation and instead puts forward music ensembles, which have better visibility on the global stage.

Relevant to our discussion on cultural brokers here, turning to ensembles, During argues, offers more opportunities for local musicians to experiment with new sounds and to participate in cross-cultural collaborations. Both of these are important assets to have in order to woo international cultural patrons like NGOs, development agencies, and institutions such as UNESCO, who determine the terms of recognition, legitimization and funding in a global musical market along with multinational music production companies. For these institutions, ensembles make a stronger impact as cultural ambassadors than individual artists. They are also more attractive for global audiences looking for something different but not alienating.

Inevitably these changes in the context of performance have an important impact on the aesthetics of performance. As During has remarked in his research with musicians from Central Asia, playing in a group tends to encourage the use of polyphony, which in turn leads to less attention to regional and local aesthetic idiosyncrasies. It also leads to effect-driven performance styles that eliminate subtle dynamics, as well as heterophonic and modal nuances that are the cornerstones for musical practice in the Middle East and Central Asia. Some of these trends are discernible in contemporary Arabic music and in Palestinian music since the 1990s, as we have seen with some of the examples cited above. However, it should be noted that the pressure to fall into the global aesthetic flow described by During is mitigated in the Palestinian context by the unresolved political situation. Palestinian musicians and artists today are more entangled than ever in the discourses surrounding culture as they strive to move beyond political music toward a more subjective aesthetic project in a context where such a project implicates dealing with cultural brokers like NGOs who have their own agendas.

In many ways the trajectory of the ensemble Sabreen, in particular, resonates with the dilemmas most Palestinian musicians and artists face today. When they first entered the Palestinian music scene in the 1980s, they felt that the political theme was something the audience could relate to, which in turn enabled them to try out new musical ideas, including the integration of Western instruments, while remaining relevant to the public (El-Ghadban 2001). In their subsequent albums, however, they debated a return to Arabic instruments. As Said Murad, one of the founding members of Sabreen, recalls, "We had been using the organ (synthesizer) and drums for a long time. We faced a very serious question: Should we put Western instruments aside and use the *ʿūd* [lute] and *qānūn* [zither] instead, or both?" (cited in El-Ghadban 2001, 31). They would eventually opt for the third option by allowing both types of instruments to play a more active role in their songs: "We have several drums with which we can apply Western-inspired rhythm techniques. We divide up the music among different drums, using certain ones to play traditional rhythms. So the listener, instead of hearing just one drum, hears the bass in all the music, emanating from all the instruments" (31).

It is not so much the mixing of Western and Arabic forms and performance styles that leaves the listener with a curious sense of simultaneous familiarity and instability. It is more likely the new role that traditional instruments like the qānūn, the ʿūd, and the *ṭablah* (Goblet drum) are assigned, suddenly coming out of the shadow of the voice and taking on full characters in the making of the music (El-Ghadban 2001). If we were to consider the voice as the embodiment of the "music as resistance" discourse, then ceding some of its authority to the instruments in Sabreen's music, while never completely disappearing, is an eloquent metaphor to Palestinian musicians' ambiguous position in the current cultural context. This trend can be clearly heard in Suhail Khoury's music as well, particularly in the instrumental album *Jerusalem after Midnight* (2009), in which the clarinet enacts the daily routine of life with the checkpoint, playing short punctuated musical phrases against sound effects evoking ambulance sirens, gunshots, and the robotic voices of soldiers herding Palestinians. The political message is loud and clear; however, it is expressed through the voice of the clarinet as opposed to a human voice.

In cases where the voice is still prominent, as in Kamilya Jubran's latest album, *Makan,*[11] written and composed songs recreate a sense of improvisation, embedded in the ṭarab and maqām tradition but through an uneasy and often tense dialogue with the ʿūd. The melodic lines break some of the foundational characteristics of Arabic music performance style through quick register changes, flashes of atonality, ruptures in the maqām formal structure, heterophonic harmonics, chromatic slides, and sudden aggressive attacks.

As these examples show, while participating fully in the globalization of music by distancing themselves from rural-inspired political songs and embracing instrumental music on the international stage, since the 1990s the unresolved political situation has also pushed Palestinian musicians to engage with globalization critically by reacquainting themselves with a long tradition of commitment to maqām and ṭarab, dating back to before the Nakba, thus bringing Arab music practices to the forefront. The work of musicians like Issa Boulos, a strong critic of standardization tendencies in maqām tradition; of Ahmad Al Khatib, who continues to produce solo ʿūd performances; and archivists like Nader Jalal, whose organization, the Palestinian Institute for Cultural Development (NAWA), is unearthing precious recordings of ṭarab music from the pre-1948 era by Palestinian musicians, all testify to this.

Beyond Resistance Discourse

The place of culture in Palestinian society today is paradoxical. On the one hand, it offers an important counterweight to the dominant political discourse on offer, which is to say, it provides a much-needed re-presentation of identity, place, and time (Sherwell 2005)—what Rancière (2000) refers to as "dissensus" or a reconfiguration of the sensible, a transformation of the way of seeing the world and what is possible. On the other hand, there is a political field into which culture is subjected, not only in terms of which artists and musicians get recognition, or which cultural projects are funded and produced, but in terms of the roles attributed to culture in Palestinian society and the ideologies within which artists and musicians are pressured to insert their practices—that is, a cultural politics of art and music.

As we have demonstrated, Palestinian cultural production has moved through three important phases over the last one hundred years: (1) the folklorist movement phase, which attempted and succeeded in stopping the cultural cleansing of Palestinian society and identity through the meticulous collection and preservation of life histories and Palestinian heritage; (2) the emergence of an art as liberation and resistance movement through a generation of politically active artists and musicians who have kept the Palestinian cause on the international map and succeeded where politicians have failed; and (3) the period of globalization and ambivalence during the 1990s, which may have opened a window to an alternative path for art and music aesthetically, but at the same time has reinscribed them as instruments of social and economic development and as conduits for a new form of interventionism and humanitarianism. While the discourse on art and music as resistance can shed some light on some of the practices and creative strategies that dominated during each of these phases, it has tended to flatten out other roles and meanings attributed to cultural production among Palestinians, including culture as survival, as catharsis and most recently as a humanitarian project.

The music of the Palestinians is undoubtedly linked to their struggle for recognition of their rights and of their identity, but as we have seen with musicians in the 1990s, the creative strategies used to express that struggle cannot be limited to a unique model of cultural resistance. There is as much an element of seduction in turning to instrumental music as there is an element of subversion of the effects of globalization and the influence of cultural brokers—namely, the aid industry. Such ambiguity complicates any attempt at anthologizing Palestinian music through a single theme of resistance. Focusing on resistance as an interpretative frame, in other words, leaves many unanswered questions as to what happens when cultural production goes global and when it falls into the realm of humanitarian intervention. In our view the humanitarization of cultural production in Palestine combines and distorts existing discourses on Palestinian music, art, and culture. It is at once a form of survivalism as it constructs culture as a basic need no matter how emptied out of the dynamic and future-oriented dimensions that we summarized earlier. It provides catharsis while ignoring the causes that led to the wounds in the first place, limiting itself to the relieving of the symptoms of occupation rather than countering the disease. And, as in the case with Palestinian NGOs, which have lost touch with their grassroots and mobilizing origins, it compels artists to perform in the name of peacemaking and state making rather than resistance to occupation.

To return to our introduction, it is arguable that Jacir and Anani were well aware that by taking on the neoliberal and neo-capitalist agenda of the PNA, their public intervention was bound to be problematic for the Ramallah municipality. More important, it is equally evident that these artists had chosen to subvert the funding and organizational structure of the local art world and its demand for an anaesthetized cultural commodity. Did their work succeed? Did its proclaimed political import achieve a disruption of the fabric of consensus maintained by international NGOs and donors? This is obviously a question that is impossible to answer, never mind the works being removed soon after their installation. Yet, manifest in this exercise is the precarious existence of the musician and artist in Palestine: a place between censorship and complicity, between obscurity and notoriety, where the performance of culture is commoditized at the very moment of its creation—a game of culture borne between depoliticization and resistance.

An anthology of Palestinian music needs to take into account these fundamental changes and reflect on their repercussions, on Palestinian culture in general, and on the way we have studied it up to now.

Notes

1. Ali Abunimah, "Ramallah Municipality Censors Artist Billboards," Posterous blog, July 13, 2010, http://aliabunimah.posterous.com/ramallah-municipality-censors-artist-billboar.

2. See the essay by Stig-Magnus Thorsén in this book.

3. In this chapter we define culture as a dynamic set of values, discourses, representations, and practices that may be part of, reflect, or comment on larger social issues, while politics is defined as the relations of power concerned with the representation and governance of social life. The aspect of social life that concerns us here is cultural practices and how these relations of power structure and are structured by cultural practices—in this case, music and art.

4. The comment in the title to this section is attributed to Haitian author and journalist Dany Laferrière following the January 12, 2010, earthquake that devastated Haiti.

5. Orientalist scholars visited the land in organized expeditions, which then resulted in books such as the *Palästinischer Diwan* by German theologian Gustaf H. Dalman (1901). He had collected a repertoire of traditional songs that he then listed in the book by geographical area; context of performance; and melodic, rhythmic, and poetic form. See the essay by Rachel Beckles Willson in this book.

6. See David McDonald's essay in this book.

7. See McDonald's essay in this book.

8. See Alqam 1977, Barghouti 1986, Muhawi and Kanaana 1989, Kanaana 1992, among others.

9. See the report of the International Federation of Art Councils and Culture Agencies, *Creative Intersections: Partnerships between the Arts, Culture, and other Sectors* (2012), which documents the ways governments and funding bodies have been engaging with the arts and culture as part of their national and foreign policies on education, health, the environment, social cohesion and inclusion, business, conflict resolution, institutional capacity building, and development, among others.

10. See Prince Claus Fund for Culture and Development, "3-dimensional virtual museum in Palestine," July 25, 2012, http://www.princeclausfund.org/en/activities/3-demensional-virtual-museum-in-palestine.html.

11. Kamilya Jubran, *Makan* (CD), Harmonia Mundi, 2009.

References

Abd al-Hadi, Hashim, ed. 1984. *Al-muwsūʿah al-falasṭīnīyyah* [Encyclopaedia Palaestina]. Beirut, Lebanon: Encyclopaedia Palaestina Corporation.

Al-Kurdi, Wassim. 1994. "Artistic Inspiration from Folklore." In Sharif Kanaana, *Folk Heritage of Palestine,* 215–30. Taybeh, Palestine: Research Center for Arab Heritage.

Alqam, Nabil. 1977. *Madkhal li dirāsāt al-folklūr* [Introduction to Folklore Studies]. Al-Bireh, Palestine: Committee for Palestinian Folklore and Social Research, Inash Al Usra.

———. 1994. "Dealing with Our Folk Heritage." In Sharif Kanaana, *Folk Heritage of Palestine,* 179–215. Taybeh, Palestine: Research Center for Arab Heritage.

Al-Qush, E. 1994. "Makānat al-doktūr Tawfīq Kanʿān wa manhajuhu fi dirāsat thaqāfāt al-shaʿb al-falasṭīnī" [Tawfiq Canaan's role and contribution to Palestinian cultural studies]. *Al-Jana al-Arabi* (Arab Resource Center for Popular Arts) 2, 8–10.

Artaud, Antonin. 1964. *Le théâtre et son double.* Paris: Gallimard.

Barghouti, Abdellatif. 1963. "Arab Folksongs from Jordan." PhD diss., London, University of London.

———. 1986. *Diwān al-ʿatābah al-falasṭīnī* [Anthology of Palestinian ʿAtaba]. Birzeit, Palestine: Birzeit University.

———. 1990. *Diwan al-dalʿūnā* [Anthology of the Dalʿuna]. Al-Bireh, Palestine: Committee for Palestinian Folklore and Social Research, Inash Al-Usra.

Bisharat, George. 1997. "Exile to Compatriot: Transformations in the Social Identity of Palestinian Refugees in the West Bank." In *Culture, Power, Place: Explorations in Critical Anthropology,* edited by Akhil Gupta and James Ferguson, 203–33. Durham, NC: Duke University Press.

Canaan, Tawfiq. 1932. "The Palestinian House: Its Architecture and Folklore." *Journal of the Palestine Oriental Society* 12, 1–83.

———. 1934. "Modern Palestinian Beliefs and Practices Relating to God." *Journal of the Palestine Oriental Society* 14, 59–92.

Castelo-Branco, Salwa E. 2002. "Performance of Arab Music in 20th Century Egypt: Reconciling Authenticity and Contemporaneity." In *Garland Encyclopedia of World Music: The Middle-East,* edited by Virginia Danielson, Dwight Reynolds, and Scott Marcus, 557–61. New York: Routledge.

Clayton, Michael, Trevor Herbert, and Richard Middleton. 2012. *The Cultural Study of Music: A Critical Introduction.* 2nd ed. New York: Routledge.

Clifford, James, and Georges E. Marcus. 1986. *Writing Culture: The Poetics and Politics of Ethnography.* Berkeley: University of California Press.

Craissati, Dina. 1998. *Social Movements and Democracy in Palestine: A Future for Radical Politics in the Arab World?* PhD diss., Hamburg, Universitaet Hamburg.

———. 2005. "New NGOs and Democratic Governance in Palestine: A Pioneering Model for the Arab World?" In *NGOs and Governance in the Arab World,* edited by Sarah Ben Nefissa, Nabil Abd Al-Fattah, Sari Hanafi, and Carlos Milani, 181–208. Cairo: American University in Cairo Press, 2005.

Dalman, Gustaf H. 1901. *Palästinischer Diwan. Als Beitrag zur Volkskunde Palästinas.* Leipzig: J. C. Hinrichs'sche Buchhandlung.
Delvicchio-Good, Mary-Jo, and Byron Good. 2008. "Indonesia Sakit: Indonesian Disorders: Subjective Experiences and Interpretive Politics of Indonesian Artists (1999–2006)." In *Postcolonial Disorders,* edited by Delvicchio-Good, Sandra Hyde, Sarah Pinto, and Byron Good. Berkeley: University of California Press.
During, Jacques. 2011. "Globalisations à l'ère préindustrielle et formatage de l'oreille du monde. L'écoute de l'ethnomusicologue." In *Musique et globalisation: Musicologie-ethnomusicologie,* edited by Jacques Bouët and Makis Solomos, 39–68. Paris: L'Harmattan.
El-Ghadban, Yara. 2001. "Shedding Some Light on Contemporary Musicians in Palestine." *Middle-East Studies Bulletin,* 28–34.
———. 2004. "Palestines imaginaires. La scenographie comme ethnographie." *Anthropologies et sociétés,* 28 (3):15–37.
Eriksen, Thomas H. 2001. "Between Universalism and Relativism: A Critique of the UNESCO Concepts of Culture." In *Culture and Rights,* edited by Jane Cowan, Marie-Bénédicte Dampour, and Richard Wislon, 127–48. Cambridge, UK: University of Cambridge Press.
Fabian, Johannes. 1983. *Time and the Other: How Anthropology Makes its Object.* New York: Columbia University Press.
Farah, Randa. 1999. *Popular Memory and Reconstructions of Palestinian Identity: Al-Baqʿa Refugee Camp, Jordan.* PhD diss., Toronto: University of Toronto.
Fassin, Didier. 2009. "The Humanitarian Politics of Testimony: Subjectification through Trauma in the Israeli-Palestinian Conflict." *Cultural Anthropology* 23 (3): 531–58.
———. 2010. "*Noli Me Tangere:* The Moral Intouchability of Humanitarianism." In *Forces of Compassion. Humanitarianism between Ethics and Politics,* edited by Erica Bornstein and Peter Redfield, 35–53. Santa Fe: School of Advanced Research Press.
Feldman, Ilana. 2010. "Ad Hoc Humanity: UN Peacekeeping and the Limits of International Community in Gaza." *American Anthropologist* 112 (3): 416–29.
Furani, Khaled, and Dan Robinowitz. 2011. "The Ethnographic Arriving of Palestine." *Annual Review of Anthropology* 40, 475–91.
Gabiam, Nell. 2012. "When "Humanitarianism" Becomes "Development": The Politics of International Aid in Syria's Palestinian Refugee Camps." *American Anthropologist* 114 (1): 95–107.
Granqvist, Hilma N. 1931. *Marriage Conditions in a Palestinian Village.* Helsingfors, Finland: Akademische Buchhandlung.
———. 1947. *Birth and Childhood among the Arabs: Studies in a Muhammadan Village in Palestine.* Helsingfors, Finland: Söderström.
Hanafi, Sari, and Linda Tabar. 2005. *The Emergence of a Palestinian Globalized Elite: Donors, International Organizations, and Local NGOs.* Jerusalem, Palestine: Muwatin, Palestinian Institute for the Study of Democracy and Institute of Jerusalem Studies.
Kanaana, Sharif. 1992. *El-dār dār abūna. Dirāsāt fi al-turāth al-shaʿbī al-falasṭīnī* [This is our father's house. Studies in Palestine Folklore]. Jerusalem, Palestine: Markaz al-quds al-ʿalamī lil dirāsāt al-falasṭīnīyyah.
Khoury, Suhail, et al. 2009. *Jerusalem after Midnight.* Ramallah, Palestine: Edward Said National Conservatory of Music Productions.
Kristeva, Julia. 1982. *Powers of Horror: An Essay on Abjection.* New York: Columbia University Press.

Laaksonen, Annamari. 2012. *Creative Intersections. Partnerships between the Arts, Culture, and other Sectors.* Annual Report. International Federation of Art Councils and Culture Agencies. Sydney.

Libbis, Naᶜilah A. 1989. *Al-aghānī al-fulklūrīyyah al-nisāʾīyyah li munāsabāt al-khuṭbah wa al- zawāj* [Women's Wedding Songs]. Nazareth, Israel: Dāʾirat al-thaqāfah al-ᶜarabīyyah, Wizarat al-maᶜārif.

———. 1994. *Aghānīna al-naṣrawīyyah, shāmīyyah wa jay min al-shām* [Our Nazarene Songs]. Nazareth, Israel: Dāʾirat al-thaqāfah al-ᶜarabīyyah, Majlis al-thaqāfah wa al-funūn.

Lutfiyya, Abdulla M. 1996. *Baytin: Jordanian Village: A Study of Social Institutions and Social Change in a Folk Community.* The Hague: Mouton.

Marcus, Georges E., and Fred R. Myers. 1995. *The Traffic in Culture: Refiguring Art and Anthropology.* Berkeley: University of California Press.

Muhawi, Ibrahim, and Sharif Kanaana. 1989. *Speak Bird, Speak Again: Palestinian Arab Folktales.* Berkeley: University of California Press.

Nakhleh, Khalil. 1975. "Shifting Patterns of Conflict in Selected Arab Villages in Israel." PhD diss., Ann Arbor, University of Michigan.

———. 2012. *Globalized Palestine. The National Sell-out of a Homeland.* Trenton, NJ: Red Sea Press.

Nooshin, Laudan, ed. 2009. *Music and the Play of Power in the Middle East, North Africa, and Central Asia.* Surrey, UK: Ashgate.

Oliver, Anne Marie, and Paul Steinberg. 2002. "Popular Music of the Intifada." In *Garland Encylopedia of World Music: The Middle-East,* edited by Virginia Danielson, Dwight Reynolds and Scott Marcus, 635–40. New York: Routledge.

Peteet, Julie M. 2005. *Landscape of Hope and Despair: Palestinian Refugee Camps.* Philadelphia: University of Pennsylvania Press.

Poché, Christian. 2001. "Palestinian Music." In *New Grove Dictionary of Music and Musicians,* edited by Stanley Sadie and John Tyrell, 935–37. London: Macmillan.

Racy, Ali J. 2003. *Making Music in the Arab World: The Culture and Artistry of Tarab.* Cambridge, UK: Cambridge University Press.

Rancière, Jacques. 2000. *Le partage du sensible. Esthétique et politique.* Paris: La Fabrique.

Rousseau, Phillip. 2011. *Les cultures fragiles. L'UNESCO et la diversité culturelle (2001–2007).* PhD diss., Montréal, Université de Montréal.

Sirhan, Nimr. 1989. *Mawsūᶜāt al-fulklūr al-falasṭīnī.* Encyclopedia of Palestinian Folklore] 3 vols. Amman: Dāʾirat al-Thaqāfah.

Sherwell, Tina. 2005. "Contemporary Palestinian Art: Trends and Transformations." Art School Palestine. http://www.artschoolpalestine.com/index.php?option=com_content&task=view&lang=en&id=513&Itemid=0.

Stone, Christopher R. 2008. *Popular Culture and Nationalism in Lebanon: The Fairouz and Rahbani Nation.* New York: Routledge.

White, Bob W., ed. 2012. *Music and Globalization: Critical Encouters.* Bloomington: Indiana University Press.

Winegar, Jessica. 2008. "The Humanity Game: Art, Islam, and the War on Terror." *Anthropological Quarterly*83 (3): 651–81.

Yudice, George. 2003. *The Expediency of Culture: Uses of Culture in the Global Era.* Durham, NC: Duke University Press.

Contributors

Sylvia Alajaji received her PhD in musicology from the University of Rochester's Eastman School of Music. She specializes in music of the Middle East and is particularly interested in the intersections of music, popular culture, and politics in the Palestinian-Israeli conflict and in the Armenian diaspora in Lebanon. She has conducted research in Lebanon, Rwanda, and Palestine. She is currently an assistant professor of music at Franklin and Marshall College in Lancaster, Pennsylvania.

Janne Louise Andersen is a multimedia journalist with an MA in journalism from Hofstra University, New York, and a BA in anthropology from Copenhagen University and Birzeit University in Palestine, where she studied two semesters of anthropology and Arabic. She mainly writes about culture and politics among Arab diaspora communities in the United States and Denmark for Danish, American, and Arab media. From 2009 to 2010 she worked as a project manager for Project Hip-Hop Palestine with the Sabreen Association for Artistic Development, a program attempting to support the segregated Palestinian hip-hop scene. This experience has since led her to cover the Arab hip-hop scene extensively in her work, primarily for *Rolling Stone* Middle East.

Rachel Beckles Willson is Professor of music at Royal Holloway, University of London. She has published widely on music politics, referring especially to the former Eastern Bloc and Israel/Palestine. She is author of *Ligeti, Kurtág, and Hungarian Music during the Cold War* and *Orientalism and Musical Mission: Palestine and the West.* Rachel studied as a pianist at the Royal Academy of Music in London and the Liszt Academy of Music in Budapest before reading for a PhD at Kings College, London. During 2008–2010 she was based at the Humboldt University in Berlin thanks to a Fellowship for Experienced Researchers from the Alexander von Humboldt Foundation. Rachel is an active musician, performing as a pianist (western classical music), saxophonist (Cuban traditions), and *ʿūd* player (Arabic and Turkish repertoire).

Carin Berg is a PhD student in Peace and Development Research at the School of Global Studies at the University of Gothenburg, Sweden. She has published about different issues concerning the Middle East, and in particular the Israeli-Palestinian conflict. Her publications include "Lebanon and Syria" in Joel Peters, ed., *The European Union and the Arab Spring,* and "Civilisation of the EU: A Way for the EU to Do More for the World Peace?" in *Cogito.*

Issa Boulos was born in Jerusalem in 1968. He studied piano, *ʿūd,* and voice at an early age and later pursued music composition in the United States, where he studied with Gustavo Leone, Robert Lombardo, Athanasios Zervas, and Ilya Levinson. He has composed music for full orchestra, chamber, mixed ensembles, and traditional ensemble (*takht*) and has written hundreds of songs, including several hits. Among his commissions are four pieces for the Chicago Symphony Orchestra; composition/performance for the Silk Road Ensemble and original scores for award-winning documentaries, plays, feature films, and musicals. He acted as lecturer at the University of Chicago, where he directed the Middle East Music Ensemble, and is currently the head of Arab Music at the Qatar Music Academy.

Heather Bursheh, originally from Scotland, graduated in flute performance from the Royal Northern College of Music in Manchester, England, in 1998, and immediately afterward moved to Palestine, where she has been living and working ever since. As well as teaching flute at the Edward Said National Conservatory of Music and being an active performing musician, she has also worked for the conservatory in various other capacities: academic director of the Ramallah branch; deputy director for academic affairs; musical director of the Palestine Youth Orchestra and the Palestinian National Orchestra; and development officer for the new bachelor's degree programs. She gained her master's in ethnomusicology from the School of Oriental and African Studies in London in 2003.

Yara El-Ghadban is an anthropologist (PhD) and ethnomusicologist (MA). She is currently a postdoctoral fellow at l'Université de Montréal (Canada) in the Department of Anthropology. Her work is mainly situated in the Middle East (Lebanon, Palestinian Territories) and South Africa, but she has also conducted field research in Canada (Québec) and in Europe (France, the Netherlands). Her publications focus on cultural practices, particularly music, and how struggles of belonging and of recognition are mediated through music against a backdrop of inequality, histories of violence, and of competing strategies and discourses of inclusion and exclusion. Aside from her academic work, Yara El-Ghadban is also a fiction writer, publishing the novel *L'ombre de l'olivier,* set in the Palestinian refugee camps of Lebanon during the civil war.

Nader Jalal was born in Jerusalem and is a graduate of Birzeit University. He was director of the Music and Folklore Department at the Palestinian Ministry of Culture until 2010. He now directs the Palestinian Institute for Cultural Development—NAWA—and is a researcher in Arabic music and Palestinian cultural heritage. He was exposed early to practical musicianship as a folkloric dancer, a musician, and a co-founder of many folkloric music bands. He has also established popular festivals, including Ramallah and Sebastia festivals and the Palestinian Heritage Day. He has led Palestinian cultural weeks all over the world and supervised CD productions of the new edition of the Palestinian national anthem, Al-Hallaj album, Shams ou Hawa album, and Huna Al-Quds album, which comprises compositions by the late Palestinian composer Rawḥī al-Khammāsh.

Moslih Kanaaneh graduated with a Dr. Polit. from the University of Bergen in 1995 and with his BA in philosophy and Middle East history from Haifa University in 1980. He was the director of NORPAS—Norwegian Center for Research and Development in Palestinian Society—between 1997 and 2003 and since has been teaching at the Department of Sociology and Anthropology, Birzeit University, on the West Bank. From 2008 to 2011 he was chairperson of the department, as well as a member of the academic council. His main fields of interest include Palestinian national identity, Arab culture and society, community psychology, folklore, and comparative religion. He has given lectures and keynote speeches in conferences around the world and published a number of books and articles in Arabic and English.

David A. McDonald is an ethnomusicologist whose teaching and scholarly work intersects with the fields of cultural anthropology, ethnomusicology, folklore, and Middle Eastern studies. Since 2000 he has worked closely with Palestinian communities dispersed throughout Israel, Jordan, North America, and the Occupied Territories. Specifically, his work involves understanding the cultural dynamics of music performance, politics, and identity among Palestinian refugee communities. In addition to his book *My Voice Is My Weapon: Music, Nationalism, and the Poetics of Palestinian Resistance,* he has published research on music and nationalism, violence, and the body in Israel/Palestine. His most recent book project chronicles the federal prosecution of the Holy Land Foundation 5 and its impact among Palestinian communities in Dallas, Texas.

Randa Safieh, originally from Jerusalem, is an ethnomusicologist and secondary music teacher based in London. Having gained an MA in music and culture from Roehampton University, Randa specializes in issues of cultural identity, diaspora, and resistance in Palestinian music; has written for the Palestinian *Youth Times* newspaper, SOAS *Middle East in London* magazine; and has presented lectures—most recently, at Leighton House Museum on hip-hop of the Arab world—as part of the Nour Festival of Arts. She was interviewed live on BBC World News by Zainab Badawi, as well as on Voice of America and world music radio station Sheffield Live. She has also emceed Palestinian cultural events such as Poetic Resistance, featuring Palestinian poets Remi Kanazi and Rafeef Ziadah.

Michael Schulz is Associate Professor in Peace and Development Research at the School of Global Studies, University of Gothenburg, Sweden. He has been involved in various research projects and has published extensively on issues concerning the Middle East, and in particular the Israeli-Palestinian conflict. His publications include "Whose Security in Palestine? An Analysis of the Impact on Human Security of the EU's Security Sector Reform in Palestine" (*Development Dialogue*); "Palestinian Civil Society," in Joel Peters and David Newman, eds., *The Handbook of the Israeli Palestinian Conflict*; and "Palestinian Public Willingness to Compromise: Torn between Hope and Violence" (*Journal of Security Dialogues*).

Kiven Strohm is a PhD candidate in the Department of Anthropology, Université de Montréal. His research explores the politics of contemporary art among Palestinians in Israel. More broadly, his interests include the history of anthropology, aesthetics and politics, and contemporary art and popular culture in the Arab world. He received an MA in Philosophy and Cultural Analysis from the Universiteit van Amsterdam and has been a visiting researcher at the Sociology and Anthropology Department at Birzeit University (Palestine) in 2011 and the Department of Sociology and Anthropology at Central European University (Budapest, Hungary) in 2012. In the fall of 2012 he began postdoctoral research on the reconfigurations of place and politics within contemporary Palestinian art.

Reem Talhami was born in Shefaʿamr in 1948 Palestine and moved to Jerusalem at age seventeen to pursue her BA in music at the Hebrew University. She participated in establishing the musical group Ghurbaih and sang her first original song in 1987, written by Ibrahim al-Khatib. She has participated in all the major Palestinian festivals and has given concerts in many Palestinian cities, villages, and refugee camps. As an actress and a singer, she has appeared both at home and abroad in many albums, films, television shows, and plays, including the production of *Jidārīyyah* by Mahmoud Darwish. She teaches voice in the Drama Academy in Ramallah and has been working recently on her first personal new music project with the poet Khaled Juma from Gaza city and the composer Said Murad.

Stig-Magnus Thorsén, Professor in music and society at the Academy of Music and Drama, has been employed at Gothenburg University since 1971. His scholarly interests began with music technology and research with a natural science perspective on music. He moved over to the field of sociology and anthropology of music and in 1980 wrote a dissertation on music and religion. He has built up courses in multiculturalism, world music, globalization, and a master's program in music performance. Since 1994 he has been working with international relations in music and music education, mainly connected to South Africa and Palestine. His publications are related to sociology of music and postcolonial perspectives on music, including topics like music and work, music and mission, and intercultural music.

Index

Page references in italics refer to figures.

www.ingramcontent.com/pod-product-compliance
Lightning Source LLC
Chambersburg PA
CBHW061728270326
41928CB00011B/2157
9780253011060